THE
Universal Chronicle
OF
RANULF HIGDEN

Oxford University Press, Ely House, London W. 1

GLASGOW NEW YORK TORONTO MELBOURNE WELLINGTON
CAPE TOWN SALISBURY IBADAN NAIROBI LUSAKA ADDIS ABABA
BOMBAY CALCUTTA MADRAS KARACHI LAHORE DACCA
KUALA LUMPUR HONG KONG

THE

Universal Chronicle

OF

RANULF HIGDEN

BY

JOHN TAYLOR

OXFORD

AT THE CLARENDON PRESS

1966

TO E. T.

PREFACE

THE following study is an attempt to examine the most popular history of fourteenth-century England, the *Polychronicon* of Ranulf Higden. Such a study involves a consideration not only of Higden's text, but of the continuations of the *Polychronicon*, which include many of the important chronicles of the period.

The subject of the *Polychronicon* was suggested several years ago by Professor V. H. Galbraith. His own writings on fourteenth-century chronicles constitute the starting-point for this work, and I am particularly indebted to him for his advice over many years, for reading the book in typescript, and for suggesting many improvements. I am indebted to Professor Sir R. A. B. Mynors for the use of his catalogue of surviving manuscripts of the *Polychronicon* which made possible the present study, and I would like to thank the various libraries and colleges which supplied microfilm of manuscripts in their possession.

I should also like to thank Professor John Le Patourel for reading the book in typescript; Miss Beryl Smalley, Mr. Richard Hunt, and Dr. P. J. Jones for reading Chapter V; and Professor R. W. Southern for reading the first part of Chapter VII, which is reprinted by permission of the editor of the *English Historical Review*. Mr. K. R. Rowe assisted me with the Latin text. I should finally like to thank my wife who gave me advice and help at every stage.

JOHN TAYLOR

CONTENTS

ABBREVIATIONS

Brie	F. W. D. Brie, *Geschichte und Quellen der Mittelenglischen Prosachronik, 'The Brut of England' oder 'The Chronicles of England'* (Marburg, 1905).
B.J.R.L.	*Bulletin of the John Rylands Library*, Manchester.
B.M.	London, British Museum.
C.P.L.	*Calendar of Papal Letters.*
C.P.R.	*Calendar of Patent Rolls.*
C.S.E.L.	*Corpus scriptorum ecclesiasticorum latinorum* (Vienna, 1866–).
C.S.	*Camden Society.*
E.E.T.S.	*Early English Text Society.*
E.H.R.	*English Historical Review.*
English Friars	Beryl Smalley, *English Friars and Antiquity in the Early Fourteenth Century* (Oxford, 1960).
F.S.	*Fritz Saxl, A Volume of Memorial Essays*, ed. D. J. Gordon (London, 1957).
H.L.Q.	V. H. Galbraith, 'An Autograph Manuscript of Ranulf Higden's *Polychronicon*', *Huntington Library Quarterly*, xxiii (1959).
Kingsford	C. L. Kingsford, *English Historical Literature in the Fifteenth Century* (Oxford, 1913).
M.G.H.S.	*Monumenta Germaniae Historiae: Scriptores.*
P.L.	J. P. Migne, *Patrologiae cursus completus series latina* (Paris, 1844–55).
R.S.	Rolls Series.
T.E.	*Testamenta Eboracensia*, Surtees Society.
Tout, *Chapters*	T. F. Tout, *Chapters in the Administrative History of Medieval England*, 6 vols. (Manchester, 1923–35).

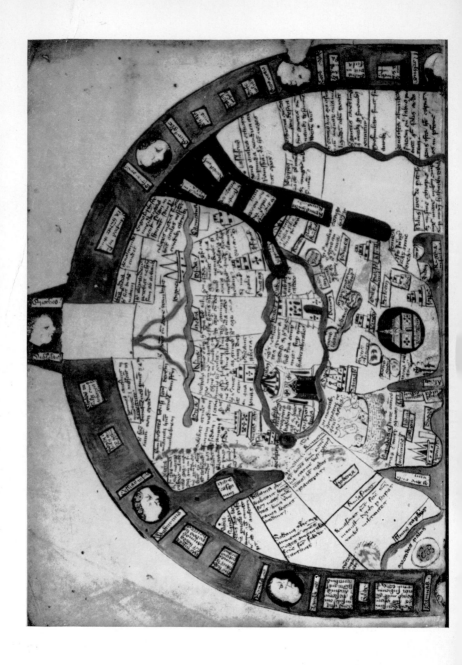

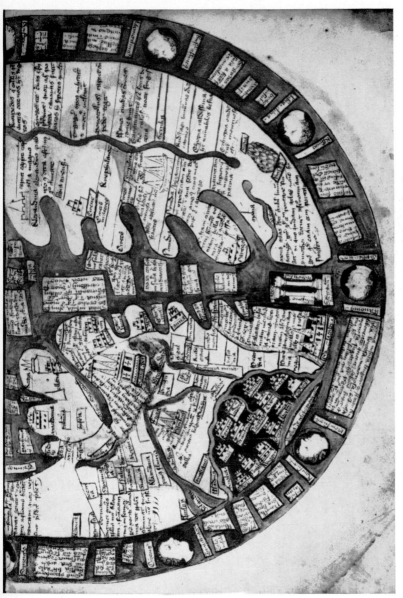

Higden's world map. B.M. MS. Royal 14. C. ix. ff. 1ᵛ–2.

I

INTRODUCTORY

I

OF Ranulf Higden, the author of the *Polychronicon*, and one of the most industrious historians of the fourteenth century, we know little. From the contents of his history he appears to have been a Cheshire man, with a great interest in his native county. According to a colophon in a copy of the *Polychronicon* (B.M. MS. Laud Misc. 619, which is also found on the fly-leaf of the New College, Oxford, MS. 152) Higden entered the Benedictine abbey of St. Werburgh, Chester, in 1299. There is no evidence from his chronicle that he studied at a university, or that he ever travelled extensively beyond Cheshire. His observations from direct experience are almost all concerned with local affairs. Though there were troubles at St. Werburgh's during his lifetime there is no evidence that he was concerned in them. The one reliable fact for the later years of his life is that in 1352 he was summoned by Edward III to appear at court with his chronicles.[1] By that time his reputation as an historian was evidently well established. According to the terms of the entry on the Close Roll for August 1352, 'Father Ralph, a monk of the abbey at Chester' was summoned to Westminster on 21 August, and he was ordered to come 'with all your chronicles, and those which are in your charge to speak and take advice with our council on certain matters which will be explained to you on our behalf'. It is not known what the business was that made the king require his presence,[2] and there is no evidence that he ever

---

[1] J. G. Edwards, 'Ranulf, Monk of Chester', *E.H.R.* xlvii (1932), 94.

[2] This may have been in connexion with affairs in France or Scotland. Chronicles were valued, as Edward I's search of the chronicles showed, for their part in strengthening political demands. F. Palgrave, *Documents Illustrating the History of Scotland* (Record Commission), i. 56–137.

again strayed into the affairs of state. The note in the manuscripts that have already been mentioned (MS. Laud Misc. 619 and New College, Oxford, MS. 152) suggests that he died in 1363/4 in a 'good old age', after living over sixty years in religion. 'At last, after living for sixty-four years in the religious life, he died at an advanced age about the feast of Saint Gregory 1363.' His tomb in Chester Cathedral, near the gate of the south choir aisle, is still to be seen.

These are the known facts of Higden's life. He was a scholar who apparently spent much of his life in the monastic *scriptorium*. The reference to his chronicles in 1352 may indicate that 'he was probably the official custodian of the abbey's library and the head of the *scriptorium*'.[1] Higden's chief literary memorial is the *Polychronicon*, a universal chronicle,[2] which gave to the educated and learned audience of fourteenth-century England a clear and original picture of world history based upon medieval tradition, but with a new interest in antiquity, and with the early history of Britain related as part of the whole. Higden's chronicle was an immediate and unprecedented success; it appealed to the changing interests of the times, when monks and friars were becoming interested in the classics, when in his old age Walsingham graduated from chronicle writing to classical commentary, and when schoolmasters like John Seward would soon be writing classical epigrams.[3] Higden almost certainly wrote the first version of his chronicle during the 1320's, the high political moment of the Middle Ages, but the vogue of the *Polychronicon* lasted for two centuries after this. So great was its success that Trevisa translated it into English during the 1380's, and it was

---

[1] *E.H.R.* xlvii (1932), 94.

[2] Apart from the publication by T. Gale, *Historiae Britannicae Scriptores XV* (1691), i. 179–287, of extracts from the chapters relating to English history in Book 1 and other books, the Latin text of the *Polychronicon* was published for the first time in the Rolls Series. It was originally entrusted to Canon Hardwick, and on his death to Churchill Babington, who published two volumes (1865–9). It was finished in nine volumes by J. Rawson Lumby in 1886. The edition is unsatisfactory in many ways.

[3] See Chapter V. On Seward see the remarks of V. H. Galbraith, 'John Seward and his Circle', *Medieval and Renaissance Studies* (1943), pp. 151–5.

again translated by an unknown author in the fifteenth century. Caxton printed chapters from the first book of Trevisa's translation in 1480, and in 1482 he printed the whole of Trevisa's text with a continuation of his own. The universalizing trend in historical thought lived on into Tudor times. Writers such as Fabyan and Stowe quoted Higden. William Cecil, Lord Burghley, possessed a manuscript of Trevisa's text, and no work fully replaced it until Sir Walter Raleigh wrote his *History of the World* in the seventeenth century. The *Polychronicon* formed part of the medieval legacy to Renaissance times.

II

Among minor writings which can definitely be attributed to Higden are two works classified as aids to preaching. Though the fourteenth century was not a great period for the monastic sermon, monks preached inside the abbey church, and within the churches of the city. They delivered sermons at clerical synods, and at the time of visitations. Delivered as they were in Latin on such formal occasions, monastic sermons all too often contained little that was original. Higden's writings reveal, none the less, that within the field of homiletic literature Benedictines could still produce works of some interest.

A collection of sermons written in Latin, which has been attributed to Higden, survives in a manuscript of the fifteenth century,[1] but of greater interest is the *Ars Componendi Sermones*, a guide to sermon literature, which was popular during the fourteenth century.[2] As its title suggests, the *Ars Componendi Sermones* is concerned with the selection and composition of sermons. The medieval sermon was strictly organized with a text taken from the epistle or gospel of the day. The subject could be developed through a consideration of various symbolic meanings, or through

[1] The sermons are in MS. Latin Rylands 367. For a description of Higden's writings see Appendix V.
[2] Bodley MS. 5. For the other manuscripts of this text see Appendix V. G. R. Owst, *Preaching in Medieval England* (1926) has many references to the *Ars Componendi Sermones*.

images drawn from the Fathers and history. The selection of the text was a matter of some importance. In his work Higden suggested texts for every occasion, for visitations, elections, synods, processions, and funerals. To interest the medieval audience, illustrations and *exempla*, such as are to be found in the *Polychronicon* itself, might be used. With its selection of texts, its notes upon sermon divisions, and its warnings against inordinate length, the *Ars Componendi Sermones* was a useful guide to the medieval preacher.

The *Speculum Curatorum*, compiled as an aid to preaching, reveals more clearly the encyclopaedic nature of Higden's mind.[1] Higden's authorship of the *Speculum Curatorum*, as well as of the *Ars Componendi Sermones*, is established by the fact that in both works the initial letters of the opening chapters spell out his name, while in the *Speculum Curatorum* the date of composition, 1340, is also given.[2] The *Speculum Curatorum* deals with a variety of subjects including the articles of faith, the Lord's prayer, the beatitudes, the virtues and the vices. The character of the work can be deduced from the chapter on *sortilegium* or divination,[3] in which Higden dealt with the various methods of divination, the cult of devils, of heavenly bodies, of elements, idols, images, and figures. On the subject of divination by heavenly bodies Higden wrote, 'The signs of great coming events do appear in the air from time to time—comets, points of fire, and eclipses—and it is perfectly lawful to foretell from the stars such future events as droughts, fair weather, winds, rains, and the seasons for sowing, dosing, and blood-letting, caused by the irruption of heavenly

---

[1] Balliol College, Oxford, MS. 77, Cambridge U.L. MS. Mm. 1. 20, and Durham Cathedral Chapter MS. B. iv. 36 are the three main manuscripts of this work. See R. A. B. Mynors, *Catalogue of the Manuscripts of Balliol College, Oxford* (1963), p. 62.

[2] In the *Ars Componendi Sermones* (MS. Bodley 316, ff. 176–83) Higden writes at the end, 'Explicit ars componendi sermones. Nota quod littere capitanee huius artis syllabatim invicem tantum sonant Ars Ranulphi Cestrensis.' In the *Speculum Curatorum* the initials of the first eighty chapters read: 'Cestrensis monachus frater Ranulphus compilavit hoc speculum anno Domini MCCC quadragesimo.' See Appendix V.

[3] See G. R. Owst, '*Sortilegium* in English Homiletic Literature of the Fourteenth Century', *Studies Presented to Sir Hilary Jenkinson* (1957), pp. 272–303.

bodies. Dreams too, may be used likewise in certain situations ....'
On the cult of elements he wrote, 'To cause children to pass
through fire for the sake of their health, or to venerate bonfires
kindled from the bones of horses on St. John the Baptist's Night
is superstition. Tapers and candles blessed at the feast of the
Purification are believed to protect the animals which they burn;
but this protection is not due to the virtue of the wax but to the
Church's benediction . . ..'[1]

The *Speculum Curatorum* reveals the nature of Higden's mind,
a mind 'equally at home in the lore of constellations, the "properties of things", the psychology of dreams, and some of the
typical sources of popular habits and ideas'.[2] The work is compilation, taken, without acknowledgement, mainly from the *De
Universo* and *De Legibus* of William of Auvergne. In the *Polychronicon* Higden adopted similar methods, quoting without
acknowledgement the work of John of Wales and Bartholomaeus
Anglicus. His minor writings reveal that he was an encyclopaedist, an omnivorous reader, who set down rather in the fashion of
Vincent of Beauvais what he knew of the marvels of nature and
the history of men.

Apart from the *Ars Componendi Sermones* and the *Speculum Curatorum* Higden has been credited with certain other writings of
little importance,[3] and in Tudor times his name was linked with
the Chester cycle of Whitsuntide plays, written in English during the fourteenth century. What has been described as 'a
persistent tradition', which arose during the sixteenth and
seventeenth centuries, says that Higden devised or invented
these plays.[4] It is not difficult to imagine the manner in which

[1] Owst, pp. 284–5. This chapter in the *Speculum Curatorum* occurs in Durham
MS. B. iv. 36, ff. 23–26ᵛ, and is followed by one on the tricks of devils, *De ludi-
ficationbus demonum* (ff. 26ᵛ–29ᵛ).

[2] Owst, p. 279.   [3] See Appendix V.

[4] In Appendix W of *The Medieval Stage* (1903), ii. 348–52, E. K. Chambers lists
in some detail the evidence for the tradition concerning the composition of the
Chester cycle of Miracle Plays. See Hardin Craig, *English Religious Drama of the
Middle Ages* (1955), pp. 168 ff. There are scholars who believe that Sir Henry
Francis wrote the Chester plays. See F. M. Salter, *Medieval Drama in Chester*
(University of Toronto Press, 1955). E. K. Chambers, *English Literature at the
Close of the Middle Ages* (1947) argues, mainly on linguistic grounds, that 'the

a 'tradition' of this kind arose among the 'legend-hungry' antiquaries of Tudor times.[1] Higden was the one Chester author
belonging to the first half of the fourteenth century whose work
they knew. As he was a Chester monk who had written a
universal history it was natural to suppose that it was he who
had written a cycle of plays which 'typify the ecclesiastical conception of universal history from the day of creation to the day
of judgement'. On the other hand, since the plays are written in
English it may well be doubted whether Higden or any monk of
St. Werburgh's wrote them during the first half of the fourteenth
century.[2] Though a Benedictine monk might be trilingual his

ascription to Higden is not very plausible' (p. 25). The standard text of the
Chester plays is by H. Deimling and G. W. Matthews (E.E.T.S. 1892, 1914,
vols. lxii, cxv). For the bibliography of the Chester plays see *English Literature at
the Close of the Middle Ages*, p. 213.

[1] The banns or public announcements which were recited on St. George's
Day by the town crier in Chester state that in 1551–72 John Arneway 'sett out
in playe The devise of one dom Rondall, moonke of Chester abbe'. *The Breauarye
of Rogers* (1609), in a list of mayors under the mayoralty of Sir John Arneway
which it gives as 1328, has the reference 'The whitson playes invented in
Chester by one Rondoll Higden, a monke in Chester abbaye'.

In the two sources which have been mentioned the name associated with
Higden is that of John Arneway, whose dates as mayor of Chester are tradition-
ally 1268 to 1277. It is obvious that if these dates are correct Arneway could not
in fact have been associated with Higden, who only took his monastic vows in
1299. To explain this inconsistency Professor E. K. Chambers has suggested that
the name Arneway has been confused with that of Richard Erneis or Herneys,
who was mayor from 1327 to 1329. More recently reasons have been advanced
for questioning the dates of Arneway's mayoralty. From the evidence of B.M.
Add. MS. 29777, and MS. Harley 2013, it appears that Arneway may have been
Mayor of Chester during the years 1327–8. See Arthur Brown, 'A Tradition of
the Chester Plays', *London Medieval Studies*, vol. ii, pt. 1 (1951), 68–72.

A third name associated by tradition with the Chester Corpus Christi plays is
that of Sir Henry Francis, who by 1377 had become a senior monk in the monastery of St. Werburgh. William Newhall's proclamation for the plays written
in 1544 ascribed their authorship to Sir Henry Francis. A sixteenth-century
tradition says that Francis went three times to Rome before he secured from
Pope Clement, possibly Clement VI (1342–52), a grant of forty days' pardon to
everyone who resorted to the plays in a peaceable manner, and ten additional
days of pardon from the Bishop of Chester on the same terms. The banns of 1544
state that Sir Henry Francis, 'somtyme monk of this dissolved monastery',
devised the plays.

[2] Behind the plays may lie a primitive version similar to 'the Tergernsee
Ludus de Antichristo and the Anglo-Norman *Adam* of the twelfth century, the
Benediktbeuern and Riga *Prophetae* of the thirteenth, and the Rouen *Prophetae* of
the fourteenth'—E. K. Chambers, p. 26. This primitive version might have been

natural literary medium at that time was still Latin or French. The translations into English that were made by Benedictines during the fourteenth century were writings of an order different from that of the miracle play.[1] It is unlikely that a monk at St. Werburgh's would have written a cycle of plays of a type that so openly appealed to a popular audience, and was so strongly condemned by many within the Church.[2] The undertaking of such a work ran counter not only to the deep conservatism of medieval monastic life, but also to what is known of Higden's own interests. The author of the Chester plays, if there was but one, should probably be sought rather among the secular clergy of the city than among the members of its wealthy and privileged religious house.

III

The Benedictine monastery of St. Werburgh at Chester was for sixty years the setting of Higden's life. Although a period of unrest in Cheshire, the fourteenth century marked the height of Chester's medieval prosperity, and within the city the wealthy Benedictine abbey of St. Werburgh was an important institution. The wealth of the monastery came from its extensive property in various parts of Cheshire, especially in the Wirral peninsula; from the appropriated revenues of several churches; and from properties and rights within the city walls.[3] In

written in Latin, French, or English. In the opinion of E. K. Chambers Higden may have written the Latin or French but not the English version; 'all his [Higden's] known or suggested writings are in Latin, and in the *Polychronicon* he tells us that in his day English *in paucis adhuc agrestibus vix remansit*. He may have exaggerated, but probably his own vernacular was Norman French' (*English Literature at the Close of the Middle Ages*, p. 25).

[1] For a survey of these writings see W. A. Pantin, *English Church in the Fourteenth Century* (1955), pp. 220–43.

[2] Grosseteste in the thirteenth century had urged his clergy to stamp out Miracles, 'William of Wadington, and Robert Mannyng his translator, while allowing plays on the Resurrection and the Nativity if decently presented in the church, condemn the Miracles played in open places . . . .'—K. Sisam, *Fourteenth Century Verse and Prose* (Oxford, 1937), p. xxiii; see also E. K. Chambers, pp. 12–14.

[3] On St. Werburgh's see R. V. H. Burne, *The Monks of Chester* (1962); J. Tait, *The Chartulary of St. Werburgh* (Chetham Society, vol. lxxix, 1920); D. Jones, *The Church in Chester, 1300–1540* (Chetham Society, third series, 1956).

Higden's time the abbots of St. Werburgh's were persons of consequence. They entertained kings and archbishops on the occasion of their visiting and passing through Chester, and at the great annual Chester fair licensed by the abbey, and held on the feast of St. John the Baptist, the abbot levied a tax upon all transactions, and had cognizance of all crimes except homicide. The abbot held his courts, and the abbey tenants, who were numerous both within and without the city, owed suit to St. Thomas' court on the south side of the abbey gate.

Though the abbey was a wealthy and powerful institution it had its troubles. Chief among these was the question of exemption from episcopal visitation and control. Exemption from episcopal visitation was obtained for St. Werburgh's by Abbot William de Bebington (1324–49) in 1345, but it was opposed by several of the monks, who feared that it placed too much power in the hands of the abbot.[1] Bebington's successor, Richard de Seynesbury (1349–62), was compelled to resign in 1362 after a visitation by commissioners of the Benedictine general chapter,[2] and Newport, who succeeded him, obtained in 1363 a revocation of the order of exemption.[3] Apart from the struggle over exemption the internal life of St. Werburgh's was disturbed in other ways. In the time of Seynesbury 'the monastery entered upon a period of lawlessness and violence which continued for a century or more'.[4] In 1362, after a dispute with the abbot, three of the monks sought the Black Prince's protection, saying that they dared not remain in the abbey for fear of perpetual imprisonment or loss of their lives.[5] Throughout the period the number of monks diminished,[6] and despite its wealth St. Werburgh's appears already to have passed the peak of its influence in the fourteenth century.

It was at this time that, outwardly rich and powerful, though

---

[1] Burne, p. 79.
[2] W. A. Pantin, *Chapters of English Black Monks* (C.S., third series), iii. 35.
[3] *C.P.L.* iv. 88.   [4] Burne, p. 84.   [5] Burne, p. 93.
[6] The commissary of the provincial chapter visiting the house in 1393 found the number of monks to be insufficient. Pantin, *Chapters of English Black Monks*, ii. 92.

inwardly attacked by dissension and the beginning of a decline,
St. Werburgh's produced in the *Polychronicon* of Ranulf Higden
its greatest contribution to medieval learning. Though not a
house of any particular intellectual distinction St. Werburgh's
had not been entirely devoid of learning or of literary traditions
in earlier times. In the person of the twelfth-century monk who
called himself Lucian, St. Werburgh's had produced an author
in the twelfth century. Lucian wrote a work, *De Laude Cestrie*,[1]
for a patron who was a member of the College of St. John the
Baptist outside the walls of Chester. The *De Laude Cestrie* is a
description of Chester, and an early example of this form of
literature. It describes the town as it was in Lucian's day. Amid
a good deal of moralizing, the work, in the fashion of a guide
book, describes the principal buildings of the city, including the
market and churches. The *De Laude Cestrie* was known to Camden, who quoted it in the 1600 and subsequent editions of the
Britannia, but Higden, a member of the same monastery writing
little more than a century later, did not quote Lucian's work in
his chronicle or mention it in his list of authorities. The omission
is surprising in as omnivorous a reader as Higden unless it was
that the *De Laude Cestrie* remained in a single copy in the College
of St. John the Baptist. Though Higden had much to say about
Chester his information was original and came mainly from his
own observations.

After Higden St. Werburgh's produced one more author of
note in the person of Henry Bradshaw, who wrote a Life of St.
Werburgh in English verse.[2] The little that can be said of

---

[1] *Liber Luciani de Laude Cestrie*, ed. M. V. Taylor (Record Society of Lancashire
and Cheshire, vol. lxiv, 1912). The text is in MS. Bodley 672.

[2] On Bradshaw see A. B. Emden, *A Biographical Register of the University
of Oxford to A.D. 1500* (1957–9), i. 244. According to Anthony Wood, Bradshaw
spent some time at Gloucester College, where, after he had passed his course
in theology, he returned to his cell at St. Werburgh's, but Wood gives no authority
for this statement.

Bradshaw's poem was first printed by Pynson in 1521. It was printed for the
Chetham Society in 1848, and edited by F. Hawkins. It was edited by Horstmann
for the E.E.T.S., O.S. lxxxviii (1887). Bradshaw wrote the '*De Antiquitate et
magnificentia Urbis Cestriae*', and the date of his death is fixed at 1513 by '*A Balade
to the Auctour*' printed with the *Life*.

Bradshaw is that he was the author of several works, including this *Life* and that he died early in the sixteenth century. As befitted a monk of Chester, Bradshaw quoted Higden in his *Life* of St. Werburgh, which was a translation of a Latin *Life*, written in rhyme-royal, with acknowledgements to Chaucer and Lydgate, and to his own contemporaries,

> To pregnant Barclay now being religious
> To inventive Skelton and poet-laureate.

Apart from these authors St. Werburgh's must at one time have possessed a library of considerable size. As well as the usual theological works the library probably contained a number of classical authors such as Ovid, Seneca, and Virgil,[1] as well as copies of medieval chronicles. From the contents of the medieval library only a few manuscripts survive. Among them are annals and the remains of a chronicle;[2] a psalterium (Bodleian MS. Tanner 169) which contains a list of obits of abbots and founders;[3] a Latin and an English version of the *Polychronicon*;[4] a grammatical work (Misc. grammatica, Berlin, Stadtsbibl. MS. lat. 194); and a work entitled 'Speculum spiritualium' (Dublin, Trinity College, MS. 271). Of teaching within the abbey we know nothing, although it is worth noting that in 1399 the Abbot of St. Werburgh's was fined by the provincial chapter for failing to maintain a scholar at Oxford,[5] and fined again for a similar offence in 1408.[6]

Chronicles were written at St. Werburgh's before Higden's time. The main chronicle of the house is found in the Mostyn manuscript and has been printed under the title of the *Annales*

---

[1] These are quoted by the Chester writer known as Lucian. It is doubtful if Higden found all his classical texts there. See Chapter V.
[2] See pp. 11–12.
[3] This is printed in *Liber Luciani de Laude Cestrie*, pp. 85–103.
[4] The English version of the *Polychronicon* is Aberystwyth N.L., DN 4923. The Latin version is Huntington Library MS. 132. See pp. 92–96. The surviving manuscripts of St. Werburgh's are listed in *Medieval Libraries of Great Britain*, ed. N. R. Ker (1941), p. 31. See now the second edition (1964).
[5] W. A. Pantin, *Chapters of English Black Monks*, iii. 175.
[6] Ibid., p. 149.

Cestrienses.[1] The Mostyn manuscript is a paper manuscript of the late fifteenth or early sixteenth century, and contains an historical account covering the sixth age of the world, i.e. from the birth of Christ to 1297. It is written in the form of annals, and, judging from the number of early entries relating to the archbishops of Rouen and to continental matters, it may have developed from a Rouen chronicle which the first abbot, Richard, who was a monk at Bec, brought with him from Normandy to Chester.[2] Later entries prove its St. Werburgh's provenance, and its favourable treatment of Simon de Montfort suggests that that section of the narrative may well have been put together during the abbacy of Simon of Whitchurch (1265–91), who was active in Montfort's support.

These annals are not the only historical entries to survive from St. Werburgh's. An eighteenth-century transcript of a shorter series of annals covering the years from 594 to 1295 is found in a manuscript bound up at the end of Bishop Gastrell's *Notitia Cestriensis*.[3] Although these annals have entries in common with the Mostyn account they appear to be more than merely a series of extracts taken from the longer chronicle. The material they possess in common implies that both sets of annals may derive from a common original, a chronicle written within St. Werburgh's, which contained a good deal of information upon the house and its patron saint.

A mutilated fragment which now forms the first two folios of B.M. MS. Cotton Otho B. iii may once have formed part of this chronicle. The manuscript that contained these folios was almost completely destroyed in the fire at Ashburnham House in 1731. The text of the surviving folios is very faint, and even under ultraviolet light much of it appears to be missing. In the view of Maunde Thompson the fragment was once part of a continuous narrative written at St. Werburgh's during the fourteenth

---

[1] *Annales Cestrienses*, ed. R. C. Christie (Record of Society of Lancashire and Cheshire, vol. xiv, 1887)

[2] *Chartulary of St. Werburgh*, ed. J. Tait (Chetham Society, vol. lxxix, 1920), p. xxiv.

[3] This is now in the diocesan registry at Chester.

century, which contained a fuller account than either of the two surviving sets of annals.[1]

In the absence of this narrative the relationship of the various Chester annals can be little more than a matter of conjecture. It seems reasonable to suppose, however, that Higden's own writing grew out of a small pre-existing corpus of Chester narratives. Certain of his entries in the *Polychronicon* are similar to entries in the *Annales Cestrienses*[2] and both may be related to the narrative of which only the fragments in B.M. MS. Otho B. iii remain.

---

[1] *Annales Cestrienses*, pp. xxiv–xxv.

[2] The entries in the *Polychronicon* and the *Annales* for 1258, 1259, 1264, 1268, 1269, and 1282.

II

THE CHRONICLE BACKGROUND

I

THE fourteenth century was the age of two popular histories, the *Brut* and the *Polychronicon*. Both were produced in an unprecedented number of copies, and appealed to a far wider public than any previous chronicle in England. To both continuations were added which were in themselves important historical works, while in their English versions the *Brut* and the *Polychronicon* were alike printed by Caxton in the course of the fifteenth century. Yet despite these parallels it would be difficult to imagine two more dissimilar histories. A comparison between the *Brut* and the *Polychronicon* reveals at the outset the contrasts latent in this period of chronicle writing.

The *Brut*, an Anglo-French compilation that extended in its earliest versions from the time of Albion and Brutus down to the battle of Halidon Hill in 1333, derived its opening from the *Historia Regum Britanniae* of Geoffrey of Monmouth.[1] Geoffrey had given what professed to be a new and authentic version of British history based on 'a book in the British tongue brought from Brittany by a learned and important friend, Walter, Archdeacon of Oxford'.[2] According to Geoffrey the historical origins of Britain began with Brutus, the great-grandson of Aeneas, who after many wanderings arrived in Britain to become the first king of the island. He called the country after his own name,[3] and

---

[1] *Historia Regum Britanniae*, ed. A. Griscom (1929). The influence of Geoffrey of Monmouth on later chronicles is studied by Laura Keeler, *Geoffrey of Monmouth and the Late Latin Chroniclers 1300–1500* (1946).

[2] T. D. Kendrick, *British Antiquity* (1950), p. 5, which gives an interesting account of Geoffrey's history.

[3] 'Primitus haec insula vocabatur Albion ab albis rupibus circa littora maris a longe apparentibus; tandem a Bruto eam acquirente dicta est Britannia', *Polychronicon*, ii. 4.

built Trinovantum or New Troy. Brutus divided the kingdom between his three sons, Locrinus, Camber, and Albanactus, but after his death the eldest son Locrinus became king of the whole island. Among the British rulers who featured in Geoffrey's account were Bladud who built Bath, Molmutius who made laws, Lud who gave his name to London, and Cassibellanus, the brother of Lud, who twice defeated Caesar. In the Roman period, which began when Arviragus submitted to Claudius, the line of British kings included Lucius, Carausius, Coel, and Constantius. After the departure of the Romans came the great victories of Arthur who conquered Denmark, Norway, Ireland, and Sweden, though 'without leaving the faintest trace of the achievement in the annals or literature of any other nation'.[1]

Such was the start of Geoffrey's remarkable history, which became more marvellous as it proceeded, though, as Gairdner says, 'how it could have been regarded as serious . . . is the greatest marvel of all'.[2] The *Historia Regum Britanniae* was, however, an immediate success. For Alfred of Beverley, who wrote a history of Britain in nine books during the twelfth century, history began with Geoffrey's 'romance'.[3] Though William of Newburgh was not misled by Geoffrey's fictitious history, and denounced what he termed its 'impudent fabrications', criticism was helpless, and the *Historia Regum Britanniae* 'swept away opposition with the ruthless force of a great epic'.[4] Its success lay partly in its literary merit, and partly in the fact that Geoffrey flattered the pride of the British peoples, for he aimed in his writing 'to establish that the British, like the admittedly senior nations of the Mediterranean and the Near East, did come into remote history, and were not barbarians deservedly left out of the main story of the ancient world'.[5]

In the fourteenth century the *Brut*, with this opening, circulated in many copies. The original French text is mostly

---

[1] J. Gairdner, *Early Chroniclers of Europe, England* (1879), p. 161.
[2] Ibid., p. 161.
[3] *Annales sive Historia de gestis Regum Britannie*, ed. T. Hearne (1716).
[4] Kendrick, p. 7.
[5] Ibid. p. 3.

unpublished,[1] though the English version which was translated from the French has been edited by Dr. Brie for the Early English Text Society.[2] His introduction, which was published separately,[3] is the standard work upon the *Brut* manuscripts, of which there are over 160, written in the original French, in English, and in Latin. As a result of Dr. Brie's investigations it can be said that there were two main prose versions of the French *Brut* extending to 1333. Dr. Brie called these the Long and the Short Version,[4] and they used common sources up to 1307. After 1307 the Short Version was based upon the *French Chronicle of London*, and was already closely connected with a London narrative. The Long Version, which was thought to have been written by William Pakington, is in fact an original account of the reign of Edward II and the early years of Edward III, written by a contemporary whose sympathies lay with the Lancastrian cause.[5] Although it is not possible to say where the Long Version was written, the absence of documents in the narrative suggests that its provenance did not lie in a record-keeping institution such as a monastic house.

In the course of the fourteenth century the *Brut* was furnished with further continuations. A standard continuation went to 1377, the full text of which is found in only one manuscript.[6] This narrative drew upon such sources as the Westminster continuations of the *Flores Historiarum*, the chronicle of Murimuth, and the first continuation that was added to Higden's text. After 1377 another continuation was added, which went to 1419, the whole of which may have been written in the 1430's. Individual continuations to the *Brut* were made after 1307 and 1333,[7]

---

[1] See J. Vising, *Anglo-Norman Language and Literature* (London and Oxford, 1923), p. 74. Lists of the manuscripts are given in Vising; P. Meyer, *Bulletin de la Société des anciens textes français* (1878), pp. 116 ff.; Brie, pp. 17 ff., 33; G. E. Brereton, *Des Grantz Geanz*, Medium Aevum Monographs, ii (Oxford, 1937), pp. vi ff.   [2] E.E.T.S. O.S. cxxxi. 136.
[3] Cited as Brie. See review by J. Tait, *E.H.R.* xxi (1906), 616–17.
[4] Brie, p. 17.
[5] See J. Taylor, 'The French *Brut* and the Reign of Edward II', *E.H.R.* lxxii (1957), 423–37.
[6] Corpus Christi College, Cambridge, MS. 174.
[7] V. H. Galbraith, 'The *Historia Aurea* and a French *Brut*', *E.H.R.* xliii (1928),

while the *Anonimalle Chronicle* at St. Mary's, York was written as a continuation of a *Brut* text.[1] Among the laity the *Brut* was probably the most popular chronicle of the day.

Equally popular, though for different reasons, was the *Polychronicon* of Ranulf Higden. Where the *Brut* was a French chronicle, possibly of lay origin, the *Polychronicon* was a Latin history written by a Benedictine monk. While the *Brut* gave a legendary account of British history based upon the story of Geoffrey of Monmouth, the *Polychronicon* offered to the most educated and learned audience in England something which they had never previously known, a clear and convincing picture of world history. Whereas in its early chapters the *Brut* provided fiction and romance, Higden struggled with a mass of classical and medieval sources to give a true picture of the Roman world.

Like the *Brut* the *Polychronicon* enjoyed an enormous success during the fourteenth and fifteenth centuries mainly among the regular and secular clergy. The interest that Higden's work aroused can be seen from the number of copies that were made for monastic houses, cathedral churches, and colleges. The number of copies of the *Polychronicon* must originally have run into many hundreds, for over a hundred manuscripts of the Latin version still survive. The *Polychronicon* killed the demand for the older histories, and religious houses that owned copies of Higden's text added continuations in the course of time. These continuations include some of the main chronicles of the second half of the fourteenth century. Many of the principal accounts of Richard II's reign, the 'Scandalous Chronicle' of Thomas Walsingham, the chronicle of the monk of Westminster, and Adam of Usk's chronicle, followed a copy of Higden's text. Other chronicles reveal the tremendous influence of Higden's work. To chroniclers in the second half of the fourteenth century the *Polychronicon* stood alone.

203–17. The account of the deposition of Edward II which is found in the short French chronicle in B.M. MS. Cotton Julius A. 1 appears after a French *Brut*. See p. 26, note 2.

[1] *Anonimalle Chronicle*, p. xxi.

II

In aim and object the *Polychronicon* was quite different from the majority of monastic chronicles which gave simply a record of contemporary events, whereas the *Polychronicon* was a world history which devoted little space to 'modern times'. The briefest survey of contemporary writing reveals the difference in purpose between most fourteenth-century chronicles and Higden's work.

In medieval England chronicle writing was particularly associated with the Order of St. Benedict. Though there was little in St. Benedict's Rule to imply work of this kind, the later emphasis upon intellectual activity facilitated the writing of history, while the genius and outlook of the Benedictines was perhaps particularly suited to the slow and laborious compilation of annals and chronicles. In the fourteenth century the Benedictines looked back on a long tradition. In Bede they had produced the first historical scholar of repute, in William of Malmesbury the most renowned historian of the Anglo-Norman State, and in Roger of Wendover and Matthew Paris the real founders of the great St. Albans school of history, whose approach has been regarded by some as the medieval equivalent of the 'Whig view of history'.[1] In the fourteenth century the Benedictine output was still important. Their houses continued to produce important chronicles and chroniclers, and in the latter part of the century Thomas Walsingham attempted to write contemporary history in the manner in which Matthew Paris had written it during the thirteenth century.

St. Albans, a day's journey out of medieval London, was the centre of historical writing during the second half of the fourteenth century. After a succession of shadowy figures, 'Rishanger', Trokelowe, and Blaneforde, men of straw after the great figure of Matthew Paris, there appeared in the 1370's the first work of Thomas Walsingham, whose chronicles are a main source of English history until the beginning of the fifteenth

---

[1] V. H. Galbraith, *Roger Wendover and Matthew Paris* (1944). On the chronicles of Matthew Paris see R. Vaughan, *Matthew Paris* (1958).

century.[1] Walsingham is first heard of in 1380 in a manuscript which he wrote, the *Liber Benefactorum*, where his name appears twenty-second in the list of monks of the abbey. Walsingham was *precentor* when he wrote the *Liber Benefactorum*, and in 1394 he left St. Albans to become prior of the cell at Wymondham. He returned to St. Albans at the end of 1396 or early in 1397, and he remained there until he died soon after 1420. Walsingham's main work was a *Chronica Maiora*, which linked the history of his own times to those of Matthew Paris. He began his *Chronica Maiora* with an account of the years 1376–7, which was once found continuing a text of the *Polychronicon*, in MS. Bodley 316.[2] In the later manuscripts of his chronicle which went down to 1420, Walsingham omitted this account of the years 1376–7, which was openly critical of John of Gaunt, and for it substituted a more moderate version. The *Chronica Maiora* as a whole has never been printed, and its text has to be discovered in the various volumes of the St. Albans chronicles printed in the Rolls Series.[3]

Apart from the *Chronica Maiora*, a work which occupied many years, Walsingham also wrote a short history from 1327 to 1422, which was partly an abbreviated version of his *Chronica Maiora*. The text of this chronicle is again distributed between the printed volumes of the Rolls Series, the *Chronicon Angliae* and the *Historia Anglicana*.[4] Apart from these histories, Walsingham wrote the *Ypodigma Neustriae*, an epitome of English history from 911 to 1419, and in the *Gesta Abbatum*, a history of the abbey, he transcribed

---

[1] On the work of Walsingham see V. H. Galbraith's introduction to *The St. Albans Chronicle 1406–1420* (1937).

[2] See V. H. Galbraith, 'Thomas Walsingham and the St. Albans Chronicle', *E.H.R.* xlvii (1932), 12–29. See pp. 124–7.

[3] The contemporary portion of the *Chronica Maiora* is printed:

1376 (Good Parliament) to 1382 in the *Chronicon Angliae*, pp. 68–354.
1382 to 1392 in the *Historia Anglicana*, ii. 70–211.
1393 to 1406 as the *Annales Ricardi II et Henrici IV* in *Trokelowe*, pp. 155–420.
1406 to 1420 in the *St. Albans Chronicle 1406–1420*, ed. V. H. Galbraith.

[4] The text for various years is as follows:

1328–76 in the *Chronicon Angliae* or 1343–77 in the *Historia Anglicana*.
1382–8 in the *Chronicon Angliae*, pp. 355–87.
1392–1422 in the *Historia Anglicana*, ii. 211 seq.

The text for the years 1327, 1377–82, 1388–92, has never been printed.

and continued the work of Matthew Paris and Rishanger.[1] Walsingham also wrote a number of minor works, and a classical treatise which reveals his later interest in the Latin classics.[2]

Among Benedictine monasteries a consistent tradition of chronicle writing is found in the royal foundation at Westminster. The transference of the Chetham manuscript of the *Flores Historiarum*, an abridgement of the work of Matthew Paris, from St. Albans to Westminster at the end of the thirteenth century, marked the beginning of a century of historical writing there, which ended only in 1394. Though the early Westminster chronicles such as the chronicle of Robert of Reading, which covered the years from 1307 to 1325, and the chronicle of John of Reading, which extended from 1346 to 1367,[3] are relatively minor works, they are important because of the scarcity of other sources, and in the reign of Richard II chronicle-writing at Westminster revived with the account of contemporary history (1381–94) by an anonymous monk of that house.[4] Like Walsingham's early history this Westminster chronicle was written as a continuation of Higden's text.[5] Already by the reign of Richard II the *Polychronicon* had become the standard account of early history, an indispensable text, and one whose narrative later chroniclers attempted to continue.

[1] The printed texts of Walsingham in the Rolls Series include the *Chronicon Angliae*, the *Historia Anglicana*, the *Annales Ricardi II et Henrici IV*, the *Ypodigma Neustriae*, and the *Gesta Abbatum*. The *Chronicon Angliae* was edited by E. M. Thompson (1874), and the remainder by H. T. Riley (1863–76). The text of Walsingham's contemporary history is confused in the first two works. Walsingham's authorship and the interrelationship of the St. Albans' manuscripts has been worked out by V. H. Galbraith, 'Thomas Walsingham and the St. Albans Chronicle' (loc. cit.), who printed another portion of Walsingham's chronicle in *The St. Albans Chronicle 1406–1420*.

[2] *The St. Albans Chronicle 1406–1420*, pp. xli–xlv. See Chapter V.

[3] The chronicle of John of Reading is printed in *Chronica Johannis de Reading et Anonymi Cantuariensis*, ed. J. Tait (1914). The chronicle of Robert of Reading is found in the Chetham manuscript of the *Flores Historiarum*, and is printed in the *Flores Historiarum*, ed. H. R. Luard, vol. iii (R.S., 1890).

[4] The Westminster chronicle is printed in the Rolls Series edition of the *Polychronicon*, vol. ix.

[5] J. Armitage Robinson, 'An Unrecognised Westminster Chronicle', *Proceedings of the British Academy*, iii (1907), 61–77. See pp. 127–9.

The Anonimalle Chronicle 1333–1381,[1] written at St. Mary's, York, is a continuation of a French *Brut*. Like the majority of Benedictine chronicles it is a record of recent history, though unlike most it was written in French. The most interesting parts of the *Anonimalle Chronicle* are those which describe the Good Parliament of 1376 and the Peasants' Revolt of 1381. So detailed is the account of the Good Parliament which is found in the *Anonimalle Chronicle* that the chronicler may well have used a London source. The connexion, dating from the time of Thoresby, between Yorkshire clerics and the Chancery which had responsibility for the Parliament Rolls after 1330, may explain the appearance of information about Parliament in a northern chronicle. The account of the Peasants' Revolt that the chronicle gives is almost certainly the work of an eyewitness. Written as it is with a measure of detachment, and with some understanding of the causes of the Rising, this 'anonymous account' comes from a new and a different world from that of the majority of fourteenth-century chronicles.[2]

Though the Benedictines wrote contemporary history Higden's universal chronicle was copied at Malmesbury in the form of the *Eulogium Historiarum*.[3] Its compiler says that his abbot asked him to do something 'by way of a chronicle', and that he set to work therefore to write a history on the lines of Higden's narrative. The *Eulogium Historiarum*, which was completed during the 1360's, is little more than a copy of the *Polychronicon*, though from 1364 it was furnished with a continuation which reveals the prevailing interest in contemporary affairs.[4] The continuation describes, among other matters, an imaginary session of Parliament in May 1374, to deal with the demand of

---

[1] *The Anonimalle Chronicle*, ed. V. H. Galbraith (1927).

[2] G. Kriehn, 'Studies in the Sources of the Social Revolt in 1381', *American Historical Review*, vii (1901), 254–85; A. F. Pollard, 'Authorship and Value of the *Anonimalle Chronicle*', *E.H.R.* liii (1938), 577–605.

[3] *Eulogium Historiarum*, ed. F. S. Haydon, 3 vols. (R.S., 1858). See p. 143.

[4] The continuation of the *Eulogium Historiarum* is found in B.M. MS. Cotton Galba E. vii. It is printed in the Rolls Series text of the *Eulogium*, iii. 333–421. The reasons for a Canterbury origin are given in the introduction to vol. iii.

Gregory XI for the arrears of papal tribute.[1] According to the continuation Archbishop Whittlesey said on this occasion that he could find no answer to the question of papal authority, whereupon the Black Prince replied, 'You ass, answer me: it is your duty to instruct us', a remark which prompted the archbishop to say, 'I am content that the Pope shall not be Lord here'.[2]

Like the Benedictines the Austin canons wrote contemporary histories. At the beginning of the century two Austin canons from Yorkshire, Walter of Guisborough of the house at Guisborough, and Peter Langtoft, a canon of Bridlington, wrote important accounts of Edward I's reign. Though they began their chronicles with the Norman Conquest and with Brutus respectively, their main concern was with the history of their times. Walter of Guisborough described the great crises of Edward's reign; and whatever the inaccuracies of his account, he possessed the gift of depicting clearly the issues upon which men were divided.[3] Peter Langtoft, who wrote in Norman French, has been described as one of 'the most violent Scotophobe historians of all time'.[4] In the last part of his chronicle, which dealt with Edward I's campaigns in Scotland, he wrote of the Scots with an extreme bitterness, which was probably representative of a good deal of contemporary feeling, and into his description of northern battles and campaigns he put extracts from songs such as the exchanges at Berwick.[5] Langtoft's

<hr/>

[1] iii. 337–9.
[2] See Aubrey Gwynn, *The English Austin Friars in the Time of Wyclif* (1940), pp. 218–20. Apart from these chronicles there are Benedictine chronicles of a more domestic kind. Examples of this type of chronicle include the fourteenth-century account of William Thorne who wrote a history of St. Augustine's, Canterbury, *Chronica de rebus gestis abbatum Sancti Augustini Cantuariae, 597–1397*, ed. R. Twysden, *Decem Scriptores* (1652), (translated by A. H. Davies (Oxford, 1934)), and the narrative of John of Glastonbury who wrote a domestic history of Glastonbury, *Historia de rebus Glastoniensibus*, ed. T. Hearne (1726), i. 5–287.
[3] *The Chronicle of Walter of Guisborough*, ed. Harry Rothwell (C.S. lxxxix, 1957). See the introduction to the chronicle.
[4] *The Chronicle of Pierre de Langtoft*, ed. T. Wright, 2 vols. (R.S., 1866–8). There are various studies of his work by Miss Dominica Legge. The section on Langtoft in her book, *Anglo-Norman in the Cloisters* (1950), pp. 70–74, is particularly valuable.
[5] ii. 234–6.

chronicle, which was popular in the north of England, was circulated in different versions.

At the end of the century appeared the chronicle of Henry Knighton, the Austin canon of St. Mary's Leicester, who wrote a history of his own times 1377–95, which he later enlarged into a chronicle beginning with the Norman Conquest, and which he never finished.¹ Knighton's chronicle, the work of a man living in an important centre of Lollardy, is an indispensable source for Richard II's reign, and is of particular importance for its picture of Leicester Lollards.² After 1340 where Knighton's copy of the *Polychronicon* ended his text is all valuable, and is distinguished by 'an unshakeable faith in the house of Lancaster, and a horror of heresy'. Though not written as a formal continuation of the *Polychronicon* Knighton's work shows the tremendous prestige which Higden's chronicle enjoyed during the latter part of the fourteenth century. A great deal of Knighton's retrospective history, from 1066 to 1340, came from the chronicle of Walter of Guisborough, and from the seventh book of the *Polychronicon*. At the point where Higden ended his chronicle Knighton wrote in his own account: 'Here ended the seventh book of the Chester writer (*Cistrensis*). Henceforth the Leicester compiler (*Leycestrensis*) proceeds alone with the task he has undertaken (*opus inceptum*).'³

In the fourteenth century the Cistercians wrote several accounts of contemporary history including the short narratives from Dieulacres and Kirkstall with their information upon the final years of Richard II's reign.⁴ A continuation of the

---

¹ *Chronicon Henrici Knighton*, ed. J. R. Lumby, 2 vols. (R.S., 1889–95). The manuscript of Knighton's chronicle is examined by V. H. Galbraith in 'The Chronicle of Henry Knighton', *F.S.*, pp. 136–45.

² The history of St. Mary's is described by A. Hamilton Thompson, *The Abbey of St. Mary of the Meadows, Leicester* (Leicestershire Archaeological Society, 1949).

³ *Chronicon Henrici Knighton*, i. 479. Quoted by V. H. Galbraith, *F.S.*, p. 144. For Knighton's use of Walter of Guisborough which escaped Lumby see the review by R. L. Poole, *E.H.R.* vi (1891), 172. A study of Knighton's sources between 1340 and 1377 might reveal more than his obvious debt to Walsingham.

⁴ An account of these chronicles is found in M. V. Clarke, *Fourteenth Century Studies* (1937), pp. 53–114. The text of the Kirkstall Chronicle and a translation is printed in the *Proceedings of the Thoresby Society*, vol. xlii (ed. Taylor). The

Polychronicon, which was written at Whalley, contains a description of a 'deposition' of Richard in 1387.[1] Though Cistercian chronicles, which were compiled in the north and midlands, provide information mainly on political events towards the end of the century, the chronicle of Meaux, written about 1400, differs in that it is an example of a domestic chronicle, built around the history of Meaux, with a section upon general history following an account of the tenure of each abbot.[2] The chronicle of 'John of Brompton' stands in a class apart. The compiler, who may have belonged to the Cistercian house of Jervaulx, wrote after 1300, and was clearly influenced by Higden's work.[3] He wrote not a record of recent history but a massive account of English affairs from the conversion of the Saxons down to the time of Edward I. The attempt defeated him, and he stopped in 1199 at the reign of John. As far as he goes, however, Brompton is more detailed than Higden on English history, and he incorporates parts of the *Polychronicon* into his work.[4]

Franciscans and Carmelites in their writings likewise recorded contemporary affairs. A Franciscan work, the 'Lanercost chronicle' extending to 1296, was revised by the Austin canons of Lanercost, and was continued down to 1346 by another Franciscan writer.[5] Parts of the final section of the chronicle, which

Dieulacres Chronicle was edited by M. V. Clarke and V. H. Galbraith in *B.J.R.L.* xiv (1930), 125–81.

[1] See pp. 132–3.
[2] *Chronica monasterii de Melsa*, ed. E. Bond, 3 vols. (R.S., 1866–8).
[3] The work is printed in Twysden, *Decem Scriptores* (1652), cols. 725–1284. The chronicle appears to have been written after 1300 for at col. 747, line 27, there is a reference to John of Ely, Bishop of Norwich (1299–1325). This John of Ely is almost certainly John Salmon, Prior of Ely, who was transferred to Norwich by papal mandate (*V.C.H. Norfolk*, ii. 237).
[4] An example is cols. 910–11 which come from the *Polychronicon*, vi. 118–28. On 'John of Brompton' see p. 144. There are Cistercian chronicles with fourteenth-century entries from Croxden (B.M. MS. Cotton Faustina B. vi, pt. 1, ff. 41–94) to 1374; Hayles (B.M. MS. Cotton Cleopatra D. iii, ff. 1–72) to 1314, and (B.M. MS. Harleian 3725, ff. 1–37) to 1366; Rushen, *Chronicon Manniae* (B.M. MS. Cotton Julius A. vii, ff. 1–52) to 1374; Woburn (B.M. MS. Cotton Domitian A. xii. i) to 1335. Tintern (B.M. MS. Royal 14. c. vi) has a continuation from 1305 to 1323.
[5] The *Chronicon de Lanercost* was edited by Joseph Stevenson for the Bannatyne Club in 1839. There is a translation by Sir Herbert Maxwell (1913). See A. G. Little, *E.H.R.* xxxi (1916), 269–79.

contains a description of Bruce and his followers climbing into Berwick in 1312, read like the account of an eye-witness, though after 1338 the chronology of events is badly confused. A Carmelite work, the *Fasciculi Zizaniorum*, which was copied in 1439 probably at the London Whitefriars for John Keninghale, Prior Provincial of the Carmelite Order, contains a connecting narrative up to 1382, which deals with the heresies of the Oxford followers of Wyclif. This connecting narrative, with its account of Oxford Lollards and its description of the part played by Carmelites as the opponents of Wyclif, was almost certainly written between 1393 and 1399, and is an invaluable source for the academic phase of Lollard history.[1]

Outside the religious houses chronicles were written by secular clerks. The best known of these chroniclers are Adam Murimuth, a canon of St. Paul's, and Robert of Avesbury, a registrar of the court of the Archbishop of Canterbury, both of whom wrote histories of the opening phase of the Hundred Years War.[2] Murimuth knew the workings of the Church and was employed on diplomatic missions to the papal curia. His chronicle is therefore an important source for ecclesiastical as well as military history. Geoffrey le Baker, a secular clerk of Oxfordshire, wrote an account of Edward II's reign at the request of his patron, Sir Thomas de la More,[3] while Adam of Usk, a lawyer, wrote a chronicle of the final years of Richard II's reign and of the early years of Henry IV, which like Walsingham's 'Scandalous Chronicle', and the chronicle of the monk of Westminster, continued Higden's text.[4] Apart from these writings there are other chronicles which were probably written by secular clerks. The *Annales Paulini* which describes the years 1307–41 is possibly the

---

[1] *Fasciculi Zizaniorum magistri Johannis Wyclif cum tritico*, ed. W. Shirley (R.S., 1858). For a study of the *Fasciculi Zizaniorum* see J. Crompton, *Journal of Ecclesiastical History*, xii. 1. 2. The *Fasciculi Zizaniorum* is in large part a collection of documents, and was put together in its present form no earlier than 1436. It may have been started or completed in 1439.

[2] *Chronica A. Murimuth et R. de Avesbury*, ed. E. M. Thompson (R.S., 1889).

[3] *Chronicon Galfridi le Baker de Swynebroke*, ed. E. M. Thompson (1889).

[4] *Chronicon Adae de Usk 1377–1421*, ed. E. M. Thompson (1904). See pp. 129–31.

work of a canon of St. Paul's.[1] It has been suggested that the *Vita Edwardi Secundi* of the so-called 'monk of Malmesbury', one of the best chronicles of Edward II's reign, was written by a clerk to the Earl of Hereford.[2] The author of the *Historia Aurea*, a popular history whose fortunes were to be linked to those of the *Polychronicon*, may have been a priest from the diocese of York,[3] while the rhyming chronicle of Thomas of Castelford, which ended with the reign of Edward II, was probably the work of a Yorkshire cleric.[4]

III

While the *Polychronicon* was a work of some significance in its own day, and Higden's treatment of ancient history is still of interest, much of its historical value comes from the continuations that were added in the course of the fourteenth century. Although the continuations which describe the reign of Richard II are the best known of these accounts, equally important are those which describe the years from 1340 to 1377. Their importance is explained by the scarcity of literary sources between 1340, the point where the *Polychronicon* originally ended, and 1377 when chronicle writing again revived.

At the beginning of the fourteenth century a number of chronicles described the events of Edward II's reign. These include the *Annales Londonienses*, the *Annales Paulini*,[5] and the

[1] *Chronicles of Edward I and Edward II*, ed. W. Stubbs (R.S., 1882–3), i. 253–70.
[2] *Vita Edwardi Secundi*, ed. N. Denholm-Young (1957). He suggests that the author was John Walwayn, D.C.L., a Herefordshire lawyer. See pp. xix–xxviii.
[3] He is called John of the diocese of York in the Durham copy of his work. V. H. Galbraith, 'Sources of the St. Albans Chronicle', *Essays in History Presented to R. Lane-Poole*, ed. H. W. C. Davis (1927), pp. 379–98. See pp. 101–2.
[4] The chronicle is unpublished, and the manuscript is at Göttingen, MS. Hist. 740. On Castelford's chronicle see M. L. Perrin, *Über Thomas Castelford's 'Chronik'* (1890). A part of the chronicle has been edited by F. Behre, *Göteborgs Högskolas Årsskrift*, vol. xlvi (1940). There are articles on the words in the chronicle in F. Behre, *Papers on English Vocabulary and Syntax* (Almqvist and Wiksell, Göteborg, 1961). I owe these references to Professor A. S. C. Ross. The chronicle is discussed in my *Medieval Historical Writing in Yorkshire* (St. Anthony's Hall Publication no. 19, 1961), pp. 18–19.
[5] *Chronicles of Edward I and Edward II*, ed. W. Stubbs (R.S., 1882–3). The *Annales Londonienses* is particularly valuable for the period to 1316, and the *Annales Paulini* covers the whole reign.

Vita Edwardi Secundi whose account extends to 1325.[1] The deposition of Edward, which his patron Sir Thomas de la More had witnessed, was recounted by Geoffrey le Baker, and also by the author of the short French chronicle bound up with the Pipewell register.[2] Several chronicles dealt also with the early years of Edward III. The canon of Bridlington's *Gesta Edwardi de Carnavan*, compiled in its present form some forty years later, contains a lengthy account of Balliol's Scottish campaigns,[3] the *Annales Paulini* extend to 1341, and the chronicles of Murimuth and Avesbury deal with the opening phase of the Hundred Years War.

After these chronicles no first-class contemporary chronicle was written between 1340 and 1377. This period, which saw the opening phase of the Hundred Years War and the development of Parliament, is from a chronicle view-point almost a lacuna in our history. Murimuth's chronicle ends at 1347, Avesbury's and Geoffrey le Baker's at 1356, and Sir Thomas Gray's at 1362. The narratives that cover the period beyond this, such as the *Eulogium Historiarum*, and the chronicle of the anonymous monk of Canterbury,[4] are, on the whole, brief and uninformative. Because of the scarcity of chronicle sources, the undistinguished narrative of the Westminster chronicler, John of Reading, must be considered an important source for the years 1356–67. Not until 1376 with the appearance of Walsingham did Edward III's reign find a real

---

[1] The account is continued down to 1348 by extracts from the *Polychronicon*.
[2] The short French chronicle is found in MS. Cotton Julius A. 1. The chronicle was used by M. V. Clarke in 'Committees of Estates', and the text was printed in *Medieval Representation and Consent* (1936), pp. 193–5. Miss Clarke assigned the chronicle to Pipewell, for the manuscript contains extracts from the register of Pipewell. On the contents of this manuscript see H. G. Richardson, and G. Sayles, 'Early Coronation Records', *Bulletin of the Institute of Historical Research*, xiv (1936), 145–8, and Miss Richardson's article on the letters to Queen Isabella concerning the rising of the lepers in France in 1321, *Medium Aevum*, x (1941), 15–25.
[3] *Chronicles of Edward I and Edward II*, ed. W. Stubbs (R.S., 1883), ii. 25–151. The chronicle must have been written in its present form after 1363 because it quotes the Bridlington prophecies.
[4] This is found in Lambeth MS. 99, and has been attributed to Stephen Birchington, a monk of Christ Church, Canterbury. It is printed by J. Tait, *Chronica Johannis de Reading et Anonymi Cantuariensis*, pp. 187–227. It is of some slight importance after 1346.

historian. Walsingham's work marks a new birth of chronicle writing, seen also in the chronicle of the anonymous monk of Westminster, Knighton's chronicle, the *Anonimalle Chronicle*, and the chronicle of Adam of Usk. These accounts contain a commentary upon contemporary events which is strikingly absent from the majority of Edward III narratives.

The reasons for the failure of the chronicle sources during the period 1340–77 must remain speculative. Several important chronicles of Edward II's reign were continuations of the *Flores Historiarum*, the abridged version of Matthew Paris. By the middle of the century, however, the age of the *Flores* continuations was passing, though contributions continued to be added, particularly at Westminster. As the tradition of Matthew Paris receded there was little to take its place apart from those continuations which were added to the *Brut* chronicle.[1] The age of Edward III saw also the opening phase of the Hundred Years War, which occasioned a considerable volume of political literature.[2] To the 1340's belongs *Le Voeu du Héron*, a grimly satirical poem that reflected external opposition to Edward's war,[3] while other poems and songs, including the works of Laurence Minot, expressed the more popular, militant spirit of the time.[4] As regards chronicle writing, however, this period lacked the political interest of both the beginning and the end of the century. In the reign of Edward III attention was concentrated upon events taking place in the provinces of France. Religious houses in England, which were still the chief centres of historical writing, were distant from these events, and relied for their information upon sources from abroad. The chronicle accounts of this period are, therefore, frequently little more than a record of campaigns,

---

[1] The *Historia Aurea* was sometimes used to cover the period from the 1320's to the 1340's.

[2] See *Political Poems and Songs*, ed. T. Wright, 2 vols. (R.S., 1859–61).

[3] It is printed by La Curne de Sainte-Palaye in *Mémoires sur l'ancienne chevalerie* (Paris, 1759–81), iii. 119–37; T. Wright, *Political Poems and Songs*, i. 1–25. See the comments of B. J. Whiting, *Speculum*, xx (1945), 261–78.

[4] See T. Wright, *Political Poems and Songs*, i. 26–40, 53–93; *The Poems of Laurence Minot*, ed. Joseph Hall (Oxford, 1898); R. H. Robbins, *Historical Poems of the Fourteenth and Fifteenth Centuries* (New York, 1959).

augmented here and there by the contents of news letters.[1] Chronicle writing only revived during the reign of Richard II when interest was again concentrated upon events at home. As in the days of Edward II, religious houses in the south of England were conveniently placed to describe the struggle between the king and the barons.

It is for the middle years of the century, therefore, from the 1340's to the 1370's, that the first continuations of the *Polychronicon* are important. Copies of Higden's work, which was the most popular Latin chronicle of the day, were quickly acquired by monastic houses and by cathedral churches. Within a few years the *Polychronicon* was furnished with a standard form of continuation which extended from the point where Higden's text ended in the 1340's to the end of Edward III's reign in 1377. Together with the chronicle of John of Reading, which ended in 1367, the first continuation of the *Polychronicon* is an important literary source for a period when chronicle accounts are few. The influence of the *Polychronicon*, however, extended beyond this. The popularity of Higden's work ended the demand for copies of the early histories, and in the second half of the fourteenth century history was written as a continuation of the *Polychronicon*. Walsingham's early history followed a copy of Higden's text, the chronicle of the monk of Westminster continued a *Polychronicon*, and the chronicle of Adam of Usk is found in a manuscript of the *Polychronicon* which Adam owned.[2] The work of Henry Knighton, which was not written as a formal continuation of Higden's chronicle, based its early chapters on Higden's seventh book. In the field of chronicle writing the second half of the fourteenth century was the age of the *Polychronicon*.

The *Polychronicon* helped, therefore, to keep historical writing alive during this period, while its later continuations include some of the most important narratives of the reign of Richard II. The main problem which concerns these later continuations is the suspicion once thought to attach to all chronicles which

---

[1] Avesbury and the *Historia Aurea* transcribe many letters in this part of their narrative.   [2] See Chapter VII for a discussion of these continuations.

described the Lancastrian seizure of the throne. Monastic chronicles were official documents, and the revolution of 1399 might well have had the effect of making English historiography conform to the Lancastrian tradition. A study of the later continuations reveals, however, that no such work of historical revision was carried out after 1399. Walsingham's contemporary history which was bitterly hostile to John of Gaunt was revised and removed from the later versions of his chronicle, but the revision was done before the deposition of Richard, and was not carried out in any general rewriting of history which went on after 1399.[1]

IV

Whatever its differences in aim and emphasis, as a monastic chronicle the *Polychronicon* was representative of the overwhelming majority of the chronicles of the time. Lay society which in the reign of Richard II was to produce a remarkable vernacular literature produced as yet few lay histories. The demand for a vernacular literature as finished as the French romances came in part from the court of the king, but the courts of Edward II and Edward III were not notable centres of historical studies. The aristocracy commissioned and read comparatively few chronicles.[2] History when known to them was known mainly in the form of the *Brut* and the historical material of the French romances. Among the few traces which remain of fourteenth-century lay libraries is one belonging to Guy, Earl of Warwick, who in 1315 left a collection of manuscripts to the Abbey of Bordesley. The list of manuscripts from his library includes 'most of the famous names of popular history:—Lancelot, Arthur and Modred', and among the romances and the Lives of Saints a *Brut*.[3]

[1] See V. H. Galbraith, 'Thomas Walsingham and the St. Albans Chronicle', (loc. cit.). See also Chapter VII.
[2] Sir Thomas de la More was the patron of Geoffrey le Baker, and Froissart, Trevisa, and Créton had aristocratic patrons.
[3] K. Sisam, *Fourteenth Century Verse and Prose*, pp. xxxi–xxxii. The works which belonged to members of the court are discussed by E. Rickert, 'King Richard II's Books', *Library*, xiii (1933), 144–7.

The middle of the fourteenth century saw the appearance of the first chronicle to be written by an English layman. Sir Thomas Gray of Heton, a soldier, wrote a history while he was imprisoned at Edinburgh in 1355. His *Scalacronica*, as the work was known, is important for its account of Border history.[1] In the prologue to the chronicle Gray explained how he came to write his work. A Sibyl appeared to him in a dream, and led him to a ladder held by the chronicler, Thomas of Otterbourne. As he climbed the ladder Gray saw various chroniclers at work including the translator of the *Brut*, Bede, John of Tynemouth, and Higden. The presence of Higden in this scheme is worth noting, for Gray began his chronicle in 1355 during Higden's lifetime. A different type of lay historian was Créton, 'a French gentleman of distinction, attendant upon Richard II with the permission of the King of France'. Créton who wrote the *Histoire du roy d'Angleterre Richard*[2] came to England in 1399 as a squire of a French knight, and by the influence of the Earl of Salisbury was attached to Richard during his Irish expedition. He was an eyewitness of the events of the Irish campaign, and he recounted from other sources the circumstances of Richard's deposition which took place after he had returned to France. Créton wrote his chronicle about 1401 at the suggestion of the Earl of Salisbury. In a letter of 1402 he said that he wrote to hold up to shame in France the lives and actions of Richard's enemies, and his later life proved his attachment to Richard's cause. A report in 1402 that Richard was alive in Scotland caused Créton to leave France and discover the truth for himself. When he found that the report was false he urged the Duke of Burgundy, regent for Charles VI, to revenge Richard.[3] Créton's chronicle was translated by Stowe, and used by Holinshed, and through Holinshed it forms one source for the

---

[1] The *Scalacronica* was edited in part by J. Stevenson (1836), and the last part has been translated by H. Maxwell (Glasgow, 1907).

[2] Ed. J. A. C. Buchon, *Collection des chroniques françaises*, xxiv (Paris, 1826), 323–466. A translation of this chronicle by the Revd. John Webb appeared in *Archaeologia*, xx (1824), 1–423. The translation was not based upon the best text.

[3] See *Archaeologia*, xx, Introduction.

sympathetic portrait of Richard which is found in Shakespeare's play.[1]

Among lay chronicles of this period must be included the fourteenth-century chronicles of London, though they lack both the importance and the interest of the later London histories.[2] The *Annales Londonienses*, written in Latin, describes the reign of Edward II, and is an early example of London entries compiled by an author who had access to documents and to corporation records.[3] The brief *French Chronicle of London* extends from the end of Henry III's reign to the early years of Edward III and is more annalistic in method.[4] Apart from these writings there are French additions to the official record of London contained in the *Liber de Antiquis Legibus*,[5] while London chronicles may survive in the sources of the *Brut* for the reign of Richard II. Apart from these examples the great majority of chronicles continued to be written within the Church. The fourteenth century was the last great century of monastic writing before

---

[1] Another source for Shakespeare's Richard was the *Chronique de la traïson et mort*, claimed to have been written by a French Benedictine monk attached to St. George's Chapel, Windsor, who was in England on the business of St. Denis, after crossing in the train of Bolingbroke (ed. with English translation by B. Williams, *English Historical Society*, 1846). Unlike Créton the author of the *Chronique de la traïson et mort* remained in England after Richard had been brought to London, and he describes the final scenes with an authenticity not present in Créton's work. A third French chronicle of Richard's deposition, equally sympathetic to Richard, is the *Chronique de Richard II (1377–1399)*, ed. J. A. C. Buchon, *Collection des chroniques françaises*, xxv, supplement ii (Paris, 1826), 1–79. The French chronicles of Richard II's reign are a reminder that French influence was strong in England throughout the century, and that French chroniclers are among those who wrote important accounts of English history. Though it would be inappropriate to discuss their work in detail, the writings of Jean le Bel and of Froissart must be included among the important chronicles of the period. Jean le Bel, canon of St. Lambert of Liège, wrote an account of English history from 1326 to 1361 in his *Vrayes Chroniques*. Jean le Bel was an eyewitness of events in England in the 1320's, and his account of conditions in York and Northumberland is valuable for that reason alone (ed. M. L. Polain, *Jehan le Bel, Les Vrayes Chroniques* (Brussels, 1863), 2 vols.). For the text of Froissart the editions are those of Kervyn de Lettenhove (25 vols., Brussels, 1867–77) and S. Luce and G. Raynaud, *Société de l'histoire de France* (to 1385) (Paris, 1869–99).

[2] For the London chronicles of the fifteenth century see Kingsford, pp. 70–112.

[3] *Chronicles of Edward I and II*, ed. W. Stubbs (R.S., 1882), i. 4–251.

[4] Ed. G. J. Aungier (C.S. xxviii, 1844).

[5] Ed. T. Stapleton (C.S. xxxiv, 1846).

the rise of vernacular histories designed to appeal to a different audience and to different interests.[1] The monastic chronicles of the fourteenth century are of particular interest, therefore, both as the last great expression of monastic history, and as a commentary 'from within' upon their age and times.

[1] The predominance of the monastic chronicle ensured the supremacy of Latin as the language of history. Chronicles written in French and in English are a distinct minority among the chronicles of this period. Those which were written in French, such as Langtoft's chronicle, the *Anonimalle Chronicle*, and the chronicle of Créton come from northern religious houses or from lay sources. Chronicles composed in English were few and unimportant. The rhyming chronicle of Robert of Gloucester, written during the reign of Edward I, ed. W. A. Wright, 2 vols. (R.S., 1887) was followed by the rhyming chronicle of Thomas of Castelford, composed by a Yorkshire cleric towards the end of Edward II's reign, see p. 25, note 4. Castelford's chronicle which survives in a single manuscript, now at Göttingen, is derived largely from the work of Geoffrey of Monmouth. A more promising field for the use of English was the translation of chronicles originally composed in Latin or French. In 1338 Robert of Brunne translated parts of Langtoft's chronicle into English with additions from Wace's *Brut* (*The Story of England*, ed. F. J. Furnivall, 2 vols. (R.S., 1887).) The *Brut* itself appeared in an English version which was written in the period 1340–70.

III

THE *POLYCHRONICON* AND UNIVERSAL HISTORIES

IGDEN's work represents in many respects the summit of medieval chronicle writing in England, and it evoked an immediate response from the educated clergy. The vogue of the *Polychronicon* was bound up with the growing study of the classics and of all things old. Though it was written in its earliest version no later than the 1320's, the Renaissance was now not far distant, and monks and bishops were beginning to take a wider and more individual view of the remoter past. Higden's chronicle gave to the most educated section of contemporary society a picture of antiquity and of early history such as they had never previously possessed. It was because of this achievement that the *Polychronicon* commended itself so quickly to a far wider public than any preceding historical work.

I

Universal history, of which in fourteenth-century England the *Polychronicon* was the outstanding example, arose within the Judaeo-Christian tradition where God was the God of all peoples.[1] Medieval history was universal because it was the record of the acts of God in history. Though universalizing tendencies were present in ancient history, classical historians had viewed the past with particular reference to Greece or Rome. The medieval chronicler, however, saw history not in relation to a particular

---

[1] For a discussion of Christian historiography see 'The Influence of Christianity' in R. G. Collingwood, *The Idea of History* (1946), pp. 46–56.
I am also indebted in these comments to C. A. Patrides's remarks on universal chronicles in his study of the rise and decline of the Christian view of history, *The Phoenix and the Ladder* (1964).

people or civilization as the ancient historians had done, but in relation to God's purpose for the whole of mankind. History written along such lines began with the Creation. It dealt with the first man, and outlined the manner in which the various nations had arisen in the course of time. Universal history broke with the cyclical theories of the Graeco-Romans, and substituted a linear view of history which began with the Creation, and moved forward to the final judgement. The birth of Christ divided the temporal process: before that event there had been a period of darkness and error; after came the period of the triumph of the faith.[1] Because the life of Christ was the central event in history, all historical divisions and periods had reference to this.

To reconcile the narratives of different peoples, and to demonstrate the unity of Christian history, a single chronological framework was needed. This was supplied by Eusebius of Caesarea (c. 260–340), whose great chronological tables gave, in parallel columns, a list of dates drawn from Assyrian, Hebrew, Egyptian, Greek, and Roman times.[2] The *Chronographia* demonstrated the universal nature of history, and in his other writings Eusebius described how the events of the pre-Christian world were but the prologue to the Christian age. If Eusebius provided universal history with its chronology, Augustine (354–430) supplied it with its philosophy. The theme of the two cities, one temporal, the other eternal, occasioned by the fall of Rome, dominated historical thinking for several centuries. In Augustine's thought only the City of God had permanence, and history progressed through the six ages.[3] These ages extended

---

[1] *Polychronicon*, i. 30.

[2] The original work of Eusebius has been reconstructed from an Armenian version published by J. B. Aucher at Venice in 1818. Jerome's translation of Eusebius is found in *P.L.* 27. 9–702.

[3] On Augustine see W. J. Oates, *Basic Writings of St. Augustine* (New York, 1948), I. ix–xl; T. E. Mommsen, 'St. Augustine and the Christian Idea of Progress', *Medieval and Renaissance Studies* (Cornell, 1959), pp. 265–98; J. N. Figgis, *The Political Aspects of St. Augustine's City of God* (London, 1921). A main contribution of Augustine to medieval historiography was the emphasis which he placed upon the periodization of history. 'To think history', says Croce, 'is to divide it into periods', but periodization owed much to Christian thought. Augustine was

from the Creation to Noah, from Noah to Abraham, from Abraham to David, from David to the Babylonish captivity, from the Babylonish captivity to the birth of Christ, and from the birth of Christ to the day of judgement.[1] Medieval chroniclers lived, as they believed, in the last age of history, and in the twelfth century the impending end of the world powerfully affected writers otherwise as different as Otto of Freising and Joachim of Flora.[2]

To the six ages was added the concept of the great empires. In the East in Hellenistic times there had developed a view of history based upon a sequence of great empires. 'Four of these empires were to follow one another, and the series was to conclude with a fifth monarchy which was to last until the end of the world.'[3] In the Christian era the prophecies of the Book of Daniel (vii. 2–27) favoured this interpretation. The Roman Empire was seen as the last in the sequence of world monarchies, and the period of the Roman Empire coincided also with the sixth age of the world. In this way a new age opened up which would last until the day of judgement.

In his own lifetime Augustine commissioned the Spanish monk, Orosius, to write one type of universal history. The *Historia adversus paganos* (417–18) was part of the Augustinian

interested in periods, which he called the *articuli temporum sive aetatum*. In his writings he speaks of the six ages of the world, which correspond to the six days of Creation. The attempt to distinguish periods in history has been called 'the mark of a mature and advanced historical thought', R. G. Collingwood, *The Idea of History*, p. 53, and the theory of the six ages held the field in Europe until it was replaced by the notion, held by the humanist historians, of a division between classical antiquity and the period which followed. On the views of the humanist historians see W. K. Ferguson, *The Renaissance in Historical Thought* (Cambridge, Mass., 1948); T. E. Mommsen, 'Petrarch's Conception of the Dark Ages', *Medieval and Renaissance Studies*, pp. 106–29; D. Hay, 'Flavio Biondo and the Middle Ages', *Proceedings of the British Academy*, xlv (1959), 97–127. For Augustine's view of the six ages see *P.L.* 34. 190 ff.; 37. 1182.

[1] In the *Polychronicon* which is organized according to the six ages, Higden described the ages as periods marked off by miraculous events, i. 30–40. Lactantius in the *Institutiones Divinae*, vii. 14 (*C.S.E.L.* xix) stated that each age was of a thousand years duration, but there is little evidence that his views were accepted in England.

[2] See p. 38.

[3] T. E. Mommsen, 'St. Augustine and the Christian Idea of Progress' (loc. cit.).

argument that the sack of Rome was not unique. As Orosius says in the dedication of his work to Augustine, 'You bade me discover from all the available data of histories and annals whatever instances past ages have afforded of the burdens of war, the ravages of disease, the horrors of famine, of terrible earthquakes, extraordinary floods, dreadful volcanic eruptions, thunderbolts, and hailstorms, and also of the cruel miseries caused by parricides and by crimes against man's better self.'[1] So well did Orosius perform his task, and so successful was he in imposing a pattern upon history, that his 'History of the World' won instant recognition, and remained popular throughout the Middle Ages.

Apart from the history of Orosius other universal chronicles appeared in the course of the fifth and sixth centuries. Sulpicius Severus (*c.* 363–425) wrote an account of world history which began with the Creation and extended to A.D. 403; St. Prosper of Aquitaine (*c.* 400–60) wrote a world chronicle to the time of the Emperor Valens (A.D. 378); Fulgentius (*c.* 480–550) wrote a universal history, *De Aetatibus Mundi*; while Victor of Tunnuna wrote a *Chronicle* from the Creation to 566. In the sixth century Cassiodorus in the *Historia Tripartita* translated with others the ecclesiastical histories of Socrates, Sozomen, and Theodoret.[2] Though he was an encyclopaedist rather than a chronicler, Isidore of Seville (*c.* 560–636), popularized the notion of the six ages and included a chronicle in his *Etymologiae*,[3] while Gregory of Tours in the *Historia Francorum*, written in the sixth century, was not alone in beginning his history with the origins of the world.

Few universal chronicles appeared in the Carolingian period.[4] The *Chronicon universale anni 741* has little value, and after 710 adopts the annalistic form. Only from the reign of Louis the Debonair do universal chronicles reappear with the writings of

---

[1] Quoted by T. E. Mommsen, 'Orosius and Augustine', *Medieval and Renaissance Studies*, pp. 330–1.

[2] For an account of these histories see J. W. Thompson, *A History of Historical Writing* (New York, 1942), vol. i.

[3] Isidore's views are given in the *Etymologiae*, v. 38–9.

[4] See the comments of J. de Ghellinck, *Littérature latine au Moyen Âge* (Paris, 1939), i. 154–9.

Freculph of Lisieux (835) and Ado of Vienne (874). The *Chronicorum libri duo* of Freculph of Lisieux was a universal chronicle that surveyed world history down to the age of Boniface III. The *Breviarium chronicorum* of Ado of Vienne was also an account of world history that progressed through the six ages. At no time, however, was the universal chronicle more popular than during the twelfth and thirteenth centuries. One example of a world chronicle of this period is the *Chronographia* of Sigebert of Gembloux (*c.* 1030–1112). Sigebert used the chronicles of Eusebius–Jerome, and the popularity of his work can be seen in the many continuations which were added to it during the twelfth century. Other universal chronicles include the *Chronica* of Hugh of Flavigny (*c.* 1065–*c.* 1111), the *Historia ecclesiastica* of Hugh of Fleury, an historical compilation beginning with Abraham which enjoyed immediate success, and the chronicle (1125) of Ekkehard of Aura, which has been described as 'the best world chronicle of the Middle Ages'. Earlier, Hermann of Reichenau, Lambert of Hersfeld, and Marianus Scotus, an expatriate Irishman who died at Mayence about 1082,[1] all wrote universal histories which employed the scheme of the six ages. In the thirteenth century the *Chronologia* of Robert of Auxerre, compiled about 1200, displaced Sigebert of Gembloux's work in popular esteem. Histories of this kind were also written by Helinand of Froidmont and Aubri of Trois-Fontaines. In Spain Bishop Lucas of Tuy, who died in 1249, wrote a *Chronicon mundi* which began with the Creation.

Among these writings it is possible to distinguish between works such as the *Chronica Maiora* of Matthew Paris which, though they might begin with the Creation, dealt mainly with the writer's times, and compilations that described at length the early history of the world. Among universal chronicles dealing at length with early history was the twelfth-century *Historia de duabus civitatibus* of Otto of Freising, which described the course

---

[1] The chronicle of Marianus Scotus is printed in Migne, *P.L.* 147. 623 seq., but with only an epitome of Books I and II. These books are printed in the Basle edition of 1559, *Germanicarum Rerum Quatuor Celebriores Vetustioresque Chronographi.*

of world history from the Creation to the writer's day. As its title suggests the *History of the Two Cities* was a version of the Augustinian theme, and Otto dealt with the early history of the Church and of the Roman state.[1] He wrote in the conviction that a Second Coming was at hand, a view shared by Joachim of Flora, who divided history into three periods, those of the Father, Son, and Holy Ghost, the third of which had yet to come. During the thirteenth century the most famous universal chronicle was the *Speculum Historiale* of Vincent of Beauvais. Vincent was a Dominican, born about 1190, whose greatest work, the *Speculum Maius*, an encyclopaedia of contemporary knowledge, included a volume on history, the *Speculum Historiale*.[2] In his chronicle Vincent gave an account of universal history beginning with the Creation, and describing the history of Rome in the greatest detail.[3] In his work eight books dealt with Roman history from the times of Caesar to the age of Constantine. Whatever the defects of this work it was a triumph of industry. Composed of extracts from a vast number of classical and medieval writings, the *Speculum Historiale* was a massive statement of contemporary knowledge, and though Vincent treated no period briefly, his account of ancient history was probably the most remarkable aspect of his work.

In England universalizing tendencies in chronicle writing were present from the earliest times. Though there were chroniclers

---

[1] The text is printed by Hofmeister in *Scriptores Rerum Germanicarum in usum scholarum* (Hanover and Leipzig, 1912). There is a translation by C. C. Mierow (New York, 1928). Otto was not concerned as Augustine had been with the mystical interpretation of the two cities. His aim was different and more historical. As he himself says, 'I have undertaken to speak of the two cities in such a way that we shall not lose the thread of history' (Mierow, p. 70). In the work of Otto of Freising there was a more historical version of the Augustinian theme. The heavenly city, after the birth of Christ, was found in the Church, and the earthly city was found in the world monarchies, where the German Empire took its place as the successor of Rome.

[2] The edition of the *Speculum Historiale* which has been used is the 1624 edition of Balthazaris Belleri.

[3] See B. L. Ullman, 'A Project for a New Edition of Vincent of Beauvais', *Speculum*, viii (1933), 312–26. E. Boutaric, 'Vincent de Beauvais et la connaissance de l'antiquité classique au treizième siècle', *Revue des questions historiques*, xvii (1875), 5–57.

such as William of Newburgh who began their writings at a definite historical date, most chroniclers began with the Creation, or with the legendary arrival of Brutus. Apart from the world history of Marianus Scotus, however, which was known in England through the continuation added to it by Florence of Worcester, no chronicler wrote a major account of world history until Ranulf Higden composed his *Polychronicon* in the fourteenth century. The *Polychronicon* was the first chronicle written in England to treat world history on an extended scale.[1] Its contents reveal just what world history meant in Higden's time.

II

The *Polychronicon* is arranged in seven books after the example, so Higden says, of the first Worker, who accomplished everything in six days, and who rested on the seventh.[2] The first book was concerned with Higden's geographical description, and the second began the account of universal history with a description of the genesis of the world.[3] Higden described Adam, the first man, created 'from the slime of the earth', his disobedience to God's command, and his exile from Eden. The list of names of Adam's progeny in the early chapters of this book indicated the unity of mankind. From the children of Adam, and the kingdoms that they had founded, had come the family of nations among which the greatest powers had been Assyria, Persia, Greece, and Rome. Higden's roll call of early man was interrupted to enable him to discourse on the longevity of the patriarchs, and the building of the Ark, and to indicate with the help of sketches the

[1] There are over 300,000 words in Higden's account.
[2] *Polychronicon*, i. 26.
[3] It should be noted that Higden's 'books' do not accord with the printed volumes of the Rolls Series. In the Rolls Series edition the books are printed:

> Book I (Vol. i. 2–430; vol. ii. 1–174)
> Book II (Vol. ii. 174–450; vol. iii. 2–104)
> Book III (Vol. iii. 104–478; vol. iv. 2–250)
> Book IV (Vol. iv. 252–474; vol. v. 2–256)
> Book V (Vol. v. 256–460; vol. vi. 2–352)
> Book VI (Vol. vi. 352–476; vol. vii. 2–246)
> Book VII (Vol. vii. 248–496; vol. viii. 2–346)

manner in which the men, birds, and animals had been arranged inside the Ark according to Augustine and to other authorities.[1]

In its later chapters this book carried Higden into a wider stream of historical events.[2] Greek history began with a discussion of the Greek myths, and a brief description of the Trojan war. This account was taken from the *De Excidio Troiae Historia* of Dares Phrygius, and followed its source in minimizing the role of Aeneas in the defence of Troy, and in providing a 'romantic interest' between Achilles and Polyxena, daughter of Priam.[3] Higden described the return of the Greeks to their home,[4] and the wanderings of Aeneas before his arrival in Italy.[5] Among the heroes of the ancient world no Greek of history or legend was more famous than Alexander of Macedon. The chapters on Alexander in the third book of the *Polychronicon* are eloquent of the Alexander legend of the Middle Ages.[6] Higden described Alexander's wars against the Persians and his expedition to India. He told of Alexander's entry into Jerusalem[7] and of his visit to the camp of Darius disguised as a messenger.[8] He mentioned the appeal 'from Alexander drunk to Alexander sober',[9] and copied the imaginary correspondence between Alexander and Dindimus, king of the Brahmans, which was well known during this period.[10] Despite the high regard in which the Greek king was held, both as a conqueror and as a source of *exempla*, no consistent view of the Greek hero emerged in Higden's chapters,

---

[1] ii. 236.

[2] In the third age from Abraham to David Higden gave an account of Isaac and Moses. He included the story of Moses and the rings of memory and forgetfulness, ii. 322–4. It is from the *Historia Scholastica, Liber Exod.* c. 6.

[3] See Chapter V.

[4] ii. 418–30. Higden was interested in the change of Diomedes' followers into birds and Ulysses' companions into swine, and he quoted William of Malmesbury and Giraldus Cambrensis on the possibility of this.

[5] For Higden's views on the possibility of Aeneas meeting Dido see Chapter V.

[6] See G. Cary, *The Medieval Alexander* (1956). For a discussion of the sources see Chapter V.

[7] iii. 418–20. The source which Higden quotes is the *Historia Scholastica* (*P.L.* 198, cols. 1490–8). This is also quoted in the *Speculum Historiale*, iv. 32. See Cary, pp. 127–30.

[8] iii. 430–2. Cary, pp. 364–5.   [9] iii. 442. Cary, p. 100.

[10] iii. 454–78.

which were an anthology of extracts taken from the Alexander books and the *Speculum Historiale* of Vincent of Beauvais.[1]

Once Higden had described the genesis of the world he was free to devote himself more fully to classical times. In the third book he began his account of Roman history. The account of the Roman world was a part of Higden's chronicle on which he bestowed much care. It remains one of the best parts of his narrative and his chapters reflect the new interest in classical studies which was developing during his lifetime.[2] In the first book of his chronicle Higden had described the city of Rome and the customs and institutions of the Roman people.[3] In the second book he described the development of Rome from its legendary foundation on the banks of the Tiber,[4] but his account became more detailed in the third book with the story of Hannibal's campaigns, and the destruction of Carthage. Finally, with the times of Caesar Rome became the principal subject of his chronicle. In successive chapters he dealt with the central epoch of Roman history, that is to say, the rule of Caesar, the rise to power of Augustus, and the establishment of the empire.[5] The story of political events, clearly told, did not prevent him from adding notices concerning Roman authors; and entries on the birth of Horace, the education of Virgil, and the banishment of Ovid found a place in his narrative.

The nature of Higden's account of Roman history can be seen from two brief extracts taken from these chapters. The first comes from a chapter composed of stories about Caesar:

Caesar fought fifty times in pitched battle. And yet no one wrote more swiftly, or read more speedily. He was accustomed to dictate four letters at once, and those whom he overcame by arms he

---

[1] See p. 73. In the case of the murder of Callisthenes Higden followed his main source, the *Speculum Historiale* of Vincent of Beauvais, in adopting a more critical attitude towards Alexander than had been customary. In the *Polychronicon* the murder of Callisthenes was associated with the murder of Cleitus, after Callisthenes had dissuaded Alexander from committing suicide in a fit of repentance. Higden also told the story of Lysimachus being thrown to the lions for helping to mitigate the tortures of Callisthenes: iii. 448–50. Cary, p. 114.

[2] See Chapter V for a discussion of Higden's sources.

[3] i. 206–52. [4] iii. 52–66. [5] iv. 188–250.

conquered through mildness. There was no day in the tumult of war when he did not write, read, or practise oratory. Julius Caesar, whose hand was no less apt with the pen than the sword, who governed the state better than anyone, in the whole of his rule ordered only one man to be slain, that is to say Domicius, to whom he had previously granted his life, but when he later saw him fighting against him a second time, though he had forsworn arms in the civil war, he said to his soldiers, 'It is enough that I have spared the life of this ungrateful man once.' He had never so much hatred against anyone, but that given the occasion he could abandon it. Caesar was a man of great patience. For the soldiers at the time of his triumph in Rome said in his hearing and without provoking his anger, 'Caesar triumphs, who has conquered the Gauls, but why is there no triumph for Nicomedes, the king of Bithynia, who has conquered Caesar?', for Caesar was said to be excessively friendly towards him. . . .[1]

The second passage is more typical of Higden's 'narrative of events', and is taken from a chapter entitled 'The civil war between Caesar and Pompey':

After the labours of ten years in which he had conquered Gaul, Germany, and Britain, Caesar asked for a triumph, or the honours which such victories merited, but Pompey, Cato, and Marcellus the consul resisted this, and ordered that he should disband his army and return to Rome. And by the order of the consul Marcellus, Pompey was sent to take charge of the legions at Liceria. Because of this rebuff, Caesar advanced with his army against his own country. While there were many offices at Rome, some of which lasted for a year, and some for two years, the greatest among them was the office of dictator, which was to last for five years. At first there was one dictator, but with the growth of the Republic there came to be three, so that if perchance a dispute arose between two of them, the third would settle it. It happened that these three, Pompey, Caesar, and Marcus Crassus, were dictators at the same time, and that Pompey because he was old, and had finished active service was left to defend the state. Crassus who had been sent to subdue the Parthians was captured by a

[1] iv. 212–14. See Appendix II.

trick and killed. Caesar was sent to the west, and stayed there for five years conquering the Gauls and the Allobroges. After that sustained by his own authority he extended his term of office for another five years during which he conquered the Britons and again conquered the Gauls. When he had reached the Alps on his return to Rome, he commanded Pompey, whose daughter he had married, to prepare a triumph for him. Pompey, however, with the consent of the senate, refused him this on account of his audacity in extending his term of office, whereupon Caesar who was furious hastened to Rome to attack Pompey.[1]

In the course of these chapters Higden spoke of the famous figures of the Roman world. One such figure was Marcus Porcius Cato, great-grandson of Cato the Censor, who had committed suicide at Utica after his defeat by Caesar. There was no excuse said Higden for Cato's act. His friends had sought to dissuade him; he had allowed his son to live under Caesar; and his action arose from the fact that he could not endure to live under Caesar's rule.[2] Concerning Caesar, Higden's chronicle reflected the two sides of medieval thought, which saw Caesar on some occasions as a tyrant and on others as a just man. Higden wrote that Caesar had acted like a tyrant and violated the liberties of Rome, yet he also noted that no one had governed better, or suffered abuse more patiently.[3] Higden quoted Eutropius to the effect that Caesar performed many cruel acts, but he included also Sallust's comparison between Caesar and Marcus Cato: 'Cato was great for the uprightness of his life, Caesar for his magnificence and liberality'.[4] On Augustus there was no such doubt. Augustus had 'found Rome brick, and left it marble'. He was an emperor 'like to a God'.[5]

In the fourth and fifth books Higden dealt with the later history of the empire, and the coming together of Rome and Christianity in the sixth age of the world. 'By a coincidence on the miraculous nature of which Christians were never tired of dilating, the beginning of Christianity had been contemporaneous

---

[1] iv. 188–92. See Appendix II.   [2] iv. 200–2.   [3] iv. 204–14.
[4] iv. 220. Sallust, *Bellum Catilinae* (ed. Rolfe), iv. 1.   [5] iv. 296, 298.

with the beginning of the empire, and Christ had been born at a moment when Rome was at the zenith of her power, when peace reigned throughout her vast dominions, and a new era was commencing under apparently the most favourable auspices.'[1] This was a narrative composed of passages concerning Roman emperors such as Titus, and early Christian saints like St. Julian.[2] Higden described the heroism of the Christian martyrs and the activities of the early popes and he concluded with an account of Constantine's conversion, and the official adoption of the Christian faith.

At the end of the fifth book Higden left the ancient world, and in his last two books concentrated upon the subject of British history. Here a place of honour was accorded to the work of Geoffrey of Monmouth. Higden recounted the well-known story of Brutus, and described the deeds of Molmutius, Lud, Cassibellanus, and Arthur. His reliance upon Geoffrey of Monmouth is evident in many parts of his chronicle. He quoted Geoffrey's account of the origins of the episcopal sees,[3] and spoke of the derivation of the name Westmorland which, following Geoffrey, he imagined came from Marius, the British king. William of Malmesbury who had supposed the name derived from Marius, the Roman consul, had erred, for he had not seen the 'British book'.[4] Despite his obvious reliance upon Geoffrey's history Higden none the less could not prevent a note of doubt from creeping into his chronicle, and he admitted that he was perplexed by several of Geoffrey's comments. He asked why Arthur, who had conquered many kingdoms, and subjugated the king of the Franks, was not mentioned by Gildas or Bede.[5] Higden's doubts, though 'mildly expressed . . . were of a kind that most of all madden the Arthurian enthusiast', and Trevisa, an Arthurian supporter, 'pointedly interrupts his English version to protest against the unexpected folly of its author'.[6]

Higden's account of British history did not stand or fall by his

[1] D. Comparetti, *Vergil in the Middle Ages* (trs. E. F. M. Benecke, 1895), p. 175.
[2] iv. 462–4.   [3] ii. 110.   [4] iv. 416.   [5] v. 334–6.
[6] Kendrick, *British Antiquity*, p. 14.

acceptance of the Arthurian story. In his sixth book he described the history of the Anglo-Saxon state. His narrative was a record of the deeds of kings, and the fortunes of the Church, and it dealt in detail with the period from Augustine's mission to England to the final defeat of the Anglo-Saxon state. Amid much that was legendary, including an account of Harold's flight to Chester after the battle of Hastings, the most famous legend was that of Alfred's foundation of the university of Oxford.[1] The story, which is found for the first time in the *Polychronicon* and in other fourteenth-century chronicles, says that Alfred founded the university at the suggestion of St. Neot.[2] Although the legend was caught up and repeated by later scholars, a marginal note in a copy of Higden's text asserting on the authority of 'J. Caius' that 'the writer [i.e. Higden] erred' reminds us that John Caius, the sixteenth-century scholar, accepted most of 'the more preposterous sorts of ancient history', but not Higden's account of Oxford's origins.[3]

In Higden's treatment of British history his concern with earlier periods is evident. Not until his seventh and final book did he reach the age of the Norman kings. As he approached his own times his entries became noticeably briefer, and less than half his final book is concerned with the more recent part of the British past. The reigns of John, Henry III, and Edward I were treated in the briefest outline, and despite an interesting character sketch of Edward II,[4] Higden had little to say about the century in which he lived. It is clear that the present and the recent past considered as history held few attractions for him, and that his interest lay in the earlier centuries.

[1] See J. Parker, *The Early History of Oxford* (Oxford Historical Society, 1884–5), pp. 5–62.

[2] vi. 354.

[3] The manuscript Cambridge U.L. Ii. II. 24, which belonged to St. Augustine's, Canterbury, has a note in the margin at this point, 'Nota, sub quo universitas Oxoniensis incepit', to which a later hand has added 'sed quantum hic scriptor erraverit, vide J. Caium de antiquitate Cantebrigiae'. See Kendrick, *British Antiquity*, p. 72, and Parker, pp. 20 seq.

[4] viii. 298. Apart from this the *Polychronicon* is of little value for the period from 1300 to 1352.

III

In the terms of its day the *Polychronicon* was an historical masterpiece of the first order. Its appeal lay not only in the historical information that it conveyed but also in its 'literary quality'. Higden was an omnivorous reader, a 'literary glutton', equally at home in the chronicles, the scientific writings of the thirteenth century, or in the great mass of medieval homiletic literature. His chronicle mirrored the reading of his life. Every conceivable kind of subject was discussed in the course of his chronicle; for example, the present resting place of the finger of John the Baptist, the symbolical significance of the colours of the rainbow, and whether devils could change men into beasts. Because of its information on these and a variety of subjects, the *Polychronicon* was a truly marvellous book to its fourteenth-century reader.

Higden's chronicle was, above all things, a story book, a mine of anecdote and of *exempla*. Higden knew how to amuse as well as how to instruct, and from his labours in the field of sermon literature he knew the need to retain the interest of his reader. Stories appeared at every stage in his chronicle; stories concerning the ancient Greeks; stories of the fountain of oil which flowed at Rome when Christ was born; and the story of the painting which Henry II had commissioned for his room at Winchester. For almost every event in history Higden had some anecdote to hand. If not all the stories which he told were edifying, most were interesting, and all, no doubt, were to the taste of his fourteenth-century readers. Many of Higden's anecdotes were the 'twice-told' tales of the Middle Ages; the story of Plato and the fishermen which came from the *De Vestigiis et dogmatibus philosophorum* of Virius Nicomachus Flavianus by way of John of Salisbury;[1] the story of Alexander and Dionides, the pirate, which is found in a general form in Chaucer, *The Manciple's Tale* (226–34), and

---

[1] iii. 350–2. *Policraticus*, ed. Webb, i. 141. 1 ff. See E. R. Curtius, *European Literature and the Latin Middle Ages* (1953), p. 52.

in more detail in Villon;[1] the story of King Cunincpert and the fly, which Higden found in the *Historia Langobardorum* of Paul the Deacon;[2] as well as several stories which he took without acknowledgement from the work of Gerald of Wales.[3] Higden's anecdotes were drawn from classical and medieval sources and were written for a literate audience who knew something of the historical personages concerned. In addition he drew on books of *exempla*.[4] Collections of *exempla* such as the *Gesta Romanorum* were the stock-in-trade of the medieval preacher, and must have been of some interest to Higden who wrote on the art of preaching.[5] Though Higden rarely generalized in the fashion of the medieval preacher,[6] some of his stories are to be found in the sermon literature of the time.[7]

In his opening chapters Higden said something about his methods. His aim was to record. History was pure memorial, Trevisa's 'great remembrancer': 'History therefore which is the witness of times, the memory of life, the messenger of age, possesses eminent dowries, has many practitioners. History renews perishable matters by the immortality of report, recalls the fugitive, preserves eternally mortal things.'[8] He admitted that

---

[1] iii. 422–4.
> Ou temps qu' Alixandre regna,
> Ung homs nommé Diomedès
> Devant luy on luy amena,
> Engrillonné poulces et des
> Comme ung larron, car il fut des
> Escumeurs que voions courir . . ..
> Le Testament, xvii (ed. Bonner, New York, 1960).

[2] vi. 144–6. *Historia Langobardorum* (M.G.H. 1878), vi.

[3] See Chapter V.

[4] On the *exemplum* see J. Th. Welter, *L'exemplum dans la littérature religieuse et didactique du Moyen Âge* (1927).

[5] See G. R. Owst, *Literature and Pulpit in Medieval England* (1961), pp. 149–210.

[6] In the books of *exempla* the story of Alexander and Diogenes, which is found in the *Polychronicon* (iii. 308–10), where Diogenes asks the king to stand out of his light becomes the tale of the philosopher and the king, who may not be specified, where the philosopher lectures the king on the need to govern the kingdom by reason, &c. In the *Polychronicon*, on the other hand, the story belongs to a definite literary tradition. See G. Cary, *The Medieval Alexander*, pp. 84, 143–62.

[7] *Polychronicon*, vii. 222–4. The passage comes from William of Malmesbury, *Gesta Regum*, i. 277. See Owst, p. 160.   [8] i. 6.

his history was compilation, taken for the most part from the work of other writers. This was justifiable; even Virgil borrowed from Homer.[1] At the same time Higden could not vouch for the truth of every extract which he quoted. Paul in the *Epistle to the Romans* did not say, 'Whatever things were written are necessarily true', but 'Whatever things were written were written for our learning'.[2] Higden's methods were basically those of the encyclopaedist. He took passages from every writer, classical and christian alike, that he could find, and arranged them in a roughly chronological sequence. In his account of ancient history medieval authors were treated as equal in value to classical ones, and elsewhere extracts from the lives of saints were placed alongside passages from chronicles. In the manner of Vincent of Beauvais he distinguished between passages which were of his own composition, and passages which he had taken from other writings, but his distinction was far from absolute, and throughout his chronicle Higden was not averse from giving under his own name extracts which were the work of another author.

In the *Polychronicon* no explicit view of historical causation was expressed. It was enough for Higden to relate the *Gesta Dei*. He accepted such orthodox medieval beliefs as those of the six ages and the four empires with little in the way of comment. As in most medieval histories there is in this work an impression of inevitability about the historical process; men 'may assassinate Caesar, but they cannot arrest the downfall of the Republic'. The ages and the empires succeed one another according to a pre-ordained pattern. Much of Higden's purpose was to illustrate not so much 'the lessons of history' as the moral qualities of its famous men. History was a great store house of *exempla*, a repository of moral tales, from which one could select the appropriate theme, such as, for example, the theme of Caesar's meeting with Cicero, taken from Pliny, which was that 'wisdom is nobler than power'.[3] It was in large part in moral terms that the past had meaning.

---

[1] i. 12.   [2] i. 18. Romans, xv. 4.
[3] iv. 216. *Natural History*, vii. 31.

IV

The *Polychronicon* was one of the last great universal chronicles of the Middle Ages. It was almost a century after Vincent of Beauvais had written his *Speculum Historiale* that manuscripts of Higden's work began to circulate in the monasteries and cathedrals of fourteenth-century England. Its impact was immediate. An interest in universal history, and in the history of antiquity, had been developing for some time, and it ensured a ready audience for Higden's work. Higden says that at first he had proposed to write a history of his own country, but that at the request of his fellow monks, he changed his plan, and enlarged the scope of his chronicle.[1] His own interests partly explain his decision. 'World history' was never far from the mind of the medieval chronicler, and Higden was a writer with a genuine interest in the remoter past.

Apart from Higden's own interests, however, the times were propitious for a universal chronicle which embraced the history of Rome. The emergent nation states of the Middle Ages, which looked back to the classical past, had acquired fictitious and legendary histories which connected their societies with those of the ancient world. The most influential history of this kind in England was that of Geoffrey of Monmouth, whose narrative linked the history of Britain to that of Troy. It was but a step from accepting Geoffrey's account to attempting to reconstruct, if even in the simplest of forms, something of antiquity itself. At the same time classical history and classical legend were increasingly present in fourteenth-century literature. Robert Mannyng of Brunne, who translated Langtoft's chronicle, introduced into his own work passages on the origins of the Trojan war. In the fourteenth century 'antiquity came to Englishmen as part of their own history. As Christians they were linked to Rome and the Holy Land through the Bible and the lives of the saints. As Englishmen they were linked to Mount Olympus and Troy

[1] i. 6–8.

town.'[1] Even without the new interest in antiquity the time was overdue for a universal chronicle to be written in England along traditional lines. Higden did in England what Vincent of Beauvais had done in France. He used the traditional sources of the Middle Ages to write a 'world history'.

[1] *English Friars*, pp. 23–24.

IV

HIGDEN'S DESCRIPTION OF THE WORLD

ALTHOUGH the *Polychronicon* was in the form of a universal history it included more than historical events and, in parts at least, it has resemblances to the thirteenth-century encyclopedias of natural science, which collected and resumed, not the advanced knowledge of the day, but traditional knowledge, which was often several centuries old at the time of compilation. It was in a tradition which included such works as the *De Proprietatibus Rerum* of Bartholomaeus Anglicus, the *Speculum Naturale* of Vincent of Beauvais, and the *L'Image du Monde* written during the thirteenth century.[1]

I

The first book of the *Polychronicon* described the countries of the world, and Higden's picture of the universe emerged also in several of his comments. Like all medieval men he believed in a universe of which the earth was the centre, and around which revolved the spheres of the seven known planets. Beyond these spheres was the sphere of the fixed stars, and beyond that again was the *primum mobile*. There is no evidence that Higden, like Vincent of Beauvais, believed in a tenth sphere composed of water,[2] but he did believe that between the earth and the sphere of the moon lay the element of fire,[3] an element that several

[1] These encyclopedias are considered by C. V. Langlois, *La Connaissance de la nature et du monde au Moyen Âge* (1911). This was reprinted as volume iii of *La Vie en France au Moyen Âge* (1927).
[2] See P. Duhem, *Le Système du monde* (1954), iii. 346–8.
[3] i. 72. See Dante,

> parvemi tanto allor del cielo acceso
> dalla flamma del sol, che pioggia o fiume
> lago non fece mai tanto disteso.
>
> *Paradiso*, i. 79–81.

medieval writers maintained was present between all the seven planetary spheres, and between the sphere of Saturn and that of the fixed stars.[1]

The planets exercised an influence upon earthly affairs, and possessed qualities which they shared with men. Higden speaks of Mars as bellicose, Mercury as covetous, Saturn as cruel.[2] The sky was divided into the twelve signs of the zodiac, and the nature of the planets changed as they entered the different signs. In the *De Proprietatibus Rerum* Bartholomaeus Anglicus had divided the twelve signs into four groups of three; Aries, Leo, and Sagittarius, which had the element of fire; Taurus, Virgo, and Capricorn, which had the element of earth; Gemini, Libra, and Aquarius, which had the element of air; and Scorpio, Cancer, and Pisces, which had the element of water.[3] These elements determined their character. The noblest group of signs were Aries, Leo, and Sagittarius. Higden said that Capricorn caused summer to come to men in the Antipodes, meaning that in December the sun entered that sign.[4]

If to a fourteenth-century scholar the sky 'was still a pictured scroll whose once familiar symbols we no longer read',[5] his picture of the earth was one that, no less, has ceased to be familiar. Higden believed that the world, like man, was composed of the four elements of earth, water, air, and fire. Each element possessed its individual qualities; earth was slow and heavy; water was fleeting.[6] Among them fire was the active element that changed the nature of things. The elements were arranged with earth at the centre, water above earth, air above water, and fire at the top.[7]

Like most medieval writers Higden accepted the view that the earth was round.[8] This was a theory developed from observation of the stars, and from arguments about the sphericity of water

---

[1] *Le Système du monde*, iii. 335.   [2] ii. 186.

[3] For a discussion of this see C. V. Langlois, *La Connaissance de la nature et du monde au Moyen Âge*, pp. 144–7.

[4] ii. 206.

[5] J. L. Lowes, *Chaucer's World* (Oxford, 1934), pp. 8 seq., gives an account of this subject.

[6] ii. 186.   [7] ii. 180–2.   [8] ii. 204.

which composed a good deal of the earth's surface.[1] The round-
ness of the earth was taken as a sign of its perfection and per-
petuity.[2] According to Higden and to the thirteenth-century
encyclopaedists whom he was quoting, the earth had a circum-
ference of 20,040 miles and the distance from the centre of the
earth to its surface was 3,245 miles.[3] The medieval writer knew
that the earth was covered with oceans, and Higden thought
that much of its surface, including the Antipodes, was unin-
habited.[4]

Higden looked out onto a world, known only in part, on which
the whole of the universe centred. To a considerable extent his
views were determined by the dictates of medieval theology, and
in accordance with that system he discussed the terrestrial position of Hell and Paradise. On the location of Hell Higden said
that if it was at the earth's centre, then it was 3,245 miles distant.[5] On the position of Paradise he wrote at greater length.[6]
Though there were suggestions that Paradise was between the
earth and the moon, Higden found this proposition difficult to
accept because it would have caused an eclipse of the moon
which had not been observed. He concluded that Paradise lay
in the extreme east of the world,[7] and consisted of a large region
untouched by the waters of the Flood. In Paradise were the four
rivers, and the Tree of Life, and the whole region was guarded
by a wall of fire. Higden's views were those of the Middle Ages,
and he simply restated the opinions of Bartholomaeus Anglicus
who was quoting Isidore of Seville.[8]

II

The description of the parts of the world in the early chapters
did little more than reproduce ideas in common currency at the

---

[1] P. Duhem, *Études sur Léonard de Vinci* (1955), i. 58–67.
[2] Langlois, *La Connaissance de la nature et du monde au Moyen Âge*, pp. 78–79.
[3] i. 44–46.   [4] ii. 204–6.   [5] i. 46.   [6] i. 66–78.
[7] '*Unde concludunt docti quod Paradisus terrestris sit in extremis finibus orientis*' . . .
(i. 74). Paradise is shown in the extreme east in the map which is found in certain
copies of the *Polychronicon*.
[8] *Etymologiae*, xiv. 3.

time. To Higden the inhabited earth consisted of three parts, Asia, Europe, and Africa, of which Asia formed half of the whole.[1] For his description of the earth Higden, who had probably never travelled farther than his journey to Westminster, was obliged to use the accounts of earlier writers, and his description of the world was indebted to the *Etymologiae* of Isidore of Seville, and the *De Proprietatibus Rerum* of Bartholomaeus Anglicus. For his description of Rome he used the twelfth-century guide-book of Master Gregory, while his account of Ireland and Wales was taken almost entirely from the writings of Gerald of Wales.[2]

His picture of the world was a traditional one. The earth from east to west ran from India to the pillars of Hercules (Gibraltar), and from north to south from the river Don to Ethiopia. There was no west, no China, and no Australia in his picture, and the description of the provinces of Asia reveals the limited and dated extent of his knowledge. The subjects of the chapters, *Scythia*, *Cappadocia*, *Numidia*, appear at first sight unfamiliar until one realizes that Higden is describing, from his authorities, the provinces of the Roman Empire as they existed in the first few centuries after the birth of Christ. There is only the slightest indication in his work that he was living at a time when the Byzantine emperors were struggling to exist, and when the Hafsid Caliphate had been established over part of north Africa.

The account of the provinces of Asia began with India.[3] To Higden India was a land of fabulous beings known through the work of Isidore and Pliny. In India there were men with no

---

[1] For an account of medieval geography see C. R. Beazley, *The Dawn of Modern Geography* (1897–1906), 3 vols.; J. K. Wright, *The Geographical Lore of the time of the Crusades* (1925); G. H. T. Kimble, *Geography in the Middle Ages* (1938). C. H. Haskins, *Studies in the History of Medieval Science* (Cambridge, 1924) is also valuable.

[2] Higden's use of these sources is considered in Chapter V. It is worth noting that Trevisa translated the *De Proprietatibus Rerum* in 1398. It was printed by W. de Worde (*c.* 1494), and there was an edition by Batman which was published in 1582 by T. East. A selection from the *De Proprietatibus Rerum* is found in R. Steele, *Medieval Lore* (London, 1907).

[3] i. 78–84.

mouths who lived by smell and others with hollow fingers. Fantasies such as these, of pygmies, and of

> the Anthropophagi, and men whose heads
> Do grow beneath their shoulders,

are found in thirteenth-century accounts, and found, no doubt, a ready audience among Higden's readers. Higden described trees which were taller than an arrow's flight, and spoke of the Cynocephali, which were baboons or dog-headed apes.

From India Higden passed to the other provinces of Asia, to Parthia, Assyria, and the region of Judaea, with the Mount of Olives, Gethsemane, and Mount Sion.[1] In the etymologizing fashion of the Middle Ages, he frequently began his account of a region with a discussion of the origin of its name, and eponymous heroes such as Asia and Egyptus found a special place in his narrative.[2] For the description of Asia his sources preserved little detailed knowledge of regions beyond the limits of the Roman Empire. Illustrative of this was the appearance of 'Scythia', partly in and partly out of Asia.[3] In the *Polychronicon* Scythia included part of Russia, but extended to Scandinavia and northern lands as well. 'Gothia' was a European part of Scythia, near to the island of Gothlandia.[4]

As regards Europe Higden's description was essentially an account of the western provinces of the Roman Empire. To Higden Germany was a country contained between the Rhine and the Danube,[5] and Spain still had something of the air of a Roman province.[6] Although the chief feudal principalities of France were mentioned,[7] in other respects he considered Europe as it was at the time of the late Roman Empire, and this gives Higden's chapters their air of unreality. He began his account of Europe with a chapter on Greece. According to his custom he said something of the ancient and modern names of the inhabitants of the country and mentioned the various provinces

[1] i. 102–18.   [2] i. 78, 130.
[3] i. 134–46. See J. S. P. Tatlock, *The Legendary History of Britain* (1950), pp. 109–10.
[4] i. 144.   [5] i. 254–66.   [6] i. 298–302.   [7] i. 288–98.

and the early history of Athens.¹ After the chapter on Greece came a shorter one on Italy describing its rivers and the boundaries and provinces of the country.² An account of the city of Rome occupied two chapters, the first of which dealt with the ancient monuments of the city, the palaces, the Parthenon, the arch of Augustus, the theatres, aqueducts, and baths.³ For these chapters Higden used a twelfth-century source, the guide-book of Master Gregory, which survives in a single copy and in Higden's work.⁴ Whoever 'Master Gregory' was, he paid particular attention to the classical buildings remaining in the city of Rome, and the quotations which Higden gives from his work reveal the remarkable interpretations placed upon classical monuments during the Middle Ages. The marble statue of the Horsetamers (*Dioscuri*) on the Quirinal was explained by reference to an episode concerning Tiberius and two philosophers. The statue, which depicted two horses of marble, was said to be a memorial to the philosophers' renunciation of all material things.⁵ A similarly ingenious explanation was found for the equestrian statue of Marcus Aurelius on the Capitol, which featured the Emperor and a conquered barbarian. The conquered barbarian was described as a dwarf called Manus. Although the pilgrims called the horseman Theodoric, the clerks of the court called him Marcus, saying that the statue commemorated Marcus going from the city, and capturing Manus, a dwarf, who had laid Rome under a spell. When he was led back to the city, the dwarf threw himself under the feet of the horse and so lost his magical power.⁶

After the chapter on Rome followed by one on Roman institutions taken mainly from the *Derivationes* of Huguccio,⁷ Higden turned to Germany and began his brief account with a description taken from Bartholomaeus Anglicus and Isidore.⁸ After mentioning the provinces of Germany in a sentence or two, he

---

¹ i. 174–96.   ² i. 198–206.   ³ i. 206–38.   ⁴ See Chapter V.
⁵ i. 226–8.
⁶ i. 228–32. See E. R. Curtius, *European Literature and the Latin Middle Ages*, pp. 405–6.
⁷ i. 238–52. See Chapter V.   ⁸ i. 254. *Etymologiae*, xiv. 4.

said something of the Scribonii who had snow in summer, and concluded with a version of the legend of the Seven Sleepers, taken from the *Historia Langobardorum*. In Germany in a cave by an ocean, sheltered by an overhanging rock, were seven men who had been asleep for many years. Their bodies and their clothes were unharmed, and by their dress they appeared to be Romans. One who attempted to remove their clothing found that his own arm was withered. It may be, the extract concluded, that God was keeping these sleepers unharmed, so that they could convert the barbarian peoples.[1]

Among European countries France was the one which Higden described in the greatest detail. Even here his knowledge was by no means remarkable, and the two chapters on France in the *Polychronicon* owed much to the *De Proprietatibus Rerum*.[2] The first chapter dealt with the early history of the Franks, who like other European peoples, he thought, had their origins in Trojan history.[3] The second chapter mentioned the various provinces of France, Normandy with its capital, Rouen, and Brittany which took its name from the Britons who had occupied it twice, once under Brennus, and a second time under Vortigern.[4] Higden did little more than excerpt from the work of Bartholomaeus Anglicus and supply an occasional story such as that of a miraculous well in Brittany which came from the *Topographia* of Gerald of Wales.[5] Higden knew little of Spain, while northern Europe was a region shrouded in mystery. In the *Polychronicon* Denmark was 'Dacia',[6] Norway was an island,[7] and Iceland was placed to the north of that.[8] Out in the Atlantic was the island of Thule, an 'island in the sun', where the sun never set.[9] Amidst the legend and romance the one example of direct observation was Higden's comment that Brabant was famous for the dyeing of wool. Though England produced the best wools it lacked the water for dyeing, but at London and Lincoln the dyers were able to produce an excellent scarlet.[10]

[1] i. 264–6. *Historia Langobardorum*, i. 4.   [2] i. 266–98. See Chapter V.
[3] i. 266–86.   [4] i. 288–98.   [5] i. 292. *Topographia*, p. 88.
[6] i. 320–2.   [7] i. 326.   [8] i. 322.   [9] i. 324.
[10] i. 288.

After describing Europe Higden turned to Britain. The last third of his geographical description was concerned with his own country, and though the account was for the most part a conventional one, drawn from Bede, William of Malmesbury, Geoffrey of Monmouth, and Gerald of Wales, this part of the *Polychronicon* aroused considerable interest in the centuries which followed. Before dealing with England Higden described Ireland and Wales. The five chapters on Ireland were little more than a summary of the remarks of Gerald of Wales,[1] and Gerald's comments on the marvels of Ireland, the islands of immortality, and the Irish saints were all faithfully copied.[2] In a similar fashion the account that Gerald gave of Wales in the *Itinerarium Cambriae*, and the *Descriptio Cambriae* formed the basis of Higden's long, rhyming chapter on that country.[3] Higden included a much shorter account of Scotland,[4] which he said, was sometimes called Albania, after Albanactus, the son of Brutus. Apart from adding that the Scots had their origins in Scythia, Higden had little more to say and did not mention the boundaries, or the topographical features of the country.

The last twenty-two chapters of the first book described the cities, countries, rivers, and natural resources of England. For these chapters Higden drew on a number of sources, including the *Historia Regum Britanniae* of Geoffrey of Monmouth. From Geoffrey he took much of his historical information including the statement that the names of the three parts of Britain came from the three sons of Brutus, Loegria (England) from Locrinus,

---

[1] The account of Ireland is found at i. 328–82, and the account of Wales at i. 394–430.

[2] The description of Ireland begins with an account of the climate and character of the country, proceeds to deal with the people, the marvellous fountains and lakes, and concludes with some notes on Irish saints. The first chapter on Ireland (Chapter 32) quotes the *Topographia Hibernica*, iii. 7; i. 1; ii. 1; i. 2; i. 4; i. 25, 26, 27; i. 7, 8, 9, 10, 11; i. 22; i. 5; i. 4; i. 18; i. 7; i. 18; i. 22, 23, 25.

[3] The chapter on Wales quotes the *Itinerarium Cambriae*, i. 2; i. 4; i. 5; i. 6; i. 9; i. 12; ii. 3; ii. 5; ii. 6; ii. 7; ii. 8; ii. 9; *Descriptio Cambriae*, chapters 4, 7, 8–19. On the rhetorical concept of poetry in the Middle Ages in praise of cities and countries see E. R. Curtius, *European Literature and the Latin Middle Ages*, pp. 145–66.

[4] i. 382–94.

Cambria (Wales) from Camber, and Albania (Scotland) from Albanactus.[1] Higden described the size and location of Britain, 800 miles long, 200 miles in width, and 50 miles from Boulogne.[2] England had many deer and sheep, but few wolves, so that sheep could be left to graze in safety.[3] There were many different kinds of fish including dolphins, porpoises, and shell-fish, some of which could be used for colouring. Among the natural resources of the island Higden spoke of white and red clay which could be used for pottery and tilestones, and the black jet which had miraculous properties. In a note under his own name he mentioned the fact that Flanders imported wool from England; Normandy, skins and velvets; Gascony, iron and lead; and Ireland, ore and salt.[4] His narrative was not always so sober, as for example, when he described the superstitions concerned with the Dee, the miraculous lakes in England, or when he told the story of the women of the Isle of Man who sold wind to fishermen contained within three knots of thread, so that the more wind the fishermen required for their ships, the more knots they had to undo.[5]

The description of England was arranged by subjects. At the beginning of these chapters Higden wrote that he intended to deal with the name and position of the country, its principal divisions, roads, rivers, cities, ecclesiastical sees, laws, and so on.[6] An account that described these matters had to deal with other than purely geographical subjects. The six chapters describing the episcopal sees contain a detailed and reasonably accurate history of the English bishoprics and began with the statement from Geoffrey of Monmouth that the episcopal sees had originated with the twenty-eight *flamines* who became bishops.[7] The account of the laws of England, which Higden also included, owed much to Geoffrey's history. Higden spoke of Molmutius, the great legislator who had made laws granting the right of sanctuary to

[1] ii. 30–32.
[2] ii. 6–12. Higden is quoting from Solinus, Pliny, and Alfred of Beverley.
[3] ii. 12–20. As usual Higden is quoting from various authorities including Pliny, Solinus, Bede, and William of Malmesbury.
[4] ii. 18.   [5] ii. 42.   [6] ii. 2–4.
[7] ii. 110. Geoffrey of Monmouth, iv. 19. See Tatlock, p. 260.

temples, and protecting the ploughs of workers.[1] The laws of
Molmutius were translated into Latin by Gildas, and into Anglo-
Saxon by Alfred, before being codified by Edward III. In the
chapters which dealt with the shires, cities, roads, and rivers of
the country, Higden used the chronicles of Alfred of Beverley and
William of Malmesbury, as well as the work of Geoffrey of Monmouth. The chapter on the shires of England listed the thirty-
two shires, and the laws by which they were governed.[2] The
cities of England were also mentioned and though Higden had
more to say about northern cities such as Edinburgh, York, and
Carlisle, than London, Canterbury, or Bath, his remarks in all
cases were purely conventional.[3] In accordance with his general
interest in etymology he mentioned the change of names in the
case of London. The city was built by Brutus and called *Trinovantum*. Lud called it *Caerlud*, the Angles called it *Lundena*, and
the name was changed by the Normans into *Loundres*, and in
Latin, *Londonia*.[4] His main source for this was still Geoffrey of
Monmouth.[5] A chapter on rivers included notes on the principal
rivers of the country, the Thames, Severn, Humber, and the
Trent and Ouse that flowed into them.[6] Some interesting details
went into the forty-sixth chapter, which had as its subject the
four royal roads.[7] Higden mentioned Watling Street which, he
said, ran from Dover through the middle of Kent to the Thames
at the west of Westminster; from there through St. Albans,
Dunstable, and Stratford to the Wrekin; thence over the Severn
to the middle of Wales, where it ended at Cardigan by the Irish
sea. Higden's own observations, as well as the accounts of
travellers who had called at St. Werburgh's, no doubt helped
him in this chapter.

[1] ii. 90–96. Tatlock, pp. 278–83. Higden says that the other laws in England
came from Marcia, Queen of the Britons, and from the Danes. Higden also explains certain legal terms, such as *sac* and *soc*, in this chapter.
   [2] ii. 84–90.   [3] ii. 52–84.   [4] ii. 56.   [5] See Tatlock, p. 30.
   [6] ii. 48–52. One example of the interest which Higden's remarks aroused in
a contemporary reader is seen in the lecture course which John Lathbury, a
Franciscan, gave in Oxford. He mentioned Higden's work, 'Scribitur enim in
historia polychronica lib. i, quod fluunt in Britannia quatuor famosa flumina,
scilicet Tamisia, Sabrina, Humbria et Trenta . . .' *English Friars*, pp. 223–4.
   [7] ii. 42–46.

Higden's description concluded with two chapters on the dialects of the English, and the characteristics of the English people.[1] Despite the fact that he wrote in Latin, he displayed an interest in the English language, and deplored the fact that the children of the aristocracy had learnt French after the Norman Conquest:

Likewise the English although in the beginning they had a language of three branches, namely southern, midland, and northern, as coming from the three Germanic peoples, nonetheless as a result of mixture, first with the Danes and then Normans, by a corruption of their language in many respects, they now incorporate strange bleatings and babblings. There are two main causes for their present debasement of the native language, one, that children in the schools against the practice of other nations, are compelled since the coming of the Normans to abandon their own tongue and to construe into French, and, secondly, that children of the nobility are taught French from the cradle and rattle.[2]

It was in this part of his translation of the *Polychronicon* that Trevisa said that John Cornwall, a master of grammar, made his boys construe into English, 'so that now, in the year of Our Lord 1385, in all the grammar schools children leave French, and construe and learn in English'.[3]

In the last chapter of this book Higden spoke of the characteristics of the English people.[4] Whatever Anglo-Saxon prejudices he may have entertained, he regarded the English as one people: 'These men be speedful both on horse, and on foot, able and ready to all manner of arms . . . and can well enough tell deeds and wonders that they have seen. The men be able to all manner sleight and wit, but before the deed blundering and hasty, and more wise after the deed, and they leave often lightly what they have begun. . . . These men despise their own and praise other men's and be scarcely pleased with their own estate.'[5]

---

[1] ii. 156–74.   [2] ii. 158. See Appendix II.   [3] ii. 161.
[4] ii. 164–74. It should be noted that although Higden began his last book at 1066 (the point at which Knighton also began his history) his remarks reveal that the Old English period was not entirely forgotten in the fourteenth century.
[5] ii. 166–70.

The contrast which Higden drew in his history was not between Norman and Anglo-Saxon, but between north and south. There were differences between north and south and between England and Scotland. 'Scots be light of heart, strong and wild enough, but by mixing with Englishmen they be much amended.'[1] So wrote a fourteenth-century 'Sassenach' who had probably never set foot in Scotland, though his comments upon his fellow northerners were scarcely more complimentary.

As a Cheshireman Higden had, none the less, his local loyalties, and scattered throughout his chapters were several notices of Chester. The origin of Chester he considered to lie hidden in the mists of British history.

> The founder of this city, as saith Polychronicon,
> Was Leon Gawer, a mighty strong giant

whose 'very name', says Camden, 'may serve to confute such plebeian antiquaries . . . seeing Lean Var, in the British Language, signifieth nothing else but the great legion'. In justice to Higden it should be stated, however, that the contemplation of the massive blocks of Chester masonry inclined him sometimes to think that the city was the work of Romans rather than of Britons.[2] Whatever his views upon its origins Higden knew that Chester had once been a Roman city, *Urbs Legionum*, an outpost of the great empire whose history he described, and he added that for one winter Chester had housed the legions whom Caesar had sent to conquer Ireland.[3] Chester was destroyed by the men of Northumbria, but restored by Aethelflaed, lady of Mercia. There were stones at Chester which, so Higden thought, had the name of Caesar on them.[4] He was alive to the beauties and the natural amenities of the region where he lived, and he spoke of the splendid thickness of the city walls, the excellence of the salmon fishing in the Dee, and the terrifying whirlpool in the Menai Straits.[5] In these comments the 'local patriotism' of the Middle Ages emerged clearly. William of Malmesbury, who had written in the *Gesta Pontificum* that Chester lacked corn and other

---

[1] i. 386–8.   [2] ii. 78.   [3] ii. 78.   [4] ii. 80.   [5] ii. 80. 28. 40.

commodities,[1] incurred Higden's indignation. He must 'have been dreaming' when he made this remark, says Higden, for Chester had a large supply of all kinds of commodities, and an abundance of the best salmon.[2] Finally, Higden quoted lines in praise of his native city, which had been so generously endowed by nature, and which had so long and famous a history:[3]

> Chester, the town of the castle as it were,
> Takes its name from the legions that were there. . . .

III

To illustrate his description of the world Higden included a map in the later versions of his chronicle. Though Matthew Paris drew maps and was interested in cartography,[4] and it was usually only in the monastic schools that the facilities were available for producing the large wall maps of the time,[5] maps were not a common feature of medieval chronicles in England.

The maps that are found in various manuscripts of the *Polychronicon* derive ultimately from the T–O kind of map, where the world was shown with the east at the top. The land was divided into three continents, of which Asia formed half of the whole, while the lower left and right sections contained the continents of Europe and Africa. The form of the map can be represented in the following manner:

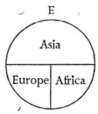

[1] *Gesta Pontificum*, ed. N. E. S. A. Hamilton (R.S., 1870), p. 308.
[2] ii. 78. [3] ii. 80–82.
[4] R. Vaughan, *Matthew Paris* (1958), p. 239. The world map of Matthew Paris is reproduced in Beazley, *Dawn of Modern Geography*, ii. 586, from B.M. MS. Cotton Nero D. v, and in K. Miller, *Mappae Nundi, Die ältesten Weltkarten* (1895), iii. 71, from Corpus Christi College, Cambridge, MS. 26.
[5] See G. R. Crone, *The Hereford World Map* (Royal Geographical Society, 1949).

The upright of the T represents the Mediterranean, and the horizontal part the western boundaries of Asia which ran from the Tanais (Don) to the Nile. This scheme was the basis not only for the world maps of Matthew Paris and Higden, but for the great 'wall' maps of Hereford and Ebstorf.[1]

A medieval world map of this kind was a combination of classical and Christian influence. From late Roman times the medieval cartographer took the picture of a world divided into three continents, orientated towards the east. From the maps of the late Roman Empire he gained some knowledge of imperial divisions. At the same time the medieval map-maker wished to provide a guide to Biblical history. Paradise was placed at the top of the map, Jerusalem was shown in the centre of the world, and considerable importance was attached to places connected with Biblical history. Within and around the map the medieval scribe placed legends describing the marvels of various countries. In the fourteenth century, however, the T-O style of map was breaking up. Though the division of continents was still present, a greater realism is evident. In the maps of the time the position of the Red Sea moved round to the upper right-hand portion, and in Africa there was an indication of a long strip of water that was possibly the Nile.[2]

The most elaborate map found in a text of the *Polychronicon* is that in B.M. MS. Royal 14. C. ix (ff. 1ᵛ–2).[3] Although like other maps in copies of the *Polychronicon* it is oval, the map derives from the T-O scheme of map-making, and presents a world orientated around Jerusalem. Like other examples of this type of world map it emphasizes places connected with Biblical history such as the Mount of Olives and Mount Sion; it describes episodes such as that of the Jews crossing the Red Sea; and it mentions the

---

[1] M. C. Andrews, 'The Study and Classification of Medieval *Mappae Mundi*', *Archaeologia*, lxxv (1924–5), 61–76.

[2] I am indebted to Mr. M. Kirk for these comments.

[3] This is reproduced in Dr. Konrad Miller, *Mappae Mundi, Die ältesten Weltkarten* (1895), vol. ii. Dr. Konrad Miller also reproduces the smaller map found in B.M. MS. Royal 14. C. ix, and the maps in B.M. MS. Royal 14. C. xii, and Corpus Christi College, Cambridge, MS. 21. See plate between pages xvi and 1.

achievements of Alexander the Great.[1] In this map the provinces of Parthia, Assyria, Media, are divided from each other by straight lines; rivers and mountains are roughly drawn; and important cities such as Jerusalem are depicted by a church or castle. The Caspian Sea and the Red Sea are shown in the top left- and right-hand corners of the map respectively. As regards Europe which is found in the bottom left-hand section, the Alps are relatively accurately placed, and some attempt is made to show rivers such as the Rhine. The islands of the Mediterranean are rectangles and squares, and along the outer margin of the map are notices of such places as the Canary Islands. At the top, in Asia, and along the right-hand side in Africa, are legends of monsters found in those parts of the world.

The map in B.M. MS. Royal 14. C. ix also draws a rough outline of the British Isles to which emphasis was given by the colouring which was used. In comparison with the outline of the British Isles given in the Hereford map, this map gives little indication of the size and shape of the country, though it shows the Thames, and some of the principal cities, none further north than York. The outline of the British Isles in the *Polychronicon* map is of the simplest kind, and in comparison with the maps of England and Scotland, drawn by Matthew Paris, which 'represent a genuine attempt at a map, rather than a mere diagrammatical representation',[2] it is elementary in the extreme. The Gough map, which gives the rivers, towns, and other settlements of England and Wales,[3] was compiled not much later than the map in the *Polychronicon* manuscript; at this time it was possible to compute latitudes, and to use them to obtain the north–south accuracy of a map;[4] yet in spite of this, the *Polychronicon* reveals that in ecclesiastical circles much the same

---

[1] This is in the top corner of the map.

[2] R. Vaughan, p. 243, who discusses the maps of Matthew Paris. The maps by Matthew Paris of the British Isles have been reproduced in colour by the British Museum, 1928.

[3] *The Map of Great Britain Circa A.D. 1360 known as the Gough Map*, ed. M. J. S. Parsons (1958).

[4] J. K. Wright, 'Notes on the Knowledge of Latitude and Longitude in the Middle Ages', *Isis*, no. 13 (1922), 75–98.

picture of Britain was held as had been held in previous centuries.

The map in B.M. MS. Royal 14. C. ix (ff. 1ᵛ–2) is the most detailed map to survive in manuscripts of Higden's work, but less elaborate maps of the same general kind are to be found. In the same manuscript, B.M. MS. Royal 14. C. ix, is a second map (f. 2ᵛ) which gives less detail. The countries and provinces are shown as subdivided strips of the three continents, and islands are depicted as rectangles with the name inscribed in a similar fashion to the larger version. There are, however, no legends, and the British Isles are not shown. A still simpler form of the map is to be found in Winchester College MS. 15, a copy of Higden's text which was given to the college by William of Wykeham, and which was probably made during the second half of the fourteenth century. In this map,

Jerusalem is in the centre of the earth. . . . The earth is surrounded by the green ribbon of ocean. At the foot of the page [the west] are some Western European names, such as Hispania and Aquitania. In the ocean stream in this quarter are the names Anglia, Scotia, Thule. Among the few features other than names is a wavy line in the African quarter of the map, marked 'Mons Athlas'; given a particular importance presumably by the classical legend of Atlas supporting the heaven, and having thus a cosmological rather than a geographical significance. The band of ocean is a pointed oval in form, compressed no doubt from a circle to fit suitably in a page rectangular but not square. The inlet of the Mediterranean is not indicated, as it is on the so-called T–O maps of the period. In the Far East, beyond 'Babilon' and India, is marked Paradise.[1]

Apart from this smaller version, there are maps (in Corpus Christi College, Cambridge, MS. 21, and B.M. MS. Royal 14. C. xii) which are little more than lists of names within an oval. In all cases the orientation is similar to the larger maps. Jerusalem is in the centre, Rome half-way below that, and the Alps are

---

[1] Walter Oakeshott, 'Some Classical and Medieval Ideas in Renaissance Cosmography', *F.S.*, p. 247.

below Rome and placed to the left. In these less-detailed maps no attempt is made to show the boundaries of continents, and the distinction between water and land is indicated only in the case of the Red Sea.[1]

There are at least eight maps to be found in manuscripts of the *Polychronicon*. Dr. Konrad Miller in his work on medieval *mappae mundi* considered the larger of the two maps in B.M. MS. Royal 14. C. ix to be the original from which the others, which are smaller in size and simpler in design, were derived.[2] He represented the relationship as follows:

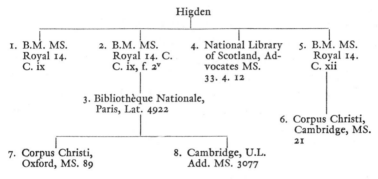

The large map which is found in B.M. MS. Royal 14. C. ix belongs to a manuscript that was once in the possession of the Abbey of Ramsey, but the map which is most closely connected with the text of Higden's work is that found in Huntington MS. 132, which was written at Chester, and which was not known to Dr. Miller. This map is similar to the smaller map found in B.M. MS. Royal 14. C. ix and it shows the earth surrounded by ocean, within which the various countries are drawn and labelled.[3] There is every reason to suppose that this was the map which Higden himself caused to be drawn. Maps similar to the one in the Huntington manuscript are found in four copies of the

---

[1] The map in B.M. MS. Royal 14. C. xii is reproduced in Bagrow, *Die Geschichte der Kartographie* (1951), p. 33, who also gives the larger map in B.M. MS. Royal 14. C. ix in his list of plates (no. 20).

[2] Dr. Konrad Miller, *Die ältesten Weltkarten, Die kleineren Weltkarten*, vol. iii.

[3] V. H. Galbraith, *H.L.Q.*, p. 17, note 26.

Polychronicon: (1) B.M. MS. Royal 14. C. ix, f. 2ᵛ; (2) Bibliothèque Nationale, Paris, lat. 4922; (3) MS. Corpus Christi College, Oxford, MS. 89; (4) Cambridge U.L. Add. MS. 3077. In addition to these a map of a simpler design similar to Winchester College MS. 15 is found in National Library of Scotland, Advocates MS. 33. 4. 12, while the simplest form of map which consists simply of a list of names written within an oval framework with no attempt made to draw in the outline of the land, is, as already mentioned, found in B.M. MS. Royal 14. C. xii, and Corpus Christi College, Cambridge, MS. 21.[1]

Whatever the relationship of these maps, Higden's attempt at cartography was entirely traditional. Dr. Miller believed that the map in the *Polychronicon* was little more than a copy of a wall map considerably older than Higden's time.[2] The *Polychronicon* map is of some interest, none the less, in indicating the monastic picture of the world in the fourteenth century. Like Higden's geography it was a mixture of fact and fantasy. Nothing of the increase in knowledge concerning the coastline of Europe and England, or of the roads of England, is evident. This development appears to have taken place mainly in lay society, for ecclesiastics, who were for the most part uninterested in exact geography, still held to a picture of the world fashioned in late Roman times.

IV

As well as the world Higden described man. In accordance with the traditional medieval doctrine he regarded man as composed of four elements, earth in his body and bones, water in his blood and humours, air in his lungs, and fire in his heart.[3] The doctrine of the four elements persisted far beyond Higden's times. 'Does not our life consist of the four elements?' asks Sir Toby Belch in *Twelfth Night*.[4] In addition to these elements Higden believed that man was compounded of the four humours

---

[1] These are discussed in Dr. Konrad Miller's work.
[2] *Die ältesten Weltkarten*, vol. iii.   [3] ii. 182.
[4] *Twelfth Night*, II. iii. 10.

of blood, phlegm, bile, and melancholy, which needed to be present in their correct proportions.[1]

The idea of the four elements, which were present in both man and the world, reinforced the further conception of man as the microcosm of the world. In a chapter on this subject Higden laboured the correspondences between man and the world.[2] The little world of man summed up the properties of earthly phenomena. Man was slow and heavy as the earth, fleeting as water, evanescent as air, burning as fire.[3] The world and man both had their miracles, and their separate parts. Both had their ages, and their existences. If Higden appears to labour these correspondences, and in considering the 'great toe of Pyrrhus' to labour them to the point of absurdity, this came from his belief in an ordered universe where all phenomena had their place. Because of the order and plan within the universe man reflected the world down to the smallest detail. There was order in the heavens, and the elements themselves were ranged in the sequence, earth, water, air, and fire.[4] The forms of created life stretched in a chain of being, from oysters which were the lowest form of life in the animal class and hardly distinguishable from plants, up to man himself. Man was the bridge between the material and spiritual orders. He stood at the bottom of the spiritual order of angels and pure intelligences. The human body, says Higden, when its humours are evenly balanced, reaches the edge of the next category above it, which is the human soul, and which occupies the lowest place in the spiritual order. The human soul is called the horizon where corporeal and incorporeal meet, and when it is cleansed of earthly things it can attain to a purely spiritual state.[5] Higden's belief in a chain of being and in an ordered universe were to prove more enduring than his historical axioms. Essentially the same views are present in the work of Elizabethan scholars.[6] One consequence of Higden's belief in an ordered universe was his

[1] ii. 180.   [2] ii. 174–200.   [3] ii. 186.   [4] ii. 180–2.
[5] ii. 182.
[6] On this subject see E. M. W. Tillyard, *The Elizabethan World Picture* (London, 1943); A. O. Lovejoy, *The Great Chain of Being* (Cambridge, 1936); Hardin Craig, *The Enchanted Glass* (Oxford, 1950).

concern with the reported change of men into other creatures.[1] In the description of the return of the Greeks to their home he dwelt at some length upon this topic. In his remarks on the change of Ulysses' companions into swine Higden concluded that devils could not change the nature, body, or soul, of those things that God had created, though, with God's permission, they might appear to change their appearance.[2]

In a work such as the *Polychronicon*,

> Talking of stones, stars, plants, of fishes, flies;
> Playing with words and idle similes,

there were naturally many marvels to be recounted, and Higden shared to the full the popular medieval beliefs in demons, monsters, and creatures of strange and varied form. The *Speculum Curatorum* which he wrote, devoted a chapter to the tricks of devils, *De ludificationibus demonum*, and dwelt with evident interest on such matters as the habits of devils in Wales,[3] for information on which Higden used the *Itinerarium Cambriae*. In the *Polychronicon* Higden concerned himself particularly with the subject of monsters, and a chapter at the beginning of the second book concerned itself with a description of monsters found in different parts of the world.[4] Higden recounted the usual stories of the Cyclops with one eye, and the Sciapodes who were so thin that when they lay on the ground they covered themselves with the shadow of their foot. He described a creature, the upper part of which was a man, and the other parts of which were made up of different shapes which recalled the Manticore, found in the bestiaries and encyclopedias, which had the face of a man, the body of a lion, and a tail like the sting of a scorpion. A great many of Higden's monsters, it may be noted, were found in those parts of the world of which he had little knowledge.

Nearer home, however, there were remarkable creatures to be described. Although the *Polychronicon* is not a bestiary, and Higden did not make it his task to describe in any detail the animals

---

[1] ii. 208–10.
[3] Balliol College, Oxford, MS. 77, f. 18.
[2] ii. 420–30.
[4] ii. 202–10.

found in the different countries of the world, the works with which he was familiar, the *De Naturis Rerum* of Alexander Nequam, the *De Proprietatibus Rerum* of Bartholomaeus Anglicus, the *Speculum Naturale* of Vincent of Beauvais, as well as the writings of Gerald of Wales, were all works associated with bestiary material. Higden mentioned the dragons and griffins of India, the crickets in Sicily which sang best when they were dead, and the one-eyed perch in Wales. The barnacle geese are one example of the mythical descriptions found in the *Polychronicon*.[1] The barnacle geese grew from trees, and hung by their beaks like the shellfish that clings to timber. When they were covered with feathers, they either fell into the water, or else flew away. They were eaten on fasting-days because they were supposed not to be carnally conceived, but none the less these birds were flesh.

Higden's animals are those of the bestiaries and of popular medieval belief. The other natural phenomena which he discussed, namely the miraculous lakes and precious stones, the strange pools, springs, and caverns of various countries, the mysterious islands off the coast of Ireland, express also the popular beliefs of the time. Because Higden shared on these topics the views of his contemporaries his book gives some notion of the outlook of fourteenth-century England.

[1] i. 334–6.

V

CLASSICAL AND MEDIEVAL SOURCES IN THE *POLYCHRONICON*

L IKE Vincent of Beauvais in the *Speculum Historiale* Higden was an assiduous transcriber of earlier authorities, and a study of his sources in the *Polychronicon* gives some indication of the learning of a Benedictine monk in the fourteenth century. His chronicle was a typically medieval compilation made up of extracts from chronicles, lives of saints, biblical commentaries, and encyclopaedias such as those of Isidore and Bartholomew of England. At the same time Higden was interested in antiquity; not only did he use the work of classical authors but he sought information about the writings of the ancient world. Though much of his knowledge of Roman writings came from medieval sources, from *florilegia* and encyclopaedias, his concern with antiquity took him at times beyond the standard compilations, and his chronicle reflects in its earlier sections the new interest in antiquity which was developing during this period.[1]

I

Of the authors of the Graeco-Roman world Higden knew only those of Rome. The opportunities for acquiring a knowledge of

---

[1] The 'classicizing friars' are a group whose activities have been recently studied. This group which includes Waleys, Ridevall, Lathbury, and Holcot reveal in their sermons, their aids to preaching, and their lectures on Scripture, an interest in classical history and literature which went far beyond that of most of their contemporaries. See B. Smalley, *English Friars and Antiquity* (1960), cited as *English Friars*. The bibliographical interests of Richard de Bury, author of the *Philobiblon*, are well known. On Richard de Bury see N. Denholm-Young, *Collected Papers on Medieval Subjects* (1946), pp. 1–25. For the text of the *Philobiblon*, *Philobiblon Ricardi de Bury*, ed. M. Maclagan (1960).

I am indebted for several suggestions in this chapter to Miss Beryl Smalley, Dr. R. W. Hunt, and Dr. P. J. Jones.

Greek were limited during his lifetime,[1] and for his account of Greek history he relied upon a number of Latin sources. The only historian who wrote in Greek whose work he knew was the late Jewish historian, Josephus. Higden used the Latin versions of the *Jewish Antiquities*, the *History of the Jewish War*, and also the medieval abbreviation of Josephus known as Hegesippus.[2]

For his comments on Greek history Higden quoted a number of widely different Latin accounts. His description of the Trojan wars came from Justin's abbreviation of Trogus Pompeius, and from the *De excidio Troiae Historia* of Dares Phrygius which was probably written in the second century A.D. His references to Greek mythology were taken from the *De Civitate Dei*,[3] while the chapters on Alexander came from the *Epitome* of Julius Valerius, the *De Moribus Bragmanorum*, which has been attributed to St. Ambrose, and the *Speculum Historiale* of Vincent of Beauvais.[4] Of Greek literature he knew little. Homer was a shadowy figure known only through legend and the account of Latin authors such as Valerius Maximus. The Herodotus who appears in Higden's pages is not the Greek historian but a 'pseudo-Herodotus', who is quoted in the *De Proprietatibus Rerum* of Bartholomaeus Anglicus, and is mentioned in the work of

[1] P. J. G. Lehmann, 'Mittelalterliche Büchertitel,' *Sitzungsberichte der Bayerischen Akademie der Wissenschaften*, Heft 4 (1948), Heft 3 (1953). I owe this reference to Dr. R. W. Hunt. See also R. Weiss, 'The Study of Greek in England during the Fourteenth Century', *Rinascimento*, ii (1951), 209–41. See *Polychronicon*, i. 240, where Higden attempts to give some Greek words.

[2] iv. 426–50. *De Bello Iudaico*, ii. 24, iii. 14, vii. 7, 8; vii. i, 12. The text of Hegesippus is printed, *C.S.E.L.*, vol. lxvi.

[3] The account of Mercury, Jupiter, and Apollo. ii. 336, 340, 342, 348, comes from the *De Civitate Dei* (Dombart and Kalb), xviii. 8, 12, 13 (pp. 265, 270, 273).

[4] Higden's immediate source was the account of Alexander found in the fourth book of the *Speculum Historiale*. This was an account made up from a number of sources, including the *Epitome* of Julius Valerius. This was not the only text which Higden used, and his ultimate source was the history of the pseudo-Callisthenes, which was translated into Latin by Julius Valerius. The *Epitome* was an abridgement of Julius Valerius which was often copied together with other Alexander material. See G. Cary, *The Medieval Alexander*, pp. 24 seq.; R. W. Hunt, 'A Manuscript Belonging to Robert Wivill, Bishop of Salisbury', *The Bodleian Library Record* (June 1962), p. 27.

Vincent of Beauvais.[1] On Greek medicine Higden mentioned Hippocrates and Galen, but for the rest the achievements of the Greek world faded into insignificance when set against the accomplishments of Rome.

A main part of Higden's concern with Greek history lay in the moral example and the moral precepts furnished by the lives of Socrates, Plato, Pythagoras, and Aristotle. Though the subjects belonged to antiquity Higden's material was relatively modern, for in order to write his account of the Greek sages he used the thirteenth-century treatise of the Franciscan, John of Wales. The *Compendiloquium*, as the work was known, was a significant piece of writing.[2] With its numerous quotations and anecdotes from the pagan classical world it linked the humanism of the twelfth with that of the fourteenth and fifteenth centuries.[3] Stories illustrating the lives of famous Greeks drawn from Valerius Maximus, Macrobius, Cicero, and Aulus Gellius were copied in the *Compendiloquium*, and found their way into Higden's work. From the *Compendiloquium* Higden took the story of Plato and the fishermen,[4] the story of Aristotle in Athens,[5] and the story of Aristotle ordering his writings to be buried with him where anti-Christ would find them.[6] Almost the whole of Higden's

[1] For Vincent of Beauvais's knowledge of classical writings see E. Boutaric, 'Vincent de Beauvais et la connaissance de l'antiquité classique au treizième siècle', *Revue des questions historiques*, xvii (1875), 5–57. For the influence of Vincent of Beauvais see B. L. Ullman, 'A Project for a New Edition of Vincent of Beauvais', *Speculum*, viii (1933), 312–26.

[2] On John of Wales and his writings see W. A. Pantin, 'John of Wales and Medieval Humanism', *Essays to Aubrey Gwynn* (1961), ed. J. A. Watt, J. B. Morrall, F. X. Martin, pp. 297–319; B. Smalley, *English Friars*, pp. 51–55; A. G. Little, *Studies in English Franciscan History* (Manchester, 1917), pp. 176–86.

The *Compendiloquium* was printed at Lyons in 1511. It is found in Bodley MS. Laud Misc. 603, ff. 61–98ᵛ.

I am indebted to the Public Library at Cardiff for loaning their printed copy to Leeds University.

[3] See W. A. Pantin, 'John of Wales and Medieval Humanism' (op. cit.), p. 302.

[4] iii. 350–2. *Compendiloquium*, f. clxiii. The story is found in *Policraticus*, ed. Webb, i. 141. 1 ff. The source of the story was the *De vestigiis et dogmatibus philosophorum* of Virius Nicomachus Flavianus. See E. R. Curtius, *European Literature and the Latin Middle Ages*, p. 52.

[5] iii. 360. *Compendiloquium*, f. clxiiiᵛ.

[6] iii. 366–8. *Compendiloquium*, f. clxviiᵛ. It is found in *De Naturis Rerum* (R.S., 1863), pp. 337–8. The story was quoted more than once during the fourteenth

chapters on the Greek philosophers in the third book of the *Polychronicon* came from the work of John of Wales, though without the slightest hint upon their origin.[1] The Roman world was that part of antiquity which most concerned the English monk. His account of Roman history was derived from a number of classical writings including the *Catilina* of Sallust, the *Ab Urbe Condita* of Livy, the *Facta et dicta memorabilia* of Valerius Maximus, and Suetonius' *Lives of the Caesars*, not to mention quotations from Pliny and Eutropius, and occasional extracts from Cicero, Seneca, Macrobius, and Aulus Gellius. Several of these writings were well known to the medieval world. It has been said that the *Facta et dicta memorabilia* of Valerius Maximus might have been written especially to suit the taste of the Middle Ages,[2] while the popular histories of Suetonius and Eutropius were the stock-in-trade of the medieval historian.[3] Some of Higden's extracts undoubtedly came by way of John of Wales. Quotations from Cicero, the *Tusculan Disputations*, the *De Natura Deorum*, and the *De Officiis* have their origin in that source,[4] and, in addition, the work of John of Wales introduced Higden to authors such as Aulus Gellius whose writings were scarce and difficult to obtain.[5]

century. See Miss Smalley's paper, 'A Quotation from John Ridevall on *De Civitate Dei* by William Woodford', in *Medium Aevum*, vol. xxxiii, No. 1, pp. 21–25.

[1] The chapter on Diogenes which was present in the earlier versions of the *Polychronicon* was indebted to the *Compendiloquium* in a general way. iii. 310 is from f. clii. The story of Alexander and Diogenes (iii. 308) is given in a rather different form in the *Compendiloquium*, ff. clii, cliii.

[2] *English Friars*, p. 88. There are extracts from Valerius Maximus in the *Polychronicon*, iii. 342, 352, 354, iv. 140, 222. Valerius Maximus, ed. Kempf, i. 6, ix. 12, iv. 3, iii. 4. 1, vi. 5.

[3] See M. L. W. Laistner, 'Some Reflections on Latin Historical Writing in the Fifth Century', *The Intellectual Heritage of the Early Middle Ages* (1957), pp. 3–21. There are extracts from Eutropius in the *Polychronicon*, iv. 40, 60, 104, 206, 226, 238, 310. Eutropius (ed. Ruehl), ii. 20, iii. 11, iv. 6, vi. 25, vii. 4, vii. 7, vii. 11.

[4] iii. 196, 204, 318, 322, 340.

[5] iii. 192, 280. *Compendiloquium*, ff. clxxi, cxlv. Manuscripts of the *Attic Nights* appear 'to occur complete only at Christ Church, Canterbury and at Durham, then among Duke Humphrey's gifts to Oxford University in 1439 . . .'. R. A. B. Mynors, 'The Latin Classics Known to Boston of Bury', *F.S.*, pp. 199–217. A quotation from Macrobius, *Saturnalia*, 11. 4, concerning a visit of Veteranus to Augustus after the battle of Actium may be first-hand or may equally come from some intermediary source: *Polychronicon*, iv. 304.

Whatever his use of secondary sources, Higden knew some of these authors in the original. He was acquainted with the work of Valerius Maximus, Suetonius, and Eutropius. He knew the *Natural History*[1] of Pliny the Elder in those books which were available to the Middle Ages. Among Roman authors his use of Livy is perhaps of the greatest interest, suggesting as it does a concern with ancient authors which went beyond the standard compilations. In the later versions of his chronicle Higden quoted the first and third decades of *Ab Urbe Condita* on such subjects as Tarquinius Priscus and the sons of Ancus, the establishment of the tribunes of the people at Rome, the battle at the Caudine Forks, and the measures taken at the time of the Second Punic War.[2] His Livy quotations are brief and are not easily identifiable, for in accordance with his later practice he departed with considerable freedom from the actual wording of his source. His use of Livy suggests an acquaintance with the classicizing interests of the day. Livy 'had lain right outside the school tradition'.[3] The earliest known commentary is that of Trevet compiled before Higden began his chronicle,[4] while the Dominican, Thomas Waleys, quoted Livy and saw the missing fourth decade at Bologna in 1330.[5] Higden wrote at a time, therefore, when scholars concerned themselves with the text of Livy, and when a new interest in classical studies is apparent. Whether he saw a copy of Livy remains in doubt, for texts of *Ab Urbe Condita* were rare, and are found only in the thirteenth-century catalogues of Glastonbury and Christ Church, Canterbury.[6]

A knowledge of the 'classicizing' work of contemporaries,[7]

---

[1] Higden appears to have known books two, three, six, seven, eight, and sixteen of the *Natural History*, which was found in an incomplete form in the Middle Ages. *Polychronicon*, i. 52, 54, 58, 60, 200. *Natural History* (Loeb edition), iii. 1, vi. 1, ii. 99, ii. 68, ii. 106 (pp. 5, 339, 347, 307, 355).

[2] *Polychronicon*, iii. 86, 186–8, 374–8; iv. 62–66. *Ab Urbe Condita* (ed. Conway and Walters), i. 40, ii. 33, ix. 2–4, xxvi (ed. Conway and Johnson), 35, 36.

[3] *English Friars*, p. 61.

[4] J. R. Dean, 'The Earliest Known Commentary on Livy', *Medievalia et Humanistica*, iii (1945), 86–98.   [5] *English Friars*, pp. 86–88, 94–95.

[6] R. A. B. Mynors, 'The Latin Classics known to Boston of Bury', *F.S.*, pp. 205–6.

[7] The term 'classicizing' is used throughout this chapter in the sense given to

acquired in the period between the first (CD) and the later (AB) versions of his chronicle, is further suggested by Higden's comment, made twice in the course of his narrative, that, despite Virgil's account, Aeneas could not have seen Dido, because Aeneas died more than 300 years before the foundation of Carthage.[1] Higden based his conclusion upon the date of the foundation of Carthage as given by Papias. In his commentary on De Civitate Dei, compiled in the 1330's, the Oxford Franciscan, John Ridevall, had similarly rejected Virgil's story. As Miss Smalley says: 'An Oxford Franciscan, grubbing in medieval compilations, had already the strength of will to reject the most famous of Virgil's stories'.[2] In view of the similarity between the two accounts, and the fact that Higden's entries appear only in the later versions of his chronicle, it is more than probable that at some time during the 1340's or 1350's he saw a copy of Ridevall's work.[3]

The work of Roman poets as well as of Roman historians was represented in Higden's chronicle. Virgil, famous in the Middle Ages as both a magician and a poet, appears in both roles in the Polychronicon.[4] The source for this 'medieval Virgil' was the De Naturis Rerum of Alexander Nequam, and from this work Higden took the well-known stories of Virgil's leech of gold which ended the plague at Naples,[5] of Virgil's garden surrounded by a wall of air, and of his palace with its images of different provinces and

it by Miss Smalley. 'It points to a fondness for classical literature, history and myth without suggesting that the (individual or) group played any special part in the rise of humanism': English Friars, p. 1.
[1] i. 166, ii. 432.   [2] English Friars, pp. 130–1.
[3] See Miss Beryl Smalley's paper, 'A Quotation from John Ridevall on De Civitate Dei by William Woodford', Medium Aevum, loc. cit. Ridevall's commentary was known to Woodford, but cannot have been widely read. It survives in only two copies. The wording of Ridevall and Higden is worth contrasting. 'Eneas nunquam vidit Didonem, que fundavit Cartaginem et fuit regina illius civitatis, quia Eneas fuit mortuus antequam Cartago fuit condita per trecentos annos et amplius' (English Friars, p. 320). '. . . quod Aeneas nunquam vidit Didonem . . . et obiit ante fundationem Carthaginis plusquam trecentis annis' (Polychronicon, ii. 432).
[4] See D. Comparetti, Vergil in the Middle Ages (1895); J. W. Spargo, Virgil the Necromancer (Cambridge, Mass., 1934).
[5] iv. 242. De Naturis Rerum, ed. T. Wright (R.S., 1863), 309–10.

lands.[1] Quotations from the *Aeneid* and the *Georgics* occur in Higden's chronicle. From the eighth book of the *Aeneid* came Virgil's description of Vulcan's shield,

> . . . tum lactea colla
> auro innectuntur.[2]

From the sixth book a line on souls returning to their bodies,

> . . . et incipiant in corpora velle reverti.[3]

Higden quoted lines from Horace, *De Arte Poetica*,[4] from the *Satires* of Juvenal,[5] and from the *Metamorphoses* of Ovid.[6]

In addition to his extracts from classical writings, Higden commented upon Roman authors and their works. Concerning Roman poets he stated, quoting Isidore, that the poet's task was to enhance and to transmute.[7] There were satirists like Persius, Horace, and Juvenal, and imaginative poets like Virgil and Ovid. According to Higden a writer such as Lucan fell into neither group.[8] Apart from comments such as these Higden gave details on the lives of men of letters. He mentioned the birth of Horace, the education of Virgil, and the banishment of Ovid. Though he

---

[1] iv. 242–4. *De Naturis Rerum*, 310.

[2] i. 266. *Aeneid* viii. 660. Higden wrote *humectentur*.

[3] iii. 196. *Aeneid* vi. 751. There is a quotation from the *Aeneid* viii. 313 at i. 208, and from the *Georgics* ii. 202 at ii. 38.

[4] i. 12. *De Arte Poetica* (ed. Wilkins), 304–5. There is another quotation from the *De Arte Poetica* in the *Polychronicon* (v. 56):

> bonus dormitat Homerus,
> *Verum operi longo fas est obrepere somnum.*   (359–60)

[5] iii. 316. *Satires*, x. 28–30:

> de sapientibus alter
> *Ridebat, quotiens de limine moverat unum*
> *Protuleratque pedem: flebat contrarius auctor?*

This refers to Democritus and Heraclitus, and not to Diogenes as Higden supposed.

[6] ii. 210, 362. *Metamorphoses*, x. 369; xiii. 23. The *Metamorphoses* in an allegorical form was used in medieval education. The most popular commentary was by Pierre Bersuire, written at Avignon about 1330. It was printed in 1515 by Regnault. In the *Speculum Historiale* (ed. Balthazaris Belleri, 1624), pp. 210–18, there are long quotations from Ovid.

At the end of his life Thomas Walsingham wrote a commentary on the books of the *Metamorphoses*, F. W. Hall, 'An English Commentary on Ovid', *Classical Quarterly*, xxi (1927), 151–5.

[7] iv. 406. *Etymologiae*, viii. 7. 10.   [8] iv. 408.

confused Cicero with a king of Rome,[1] in the case of Lucretius, whose work in the original was quite unknown, he transcribed the passage in the chronological canons of Eusebius, which preserved the known facts on the life of the poet.[2]

Higden's treatment of ancient authors reveals his undoubted interest in their work. He quoted from their writings, and set down what he could discover about their lives. In the terms of his day his learning was considerable. If he relied in part for his knowledge upon second-hand extracts to be found in patristic and medieval sources, his use of such sources was not unique, and considering the relative scarcity of several authors Higden was remarkable for what he knew. Apart from the actual extent of his knowledge the direction of his interests is also of some significance. Higden was a 'classicizing' monk, something of an antiquary, and he wrote his account of ancient authors in such a way as to interest readers in England for the next 200 years.

II

A chronicle such as Higden's, which combined an account of antiquity with a history of Britain, drew on a great number of medieval sources. A mere catalogue of these would make tedious reading, but some indication can be given both of the range of Higden's sources, and of the principal topics for which they were used. On the subject of antiquity the most significant of Higden's medieval sources was the *Compendiloquium* of John of Wales. Apart from its account of classical figures the treatise may well have introduced Higden to the work of John of Salisbury. The humanism of the twelfth reached the fourteenth century in an anthologized form. In the *Compendiloquium* John of Wales had popularized the *Policraticus*, 'exploiting it as a mine of stories,

---

[1] iv. 140. The source was Valerius Maximus, iii. 4. 1.

[2] iv. 148. *Euseb. Chron. ad ann. Abr. 1922*: 'T. Lucretius poeta nascitur, qui postea amatorio poculo in furorem versus, cum aliquot libros per intervalla insaniae conscripsisset, quos postea Cicero emendavit, propria se manu interfecit anno aetatis xliiii.' See J. Wight Duff, *A Literary History of Rome* (London, 1909), p. 276.

precepts, and fact about the ancient world'.[1] John of Salisbury had not intended his work to be used in this way; his book was a unified whole; but later writers selected simply those parts of the *Policraticus* that they found of value, and it was in this manner, as a source of information about antiquity, that the work of John of Salisbury was used in the *Polychronicon*. How well Higden knew the *Policraticus* it is difficult to say, for several of his quotations came by way of John of Wales. Apart from passages taken from the *Compendiloquium*, however, Higden appears to have used John of Salisbury's text for his description of Rome, and his account of the Roman emperors.[2]

If the work of John of Salisbury was valued mainly as a source of extracts about antiquity, the same was true of the writings of others. Scholars in the fourteenth century approached the work of Augustine in a similar fashion, for like the *Policraticus* the *De Civitate Dei* had its light to throw upon the ancient world. Commentaries on *De Civitate Dei* such as those of Trevet and Waleys stressed Augustine's wealth of detail on the Roman past,[3] and it was as a source of information about the history and religion of Rome that *De Civitate Dei* was used in Higden's work. The eighteenth book of *De Civitate Dei*, which was a recapitulation of the history of the earthly city, provided Higden with passages on the origin of the Greek myths and on the journeyings of the Greeks after the destruction of Troy, while extracts from Augustine on the First Punic War and the debate on the destruction of Carthage, were copied into the later books.[4]

---

[1] *English Friars*, p. 54. W. A. Pantin, 'John of Wales and Medieval Humanism', op. cit., p. 304.

[2] iv. 200, 308, 312, 400, 422. *Policraticus* (ed. Webb), iii. 14, vi. 4, iii. 14. viii. 13, iii. 14. The *Compendiloquium* was an intermediate text for extracts from medieval as well as classical sources. The use of the *De Naturis Rerum* of Alexander Nequam is one example. Though Higden used Nequam's work for his account of Virgil, passages which are elsewhere given under the name of Nequam, come from the *Compendiloquium*.

[3] *English Friars*, pp. 58, 88–100, 121–32.

[4] For examples of the use of Augustine in the *Polychronicon* see ii. 250, 252, 256, 274, 280, 296, 298, 304, 326, 336, 340, 342, 348, 360, 378, 418. *De Civitate Dei* (ed. Dombart), xviii. 2, xvi. 3, 17, xviii. 2, ii. 11, xviii. 5, 6, 5, 8, 8, 12, 12, 13, 12, 15, 16 (pp. 256, 125, 154, 257, 66, 262, 263, 262, 264, 265, 270, 270, 273, 270, 275, 276).

For the study of antiquity the *Derivationes* of Huguccio written in the twelfth century was a useful guide.[1] With its entries on classical and Christian history arranged alphabetically Huguccio's work was easy to use, and quotations from it are to be found in the commentaries of the 'classicizing friars'. For the chapter on Roman institutions in the first book of the *Polychronicon* Higden used the *Derivationes* as his principal source. Huguccio's information about such matters as the forms observed at a Roman triumph, the manner in which the Romans waged war, their principal feast days, and the fact that prostitutes were called *nonarie* because they were not allowed out until the hour of noon —all this was faithfully transcribed in Higden's work.[2] Apart from these entries other passages reveal Higden's reliance upon this source.

No account of antiquity could ignore the city of Rome, once the capital of the empire, and now the centre of Christian history and legend. For his description of Rome Higden used the twelfth-century guide book of 'Master Gregory'.[3] 'Master Gregory' was no archaeologist, and his explanation of classical monuments was bizarre in the extreme, yet he had a genuine interest in the buildings of antiquity. He described the palaces of Rome, the Pantheon, and the arch of Augustus, and listed the buildings by classes rather than topographically. If stories of the statue of Bellerophon suspended in mid-air, and legends such as that of the marble horses, appeared in the course of his narrative they served to emphasize its author's views.[4] 'Master Gregory' had clearly felt the power of Rome; antiquity had cast its spell; and Higden, the one writer known to quote his work, shared something of his interest.

[1] The *Liber Derivationum* is unpublished. The thirteenth-century manuscript in the University Library at Cambridge, MS. Ff. 5. 34 (no. 1324 in vol. ii of the *Catalogue of Manuscripts* published in 1857) has been used for this collation. Three leaves of the index or table are lost at the beginning.

[2] See the sections, *Clarus, Classis, Calon*, in the *Derivationes*, ff. 65, 65ᵛ, 78ᵛ. This is the source of the account in the *Polychronicon*, i. 240, 244.

[3] Master Gregory is edited by M. R. James in *E.H.R.* xxxii (1917), 531–54, and by G. McN. Rushforth in *Journal of Roman Studies*, ix (1919), 14–58. See p. 56.

[4] i. 226–88, 228–32. E. R. Curtius, *European Literature and the Latin Middle Ages*, pp. 405–6.

In his use of medieval sources Higden was not concerned with antiquity alone. For the description of the world with which he began his chronicle he used the *Etymologiae* of Isidore of Seville, and the *De Proprietatibus Rerum* of Bartholomaeus Anglicus. In the fourteenth century the *Etymologiae* still provided a chronicler with information on the countries of the world.[1] On Isidore's authority the eponymous heroes of antiquity were cited, and the etymology of place names was explained. Higden used the fourteenth book of the *Etymologiae*, entitled *De Terra et Partibus*, for his account of Parthia, Judaea, Egypt, Scythia, Italy, and for his description of Spain and the Mediterranean islands.[2] As well as the *Etymologiae*, the *De Proprietatibus Rerum* of Bartholomaeus Anglicus was used extensively throughout the first book of the *Polychronicon*. Bartholomaeus, of whom little is known, and who has been claimed both as a Frenchman and an Englishman, probably wrote his work in the first half of the thirteenth century.[3] With its account of the geography and the social customs of various European countries the *De Proprietatibus Rerum* contained a traditional body of information that was used by Vincent of Beauvais and by other writers.[4] The *De Proprietatibus Rerum* is one of Higden's unacknowledged sources. It does not appear in his list of authorities, nor is it referred to in his text. He used the fifteenth book and it is possible that he knew it under the title of the *Geographia Universalis* (B.M. MS. Arundel 123, ff. 1–22^v),

---

[1] On Isidore see Jacques Fontaine, *Isidore de Séville et la culture classique dans l'Espagne wisigothique* (1959), 2 vols.

[2]

i. 84	(Parthia)	=	*Etymologiae* 14. 3. 8
i. 102	(Judaea)	=	(ed. Lindsay) 14. 3. 20
i. 130	(Egypt)	=	14. 3. 27
i. 170	(Scythia)	=	14. 4. 3
i. 198	(Italy)	=	14. 4. 18
i. 200	(Italy)	=	13. 13. 2
i. 300	(Carthage)	=	15. 1. 30
i. 304	(Sardinia)	=	14. 6. 39

[3] The Latin text was printed by Lindelbach at Heidelberg in 1488. There is a version of the text in R. Steele, *Medieval Lore* (1907). See also Lynn Thorndyke, *History of Magic and Experimental Science* (New York, 1923), vol. ii, chapter v, and C. V. Langlois, *La Connaissance de la nature et du monde au Moyen Âge*, chapter v.

[4] It was used through Vincent of Beauvais. A. Bovenschen, 'Untersuchungen über Johann von Mandeville und die Quellen seiner Reisebeschreibung', *Zeitschrift der Gesellschaft für Erdkunde zu Berlin*, vol. xxiii (1888).

for the extracts in the *Polychronicon* have features in common with this text, which is little more than a copy, with additions, of Book XV, or in some versions, Book XIV, of Bartholomew's work.[1] Bartholomew's text was the basis of several chapters. The account of the dimensions of the world and of Paradise comes almost entirely from it,[2] as does Higden's account of Cappadocia and Asia Minor, his account of Germany,[3] his description of the French provinces of Flanders and Picardy,[4] and, with certain modifications, his remarks on Normandy and Burgundy.[5]

In the fourteenth century, as previously, the Vulgate and its commentaries were fundamental sources for a universal chronicle that described the scheme of Christian history. The book of Genesis provided the medieval chronicler with his account of the origins of the world, and of the division of the earth among the descendents of Noah, while the books of the New Testament were used to describe the birth and life of Jesus. In the early chapters of the second book where Higden discussed the first age of the world the book of Genesis was therefore a principal authority,[6] while Matthew and Luke were used for the description of the life of Christ.[7] Quotations from the Vulgate occur throughout the chronicle.[8] Equally important as a source was the work of Biblical commentators, especially the *Historia scholastica* of Peter Comestor.[9] Comestor's summary of the historical books of the Old and New Testament provided Higden with information on such topics as the birth of Abraham, the colour of the

---

[1] The extract from Priscian found in this manuscript is given in the *Polychronicon*. The editors of the Rolls Series identified the *Geographia Universalis* as a source of the *Polychronicon*, but did not appreciate that it was part of the work of Bartholomaeus Anglicus.

[2] The text of the *De Proprietatibus Rerum* in B.M. MS. Arundel 123 has been used. The folio references are to that manuscript. i. 40–46 is from f. 23; i. 66–78 from f. 14^v.

[3] i. 146–54. ff. 4^v, 9, 12^v; i. 254–66. ff. 4^v, 8, 8^v, 18^v, 20, 21^v.

[4] i. 288: f. 8; i. 290: f. 17.   [5] i. 290: f. 14; i. 296–8: f. 4^v.

[6] ii. 232, 238, 240, 284, 286, 290, 292. Genesis v. 31, viii. 4, x. 22, xi. 26, xi. 28, xxv. 16, xix. 24, 37, 38. There are quotations from Exodus. *Polychronicon*, ii. 318, 324. Exodus ii. 3, 12, 21.   [7] iv, 264 Luke i. 56; ii. 1. Matthew i. 24.

[8] i 18, v. 36. Romans xv. 4. Psalms 102. 9.

[9] See B. Smalley, *The Study of the Bible in the Middle Ages* (Oxford, 1951).

Red Sea, and various incidents in the life of Christ,[1] and was a principal source for the narrative contained in the third and fourth books of the *Polychronicon*.[2]

III

Higden's account of British history formed an important part of his work, and chronicles feature largely among his sources. For his account of earlier European history he had used Jerome's translation of the chronicle of Eusebius, the *Historiarum adversus paganos* of Orosius, and the *Historia Langobardorum* of Paul the Deacon. The *Historia Langobardorum* was the source of several passages, including the account of the Seven Sleepers in Germany, King Cunincpert and the fly, and the story of Gunthram, king of the Franks, who in a dream was shown a mountain filled with gold.[3] On matters of chronology the chronicle of Marianus Scotus was consulted, but these accounts, together with the *Speculum Historiale* of Vincent of Beauvais,[4] appear to have been almost the only European chronicles known to Higden. In his list of authorities he mentioned Ivo of Chartres and a *Historia Francorum*,[5] but apart from these he knew few continental chronicles. Though he included in his list of authorities Cassiodorus' *De Gestis imperatorum et pontificum*,[6] and mentioned the work in his text,[7] he did not use this history, but in those passages that appear under the name of Cassiodorus simply transcribed parts of the chronicle of Marianus Scotus.[8] Higden's knowledge of European chroniclers, and of French chronicles in particular, contrasts unfavourably with that of a twelfth-century writer such

---

[1] ii. 290, 294, 302, 328, 330. *Historia scholastica* (*P.L.* 98), cols. 1053–1844, Cap. 50: 1097, Cap. 56: 1103, Cap. 78: 1118, Cap. 24: 1151, Cap. 30: 1157.

[2] iii. 94, 98, 106, 108, iv. 332–4. Higden mentions Bede's translation of the Gospel of St. John (vi. 224). See M. Deansley, *The Lollard Bible* (Cambridge, 1920), p. 441.

[3] i. 264–6, vi. 144–6, v. 384–8. *Historia Langobardorum*, (*M.G.H.*, 1878), i. 4, vi. 3, 17.

[4] For the chapters on Alexander, iii. 312–478, iv. 2–16.   [5] i. 24.

[6] *Polychronicon*, i. 22.

[7] iv. 344, v. 80, 236. I owe the following reference to Dr. E. Langstadt.

[8] P. Lehmann, *Erforschung des Mittelalters* (1959), ii. 39.

as William of Malmesbury, and it emphasizes the fact that little of later European history is dealt with in his work.

For his account of early British history Higden used the chronicle of Bede,[1] but apart from the *Historia Ecclesiastica* he quoted no other pre-Conquest source. He knew best the English chroniclers of the twelfth century, Alfred of Beverley, Florence of Worcester, and William of Malmesbury. Among these, the *Annales sive Historia de gestis Regum Britannie* of Alfred of Beverley, a history of Britain in nine books from its origins to 1129, was used for the description of Britain, though the passages from Alfred's history were much changed.[2] A more important source was the chronicle of Florence of Worcester which provided passages found in the later versions of Higden's text. The Huntington copy of the *Polychronicon*, which was written at Chester, contains in the margins of the chronicle several passages that were added from the *Chronicon ex chronicis*.[3] From the fact that the name of Florence of Worcester appears last in the list of authorities at the beginning of the *Polychronicon*[4] it is probable that Higden read or reread Florence's history at a late stage in his work of revision. In recording the death of Florence of Worcester in his chronicle Higden added the note, 'to whose literary labours the present work is much indebted'.[5]

The *Gesta Regum* of William of Malmesbury was an important source for both Anglo-Saxon and Norman history.[6] Long passages from the chronicle of William of Malmesbury, transcribed in the longer versions of the text, told the story of Ranulf Flambard, the Cistercian settlement, and the times of Henry I.[7] In these chapters Higden seldom used the exact wording of William of Malmesbury, but abbreviated and paraphrased his account,

---

[1] *Polychronicon*, vi. 2, 6, 50, 58, 64, 66, 70, 72, 80. *Historia Ecclesiastica* (ed. Plummer), pp. 139, 162, 142, 145, 154, 171, 177, 179, 177.

[2] *Polychronicon*, ii. 22–26, 52–54. *Annales sive Historia*, 6–8, 9.

[3] See Chapter VI.

[4] i. 24–26.

[5] vii. 454–6. There are additions from Florence of Worcester at vi, 122, 270–2.

[6] vii. 214–28, 230–44. *Gesta Regum*, ed. W. Stubbs (R.S., 1887–9), ii. 246, 280, ii. 299.

[7] vii. 382–4, 394–404, 416–28. *Gesta Regum*, ii. 368, 380–2, 470.

bringing together widely different passages in order to construct his own narrative. Two Welsh writers who influenced the content of his history were Geoffrey of Monmouth and Gerald of Wales. The *Historia Regum Britanniae* of Geoffrey of Monmouth provided Higden with the legendary framework of British history within which his own account was written, while the topographical writings of Gerald of Wales gave him the material for several chapters in the first book of his chronicle. From the account of Geoffrey of Monmouth Higden quoted the 'facts' of early British history; the list of British kings, the laws of Molmutius, and the supposed origins of the episcopal sees.[1] His use of Gerald of Wales was more extensive. The *Topographia Hibernica*, the *Itinerarium Cambriae*, and the *Descriptio Cambriae* were the main sources for his description of Ireland and Wales in the first book,[2] and without these writings his own chapters could scarcely have been written. Though copies of the *Topographia* were to be found in ecclesiastical libraries, Higden's use of Gerald's topographical writings was unusual among fourteenth-century chroniclers and is to be explained, no doubt, by his own geographical concerns.[3] Higden took passages from other works by Gerald of Wales, for example, from the *De Principis Instructione* he took the story of Henry II ordering a painting to be made for his chamber at Winchester,[4] while the account of Richard I and his three 'daughters' came from the *Speculum Ecclesiae*.[5] In neither case was the source acknowledged.

The weakest part of Higden's narrative was his account of thirteenth-century British history, and for this part of his history

---

[1] ii. 90–96, 110. *Historia Regum Britanniae*, ii. 17, iii. 5, iv. 9.

[2] See Chapter IV where Higden's sources for this part of his history are given. Chapter 32 on Ireland is from the *Topographia*, iii. 7, i. 1, ii. 1, i. 2, i. 4, i. 25, 26, 27, i. 7, 8, 9, 10, 11, i. 22, i. 5, i. 4, i. 18, i. 7, i. 18, i. 22, 23, 25.

[3] *Topographia*, p. lxxviii. There was a copy of the *Topographia* in the library of the Austin friars at York, M. R. James, 'The Catalogue of the Library of the Austin Friars at York', *Fasciculus Ioanni Willis Clark Dicatus* (1909), no. 170. An abridgement of Gerald's work was made in the early fourteenth century. Higden appears to have used Gerald's original account.

[4] *Polychronicon*, viii. 36. *De Principis Instructione*, ed. G. F. Warner (R.S., 1891), viii. 295–6.

[5] *Polychronicon*, viii. 158. *Speculum Ecclesiae*, ed. J. S. Brewer (R.S., 1873), iv. 54.

he did not use any of the standard chronicle accounts. There is in the *Polychronicon* no mention of the work of Matthew Paris, or of any other thirteenth-century chronicler. As one source for this part of his history Higden used the *Anonymous A Life of St. Edmund Rich* which circulated in many copies.[1] His use of the *Life*, from which he took a number of *exempla*, suggests that his historical interest faded at this point, and that he did not make a study of the sources of recent British history.[2] He mentions, however, a 'missing' source, a *Life* of Richard I, said to have been written by Stephen Langton.[3] From Higden's account, the *Life*, if authentic, appears to have been concerned with the course of events in England during Richard's absence and with the attacks upon the Jews. Higden says that he took 'the flowers of Stephen's excellent work', but the ascription to Stephen Langton cannot, in the absence of other evidence, be considered final.

As can be seen from this brief survey the *Polychronicon* was a great repository of classical and medieval sources. Higden's use of classical sources is the most interesting aspect of this subject, and his quotations from Latin authors put his work in the tradition of fourteenth-century 'classicizing' thought. At the same time Higden's interests extended to other forms of literature and it is no surprise to find in his chronicle extracts from Biblical commentaries, homiletic aids, and lives of the saints. The most striking omission among his sources is possibly that of the scholastic writings of the thirteenth century. There are no Oxford books in the *Polychronicon*, and no evidence of any knowledge of the scholastic writings of the time. Though extracts

---

[1] C. H. Lawrence, *St. Edmund of Abingdon* (1960), p. 60. The account of St. Edmund is found in the *Polychronicon*, viii. 214–34.

[2] There are additions in the later versions of his text on John (viii. 170–6), and on the succession to the throne of Scotland (viii. 272–80).

[3] viii. 82, 204. See the remarks of F. M. Powicke, *Stephen Langton* (1928), p. 20. '. . . it is not possible to distinguish Higden's comments from Langton's, nor without a tedious investigation, which could only give us tentative results, to analyse the possible relations between Langton's work and other contemporary accounts of Richard's reign.' Higden adds that Langton wrote a history of Mohammed (vi. 14).

from Aristotelian commentaries had, no doubt, little relevance to a work of this nature, the very completeness of their absence serves to emphasize that Higden's interests belonged not to the fashionable world of scholastic philosophy but to the older study of literary texts.

VI

THE DEVELOPMENT OF THE TEXT

THE list of surviving manuscripts of the *Polychronicon* can be divided into its short, intermediate, and long versions. In order to illustrate more clearly the details which follow it is necessary to give at the start the relationship of these three versions. The development of the *Polychronicon* text was from a short to a long version,

Short version   (*Rolls Series CD*)

Intermediate version (*Rolls Series AB*)

Long version   (*Rolls Series E*)[1]

The essential details of this process are provided by a manuscript now in the Huntington Library which is almost certainly an autograph copy of Higden's work. The manuscript reveals that Higden started with a short version of the *Polychronicon* and added to it over a number of years. At various stages copies were struck off by professional scribes. Although a medieval 'best seller' the *Polychronicon* in one sense was never completed, for it is almost certain that Higden was working upon the text of his chronicle until the time of his death in the 1360's.

I

The problems posed by Higden's text can be seen by a glance at the Rolls Series edition. Though the edition is unsatisfactory

---

[1] The lettering of the Rolls Series edition is used throughout this chapter. The AB version is, however, described as the intermediate version to distinguish it from E.

The part of this chapter which concerns the *Polychronicon* in the Huntington Library is based on the work of V. H. Galbraith published in *H.L.Q.*

in several ways, its editors did make a considerable effort to produce a sound Latin text. To do this they collected five representative manuscripts, which they called A, B, C, D, and E.

The manuscripts which are lettered in the Rolls Series edition C and D represent a short version of the *Polychronicon* which ends at 1327. The *incipits* of the seven books of this version are:

    I.   *In historico namque contextu* . . . (C omits *namque*)
    II.   *Ordo narrationis historicae* . . .
    III. *Quinta mundi aetas* . . .
    IV. *In principio igitur* 42^i *anni* . . .
    V.   *Marcianus imperator post mortem Theodosii* . . .
    VI. *Mortuo rege Ethelredo* . . .
    VII. *Willelmus igitur ut praedictum est* . . .
    ending . . . *mare tranquillitatem ecclesia libertatem.*

Two manuscripts were chosen to represent this short version of the *Polychronicon*. The first of these was Magdalen College, Oxford, MS. 181 (C), which contains a short form of the chronicle down to 1327. It is a fourteenth-century manuscript and is one of the earliest copies of Higden's work. On f. 99ᵛ is a note in a fifteenth-century hand of the founding of the canons of Dunstable in 1131. The second manuscript was St. John's College, Cambridge, MS. 12 (D), which contains a slightly different text of the short version ending in 1327. From the evidence of a note on the last leaf, this manuscript may have belonged to Hyde Abbey and it was written by John Lutton, who wrote another copy of the *Polychronicon*, B.M. MS. Arundel 86.[1]

Apart from the short version an intermediate version of the text extends to some point in the 1340's. This is the version known in the Rolls Series classification as AB. The *incipits* of the seven books of this intermediate version are somewhat different from those of the short version,

    I.   *Post praeclaros artium scriptores* . . .
    II.   *Ordo narrationis historicae* . . .

---

[1] On John Lutton in an Oxford list of 1410 see Falconer Madan, *Oxford Books* (Oxford, 1912), ii, p. 506.

III. *Quinta mundi aetas* . . .
IV. *In principium igitur 42¹ anni* . . .
V. *Marcianus copulata sibi* . . .
VI. *Aluredus quartus natu* . . .
VII. *Willelmus igitur Londoniam* . . .

The intermediate version is represented in the Rolls Series edition by two manuscripts. The first of these is Cambridge U.L. MS. Ii. II. 24 (A), a fifteenth-century text written by a scribe named Arnold who is shown in the manuscript in a miniature praying to St. Catherine. The manuscript was no. 934 in the library catalogue of St. Augustine's, Canterbury.[1] The second manuscript selected to represent this version was Gonville and Caius College, Cambridge, MS. 82 (B), which was written during the fourteenth century. A note on the fly-leaf says that it was given by Henry Osborne at the end of that century. One difficulty in establishing the development of the *Polychronicon* text comes from the fact that this intermediate version was by far the most popular one, and survives in almost seventy copies.

In addition to these two versions the editors of the Rolls Series text took in a fifth manuscript, which they perceived represented the fullest form of the chronicle, and whose readings they generally followed.[2] This is the long version known as E. The manuscript that they used which contains the text in its most complete form is Cambridge U.L. MS. Ii. III. 1. It is written in a late fourteenth-century script and, from a note on the fly-leaf (f. 275ᵛ), it appears to have belonged to J. Broke, a monk of Christ Church, Canterbury. The text in this manuscript extends to 1352. This long version was not well known, however, and survives in only a few manuscripts.

The relationship of these versions and the stages that they represent in the development of Higden's text have long been a matter of debate. The problem posed by the existence of a short and an intermediate version was known to scholars in the

---

[1] M. R. James, *Ancient Libraries of Canterbury and Dover* (Cambridge, 1903), p. 297.
[2] *Polychronicon*, I. lii, n. 2.

sixteenth and seventeenth centuries. Bale and Wanley supposed that the short version was the work of one Roger of Chester, who called his work, *Polycratica*, as opposed to the *Polychronicon*, which incorporated the shorter work. As late as 1863 Blades in his *Life of William Caxton* stated that the *Polychronicon* had its origin in a compilation by Roger, a monk of St. Werburgh's, Chester, and that his compilation was amplified by Higden, who entitled the ensuing product, *Polychronicon*.[1] The name 'Roger of Chester' does not occur, however, in any contemporary script,[2] and there is no justification, as the editors of the Rolls Series edition themselves stated, for supposing that the short version represents the work of any one other than Higden himself.[3]

While disposing of 'Roger of Chester' the editors of the Rolls Series edition held firmly to the view that the short version was an abbreviation of a longer text. The collation repeatedly contains the phrase, 'Thus abridged in C and D', with the assumption that A and B contain the original version. A manuscript of the *Polychronicon* now in the Huntington Library, and almost certainly the autograph of Higden, reveals quite clearly that the reverse process occurred, and that in fact the short version represents an early stage of a text which was expanded over the years into the later and fuller versions.

II

The manuscript of the *Polychronicon* in the Huntington Library was originally Phillipps MS. 20712 and has notes on Arthur, Bede, and Gildas on the fly-leaf.[4] Evidence that it once belonged to the abbey of St. Werburgh is found in a marginal note written in a contemporary scrivener's script at the foot of f. 183; 'Ricardus

---

[1] W. Blades, *Life and Typography of William Caxton* (1861–3), ii. 124.

[2] It is found in a later hand in several copies of the short version. B.M. MS. Royal 14. C. xiii which is a short version has a note on the fly-leaf which says 'Cronica Rogeri monachi Cestrensis'. The 'Rogeri' is crossed out and 'Ranulphi' written.

[3] *Polychronicon*, I. xv–xx.

[4] I am indebted to the authorities of the Huntington Library for allowing me to examine this manuscript.

abbas monasterii sancte Werburge'. This note refers to Richard Seynesbury, who was Abbot of St. Werburgh's from 1349 until his resignation in 1363. Other evidence suggests a Chester origin. On f. 177 there is a framed marginal note, 'De corpore sante Werburge', and on f. 195ᵛ there is a similar heading 'Translacio Werburge ad Cestr'. Taken together the evidence justifies the presumption that the manuscript belonged to St. Werburgh's abbey during Higden's lifetime. Further evidence of its Chester provenance comes from the verses written inside the back cover by a sixteenth-century owner:

> Iste liber pertinet beare it well in mynde
> Ad me Georgium Savagium Boothe curteyes and kynde
> A penis inferni Jehesu him bringe
> Ad gaudia celestia to everlastinge joye,
>
> Amen.

St. Werburgh's abbey was dissolved in 1540, and the bishopric of Chester was founded in 1541. George Savage was appointed registrar general and chancellor of the new cathedral in 1544. In that position he had plenty of opportunity for acquiring manuscripts from the monastic library. There can be little doubt, therefore, that the Huntington *Polychronicon* belonged to St. Werburgh's. From the fact that no part of the chronicle is later than about 1352, and that the writing belongs to the middle of the fourteenth century, a strong presumption exists that this was Higden's working copy, and that it embodies his final corrections to the text.

There are several features that connect the manuscript with Higden. In the first place there are certain erasures which concern the capital letters at the beginning of the early chapters. The reason for the alteration of the capital letters was to produce the acrostic found in the intermediate version of the *Polychronicon* where the initial letters of the first sixty chapters spell out: 'Presentem cronicam compilauit Frater Ranulphus Cestrensis monachus'. The acrostic is not found in the short version of the *Polychronicon*, and the words *Frater Ranulphus* were not present in the original text of the Huntington copy. In order to associate his name with the *Polychronicon* Higden thus altered the capital letters of several chapters. The alteration can be seen in the Huntington copy with the aid of ultraviolet light. In that manuscript the scribe, in order to guide the rubricator, put in the margin the original letter which he wanted done in red. With this evidence of the original opening letters it is apparent that the opening word or words of every chapter from chapter twenty-nine to chapter thirty-four (ff. 23^v–32) have been altered. Chapter twenty-nine, which originally began with *F*, now begins with *R* to make the first *R* of Frater. A small *r* still remains in the margin (f. 23^v). Chapter thirty-seven, which began with *N*, now begins with *U* to make the first *U* of Ranulphus. The least successful of the erasures was in Chapter thirty-eight, which is the chapter describing Wales. The chapter originally began with a poem whose opening lines were:

> Priusquam tangam Angliam
> Que vastam vult materiam

and it was altered to

> Libri finis nunc Cambriam
> Prius tangit quam Angliam.

It is worth noting that the alterations are concerned only with the insertion of the author's name, *Frater Ranulphus*, and for that reason they begin only at f. 23. The author had intended from the start to put in some phrase which contained the words 'presentem cronicam compilavit . . . Cestrensis monachus'. This is shown by the fact that the early chapter headings up to f. 23 are unaltered, and by Higden's comment at f. 37: 'Est et alia urbs legionum eiusdem nominis, ubi et praesens chronica fuit elaborata, sicut per capitales huius primi libri apices clarius patet'.[1]

Apart from the elaboration of the acrostic the most interesting alterations in the Huntington manuscript concern the excision of certain leaves and the substitution of others in their place.

---

[1] *Polychronicon*, ii. 76.

These excisions occur at two places, at ff. 9, 10, 11, 12, where the new folios are pasted onto the stubs of the excised leaves, and at ff. 22, 23. The reason for the excisions at ff. 9, 10, 11, 12 is not known. The text which is covered by the present folios extends from *Iudaea* (f. 9) and goes to *sunt Pannonie* (f. 11ᵛ). It may be that the excisions at this point were made simply in order to incorporate new material. The excisions at ff. 22, 23 are more interesting for they occur at a place where the alterations to the capital letters begin (f. 23), and at a place where a new chapter, twenty-eight, has been inserted. The substitutions at ff. 22, 23 were not made for the sake of elaborating the acrostic, for this was done after their insertion, and the chapter headings are altered on the new leaves as on the succeeding folios. The substitution of the new leaves at this point was probably made in order to incorporate material in a new chapter. Chapter twenty-eight, which is contained on f. 23, was a later addition. Proof of this is furnished by the fact that the provinces of Flanders, Aquitaine, and Brittany, which are described in this new chapter, were first included in chapter twenty-seven, and were indexed as such at the back of the volume. In all these cases, however, the reference in the index was altered to twenty-eight.[1]

The alterations to the acrostic, the excision of certain folios, and the substitution of new leaves, leave little doubt that the Huntington copy was a manuscript upon which Higden worked. There is also the evidence of almost 100 marginal additions written in the same hand as the text itself. Of these some twenty are prefixed by an *R*, and are author's additions. A few were rubricated,[2] and some were erased and transferred to other parts of the manuscript.[3] One of the latest additions is at f. 280ᵛ and concerns the great frost at Chester in 1339. As well as author's additions there are extracts from the chronicle of Florence of Worcester, and a large collection of miscellaneous additions is distributed fairly evenly throughout the whole volume. The nature of the additions, and the fact that several were added not long after the chronicle was composed, again suggest that the manuscript was

---

[1] ff. 284ᵛ, 285, 287.   [2] One example is at f. 51ᵛ.   [3] f. 48ᵛ.

Higden's autograph copy. Briefly it may be said that the Huntington manuscript illustrates Higden's efforts to expand and revise a short version of the *Polychronicon*, not dissimilar to C and D, into a longer text which corresponds to the E version.

III

The Huntington manuscript reveals that Higden started with a short version of his chronicle, and added to it. In the light of this knowledge we should consider the different versions of the *Polychronicon*, and their place in the development of the text.

The original form of the *Polychronicon* was almost certainly a 'primitive version' which extended to 1327. It contained a short text with no acrostic, and with probably fewer chapters than any of the surviving copies. There were possibly no chapters at all in the earliest version, which belonged to the period before the Huntington copy was made. We do not possess a manuscript of this 'primitive version'; but a copy of the *Polychronicon*, now in the British Museum, may descend directly from it. This manuscript, B.M. MS. Royal 13. E. i, which was written in the fourteenth century, was given to the cathedral church of Lincoln by a canon, John de Warsop. It is a short version of the *Polychronicon*, and after 1327 has a continuation from the *Historia Aurea*, which is found after early copies of the text. The manuscript is distinguished by having fewer chapters than any of the surviving manuscripts of the short version.[1] In the first book it has chapter headings only after the general prologue, and for the early chapters. A second manuscript that may also descend from this 'primitive version' is MS. Rawlinson B. 191, a fourteenth-century copy, once in the possession of Christ Church, Canterbury. Its text omits the whole of the prologue and begins only at page 40 of the printed Rolls Series text. MS. Rawlinson B. 191 does not give the names of Higden's authorities, and it has several alterations to the text.

---

[1] *Catalogue of Royal and King's Manuscripts* (British Museum, 1921), ii. 111, mentions that it has no division into chapters.

These two manuscripts represent an early, perhaps the earliest, form of Higden's chronicle. In addition there are a number of copies of the short (CD) version that differ only slightly among themselves. They also descend from a text that was constructed before the Huntington manuscript was written and which contained no acrostic. From these manuscripts, Magdalen College, Oxford, MS. 181 (C), and St. John's College, Cambridge, MS. 12 (D), were chosen for the Rolls Series text, but in addition the following manuscripts contain a text of Higden's short version; B.M. MSS. Harley 1728–9, which was originally one manuscript; MS. Harley 1707; MS. Harley 1751; Cotton MS. Nero D. viii, ff. 188–344; Cotton MS. Julius E. viii; MS. Royal 14. C. xiii; MS. Royal 13. C. iii; Bodleian, MS. Rawlinson B. 151; MS. Bodley 341; Merton College, Oxford, MS. 118; Edinburgh, Nat. Lib. Advocates MS. 33. 4. 12; Rylands Latin MS. 218; Lambeth MS. 104; Trinity Hall, Cambridge, MS. 25; Brussels, Bibliothèque Royale MS. 9903.[1] Several of these copies are in an imperfect condition. MS. Julius E. viii lacks Books I–III and parts of Books IV and VII, while Lambeth MS. 104 lacks the end of Book III and the beginning of Book IV.

The manuscripts that contain the short version of the *Polychronicon* preserve what is undoubtedly an early form of Higden's chronicle, but in almost all cases they show influences of the later development of the text. Although they do not contain chapter twenty-eight, the numbering of their own chapters reveals that the scribes knew of the existence of this chapter in later copies. In more than one case chapter numbers go from twenty-seven to twenty-nine, while in MSS. Harley 1728–9 the contents of chapter twenty-eight were copied on to a separate folio, and then stitched into the manuscript. A knowledge of the development of Higden's text is also suggested by the uncertainty about the map. The map appears at the end of the Prologue in the Huntington copy, and was almost certainly not present in Higden's earliest version. Copies of the map are found

---

[1] B.M. Add. MS. 10105, and Lambeth MS. 112 may also be included with this group, although they have peculiarities of their own.

exclusively in manuscripts of the intermediate (AB) version. Yet despite this in several copies of the short version a blank space has been left at the end of the Prologue where the map would normally follow (MS. Bodley 341; St. John's College, Cambridge, MS. 12), and in certain cases this space has been filled in with a curious entry about the military service of the Cinque Ports (Magdalen College, Oxford, MS. 181; Cotton MS. Nero D. viii; B.M. MS. Royal 13. C. iii).[1]

The short version of the *Polychronicon* was the form in which Higden's work first became known. Chroniclers writing in the 1340's, such as the compiler of the *Historia Aurea*, knew only this version of Higden's text. From its first appearance, however, the success of the *Polychronicon* was certain. The earliest text of the chronicle, written *c.* 1327, was warmly received; its fame spread during the 1330's and 1340's; and by the 1350's when he was summoned to the court of Edward III Higden's work had become something of a classic. In the years following his first version Higden revised his work, and some time during these years, in the period after the *Polychronicon* had become famous, but before Higden had made all his corrections to the Huntington copy, another version, the intermediate (AB) version was written.

Exactly when the AB version was first written it is impossible to say, but it was written before Higden had finished all his corrections to the text as they survive in the Huntington copy. Proof of this is furnished by the fact that entries which were included and then removed from the Huntington copy are still found in the AB version. At whatever date the AB version was written, and it probably belongs to the 1340's, it soon became extremely popular. Religious houses and cathedral churches

---

[1] A copy of the short version which belonged to Westminster should be mentioned. This is MS. Bodley 341 which has three prefaces instead of the four found in the later AB version. It has, at the foot of a folio, a passage on the royal procession at Westminster in 1248, which is taken from the AB version (viii. 238). This passage is not found in other copies of the short version, and was inserted presumably for its Westminster interest. After the three prologues a folio is left blank (f. 2), probably for the insertion of the map. The text ends in 1327, and was followed by the *Historia Alexandri Magni* of which the end is lost.

which already possessed copies of the short version, acquired in several cases copies of the AB text as well.[1]

There are almost seventy surviving copies of the AB version. Manuscripts of this version belong to the fourteenth and fifteenth centuries, and one or two are written on paper (B.M. MS. Harley 3673 and Add. MS. 39236). From among these manuscripts the Rolls Series editors selected Cambridge U.L. MS. Ii. II. 24 (A) and Gonville and Caius College, Cambridge, MS. 82 (B) for the readings of their text, but they also used a manuscript given by Wykeham to Winchester College (Winchester College MS. 15). Among copies of the AB version that deserve mention are B.M. MS. Royal 14. C. ix, a fourteenth-century copy which belonged to the Benedictine abbey of Ramsey, and was selected as an example of the AB version in the *Class Catalogue of British Museum Manuscripts*, and B.M. MS. Royal 13. D. i, which belonged to St. Peter's, Cornhill, London, and which is an example of an early copy of the AB text written during the reign of Richard II.

The version contained in these manuscripts derives from Higden's revised text at Chester. The AB text is essentially the short (CD) version with additions. A manuscript in the B.M. MS. Royal 14. C. xii, which belonged to the Hospital of St. Thomas of Acon, started as an expanded text of the short (CD) version. Though it was generally similar to the short version it contained some entries which are not found there. To this expanded text of the short version entries were added until the manuscript finally contained an almost complete text of the AB version. Other manuscripts reveal transitional stages in the process from the short CD to the intermediate AB version. A manuscript of the *Polychronicon* in the National Library of Wales, MS. Brogyntyn 40, contains a text which begins with the AB version and then continues with the text of the short (CD) version.

The AB version was taken ultimately from a narrative which Higden had revised considerably since the 'primitive version' of his chronicle. It was a narrative which contained additional material, and passages which Higden had rewritten.[2] The

---

[1] St. Augustine's, Canterbury. See p. 106.   [2] See Appendix III.

additions came from Higden's later reading of chronicles such as Florence of Worcester, while the rewritten passages came in part from his desire to revise the text in the interests of accuracy. The intermediate version contained this revised narrative. It brought the text down to some point in the 1340's, and no longer stopped in 1327 as the short (CD) version had done. Several copies of the AB version were furnished with an index, and in certain cases they contained a map. Almost all the copies of the intermediate (AB) version ignored the final corrections that Higden made in the Huntington manuscript. Almost alone among the manuscripts of this version B.M. MS. Stowe 64 omits the section on Brabant which Higden finally erased in the Huntington copy.

The AB version did not represent the final stage in the compilation of Higden's text, the stage reached, that is to say, by including all the additions that Higden made to the Huntington copy. A text, which includes all these additions, and which carries the narrative down to the 1350's, is to be found in only a few manuscripts. This final version, described as E in the Rolls Series classification, attained no great popularity, probably because the final additions were made late in Higden's lifetime when the *Polychronicon* in the form of the intermediate (AB) version was already famous. Manuscripts that contain this final version with Higden's 'last words' are relatively scarce. Apart from the Huntington copy, the best text of this version is that found in a manuscript, possibly of the fourteenth century, which once belonged to Christ Church, Canterbury (Cambridge U.L. MS. Ii. III. 1, (E) of the Rolls Series edition). Another copy of this version, B.M. MS. Egerton 871, was returned by Thomas Erdeley, Abbot of St. Werburgh's (1413-34) to John Macclesfield, a Chancery clerk.[1]

The E version of the *Polychronicon* represents the final stage in the text as written by Higden, but one other stage should be noted in the development of Higden's text. The *Historia Aurea*,

---

[1] For Macclesfield see Tout, *Chapters*, IV. 386, n. 1. The other manuscripts of this version include Bodleian MS. Laud 619 and Trinity College, Cambridge, MS. 1293 (G of the Rolls).

a popular history of the middle of the fourteenth century, gave rise to a new version of the *Polychronicon*.[1] The *Historia Aurea*, which used the short version of the *Polychronicon*, became in its turn the source of a new version of Higden's chronicle.[2] Probably in the lifetime of both Higden and the compiler of the *Historia Aurea*, what must be classed as a new version of the *Polychronicon* was compiled from it. A characteristic and early example of this version is the text found in B.M. MS. Harley 655. This manuscript contains a form of the *Polychronicon* written in the fourteenth century. It is plain, however, that this manuscript is at least three times the size of the ordinary *Polychronicon*. It is, in fact, an expanded short version of the *Polychronicon*, which adds large sections from the later books of the *Historia Aurea*, but which endeavours to present the whole of its history within the original seven books of Higden's work.

There are several manuscripts that contain this new version of the *Polychronicon*.[3] The differences in appearance between this version and the other versions of the *Polychronicon* led one scholar of the seventeenth century, Humphrey Wanley, to suppose that the version found in MS. Harley 655 was the work of the apocryphal Roger of Chester, and that the *Polychronicon* was, in fact, taken from it: 'Re vera, est Polycratica temporum, seu Polychronica Rogeri Monachi Cestrensis, quam foedissime deflorauit Plagiarorum insignissimus, Ranulfus Higden, Commonachus suus'.[4] Like the attribution of the short version to Roger of Chester there is no foundation for this view. Though it is not known how the work was compiled, it probably arose from reciprocal borrowing at the time when copies of both the *Polychronicon* and the *Historia Aurea* were being multiplied, and

---

[1] On the *Historia Aurea* see V. H. Galbraith, 'Sources of the St. Albans Chronicle', *Essays to R. Lane-Poole*, pp. 379–98.

[2] For what follows see V. H. Galbraith, 'The *Historia Aurea* and a French Brut', *E.H.R.* xliii (1928), 203–17.

[3] These include MSS. Cambridge U.L. Dd. viii. 7; B.M. Royal 13. E. 1; Balliol College, Oxford, 236, and University College, Oxford, 177. The books of Cambridge U.L. MS. Dd. viii. 7, and Balliol College, Oxford, 236, a late manuscript, represent a more advanced stage in this process.

[4] *Harleian Catalogue* (London, 1808), i. 398.

it is not likely that either Higden or John of Tynemouth was the author.

IV

Writing in the twelfth century Gervase, a monk of Canterbury, in the prologue to his chronicle distinguished between the various kinds of history written in the Middle Ages. There are, he says, on the one hand, histories, and on the other, annals and chronicles. Though both have the same aim, they vary in form. The task of the historian is to arrange and to select, and to write in an elevated style.[1] 'The task of the humbler chronicler is to get his dates right, and year by year record briefly the acts of kings and princes, and such other events, portents, and miracles as occur from time to time. There are also, alas, too many annalists and chroniclers who, swollen with pride, make broad their phylacteries and enlarge their borders.'[2]

On the basis of this distinction Higden may be reckoned an historian rather than a chronicler. His work had literary merit, and its appeal did not rest solely upon the mass of facts which he assembled. The *Polychronicon* is not a mere table of events. Higden divides up his subject-matter and presents it under various headings. Already in the earliest form of the *Polychronicon* that we can reconstruct Higden was writing a history which was divided into books, and which dealt with subjects as well as periods. Many of the changes in his text, which we should now examine, came from his desire to improve the appearance of his chronicle, to elaborate and to revise, and to rephrase extracts in a narrative which was becoming increasingly a more personal expression.

A great many of the changes in Higden's text, however, are explained solely by his further reading and by his increased

---

[1] Knighton began with a contemporary account of Richard II's reign and then attempted to write a *history* from 1066. See the elevated style of his preface in Book I, pp. 1–4.

[2] *Gervase of Canterbury*, ed. W. Stubbs (R.S., 1879–80), i. 87. On Gervase of Canterbury see V. H. Galbraith, *Historical Research in Medieval England* (1951), p. 2.

knowledge in the twenty years or so after the completion of the first version of his chronicle. Passages were omitted, particularly in the section on the early history of Britain, which Higden felt were no longer accurate. A legend concerning the early history of Chester was, for example, modified for this reason.[1] At the same time Higden added extracts from chronicles that he had been reading. Two of the chroniclers he appears to have used late in life were William of Malmesbury and Florence of Worcester. Although he had quoted the chronicle of William of Malmesbury in his first version, Higden added many extracts from the *Gesta Regum* to his later text. He did this in the part which described the early history of Britain, when a further reading of William of Malmesbury's chronicle had inclined him to incorporate more of William's narrative into his own account. Apart from the work of William of Malmesbury Higden added extracts from the chronicle of Florence of Worcester. Several of the passages which were written in the margins of the Huntington manuscript come from this source. It seems likely that Higden used Florence of Worcester after he had written the first version of his history, for Florence of Worcester's name occurs last in the list of authorities given in the front of the *Polychronicon*.[2]

As we can tell from the changes which he made to his copy at Chester, Higden was also concerned with the style of his chronicle. In an effort to improve his work he expanded his prologue, and ran the original four prefaces together into one. He added a map, and put in a list of authorities, and an index. At some stage he almost certainly divided the books of his history into chapters. It is probable that many of these changes were made at a time when the *Polychronicon* was the most famous history in fourteenth-century England, and were designed to make easier the work of reference. In the later versions of his chronicle Higden also departed more freely from the wording of his sources. Entries were rewritten in his own words, and in this he no doubt wished to add to the originality of his work. Finally, once his chronicle had become widely known Higden attempted

---

[1] *Polychronicon*, vii. 244.   [2] i. 24–26.

to associate his name with it by means of the acrostic. This was a device that he had used in other writings, and it is found in the work of John Erghome and Henry Knighton. The labour involved in the elaboration of the acrostic can be seen from the re-arrangement of the opening words of the early chapters, and the fact that Higden gave himself this labour shows his evident desire to associate his name with the chronicle.

Among the changes was one which suggests that, at a late stage in the revision of his text, Higden was still concerned with the problems of chronology. A note on f. 48^v of the Huntington copy, later erased and transferred to the fourth chapter of Book I, concerns the ages of the world and how they are computed: 'R. Hic autem nota quod etates seculi non computantur secundum equalitatem annorum sed secundum mirabilia que in primordiis etatum contigerunt (ut pote) quod prima etas incepit a mundi creacione, secunda a diluvii inundacione, 3^a a circumcisione, quarta a regum inchoatione, quinta post transmigracionem, sexta a Christi incarnatione.'

The passage reveals that Higden was still thinking of the time division underlying his chronicle long after he had written the first draft of his history.[1]

'Author manuscripts,' it has been said, 'rightly interpreted, take us behind the scribe to the mind of the author.'[2] Though this is true, the conventions of medieval historical writing and the conditions under which many of the chronicles were written forbid us to penetrate very deeply into the thoughts of the author. The personal note is not prevalent in a form of writing which began in many cases as an official record for a religious house. None the less, from the changes which Higden made to his text, it is apparent that he was a writer with some concern for the shape and structure of his chronicle. He is remarkable also for his genuine interest in early history, and many of the corrections in the Huntington copy are concerned with the first part of his narrative.

---

[1] See V. H. Galbraith, *H.L.Q.*, p. 10.
[2] V. H. Galbraith, 'The Chronicle of Henry Knighton', in *F.S.*, p. 138.

V

The enlargement of Higden's text came in response to the growing popularity of his work. The versions which appeared in the course of the fourteenth century are almost certainly explained by this process. We should now consider the evidence for the circulation and dissemination of Higden's chronicle.

In the Middle Ages most annals and chronicles were intended as a private record for a monastery or a cathedral church. Though they might on occasion have circulated among religious communities, few were written with a wider audience in mind. Occasionally the work of a chronicler attained some degree of popularity, either among houses of his own Order, or among the educated clergy; but only very occasionally and usually during the later Middle Ages did a monastic chronicle appeal to the widest possible medieval audience consisting of all sections of the educated clergy. The evidence for determining the audience of the chronicles is fragmentary. The study of fly-leaf inscriptions (where they occur) in works such as the *Polychronicon*, which survive in a great many copies, can give some indication of the circles to which they appealed. The evidence of wills gives an indication of the type of individual who owned copies of Higden's work. Sources such as library catalogues occasionally indicate the ownership of a chronicle by a religious house or a medieval college. These lines of inquiry provide only a few examples of ownership, but few though they are they show the early dissemination of the *Polychronicon*, within and beyond the great religious centres.

Higden originally wrote at the suggestion of his fellow monks, and probably with only the inmates of St. Werburgh's in mind. In the course of time, and by stages which we cannot now reconstruct, his work became known outside his own religious house. At first the *Polychronicon* probably enjoyed mainly local fame among neighbouring religious houses but it soon circulated in other parts of the country. By 1352 when Higden was summoned by Edward III to appear at court he was already famous. The dissemination of his chronicle during these years was almost certainly the work of professional scribes. Religious houses and cathedral churches desired copies of this famous book, and the services of professional scribes would be in great demand. The names of certain of these scribes survive in copies of Higden's text. John Lutton wrote one copy of the *Polychronicon* for Hyde Abbey (St. John's College, Cambridge, MS. 12), and another which belonged to the cathedral priory at Bath (B.M. MS. Arundel 86). He may also have written the copy of the English version now in Chetham's Library, Manchester.[1] A John Lutton, writer and brewer, appears in an Oxford list of 1410.[2]

In this way copies of the *Polychronicon*, which were often handsome, and which must have been expensive, were made for the monasteries and cathedral churches of the land. Among copies which can be attributed to one particular religious house, cathedral, or collegiate church, are three which belonged to St. Augustine's, Canterbury which include copies of the short and the intermediate version (MS. Brussels, Bibliothèque Royale 3097; Cambridge U.L. MS. Ii. 2. 24 (A of the Rolls Series), and Queen's College, Oxford, MS. 307). Other Benedictine monasteries that possessed copies of Higden's text include Westminster (MS. Bodley 341); Chester (MS. Huntington 132); Glastonbury (which had two copies Cambridge U.L. MS. Dd. 1. 17[3] and B.M. Add. 10105); Gloucester (Corpus Christi College, Oxford, MS. 89); Hyde (St. John's College, Cambridge, MS. 12, (D) of the Rolls edition); and Ramsey (B.M. MS. Royal 14. C. ix). A copy which may have belonged to the Irish monastery of St. Mary the Virgin, near Dublin (MS. Rylands, Latin 217), was written by Stephen Lawles, the subprior and later abbot of the house.

A group of manuscripts belonged to cathedral churches. The cathedral priory of Christ Church, Canterbury, owned a copy of the long version (Cambridge U.L. MS. Ii. III. i, (E) of the Rolls edition) which was once the property of J. Broke, a monk of the

---

[1] Chetham's Library MS. 11379.   [2] Madan, *Oxford Books*, ii. 506.
[3] N. Ker now rejects this ascription, *Medieval Libraries* (1964), p. 91.

house, and also a copy of the short version (Bodleian, MS. Rawlinson B. 191). Other copies belonged to Bath (B.M. MS. Arundel 86); Exeter (Exeter Cathedral MS. 3509 and possibly Lambeth MS. 104); Lincoln (B.M. MS. Royal 13. E. i); and Norwich (B.M. MS. Royal 14. C. xiii). Two Cistercian houses owned copies of the *Polychronicon*, Fountains (Bodleian MS. Laud 619) and Whalley (B.M. MS. Harley 3600). Three copies can be traced to the Austin priories of Barnwell (University College, Oxford, MS. 177); Gloucester (Bodleian, MS. Tanner 170); and Llanthony (Corpus Christi College, Oxford, MS. 83). Copies belonged to the hospitals of St. John the Evangelist in Cambridge (Corpus Christi College, Cambridge, MS. 21); St. John the Baptist, Exeter (B.M. MS. Harley 3671); and St. Thomas of Acon, London (B.M. MS. Royal 14. C. xii). A copy survives from the Charterhouse of Sheen (Bodleian, MS. Hatton 14), and the Charterhouse of Witham (Eton College, MS. 213). The Austin friars at London possessed a copy (Trinity College, Dublin, MS. 486), as did the Franciscan convent at London (Bodleian, MS. Laud Misc. 545). The Duke of Gloucester in the 1390's presented a copy of the *Polychronicon* (MS. Bodley 316) to the chantry college of the Holy Trinity at Pleshey,[1] and a copy (B.M. MS. Royal 13. D. i) belonged to the parish church of St. Peter, Cornhill, London.

To this list of surviving manuscripts whose provenance is known should be added the copy (MS. Winchester College 15) that the medieval catalogue in the *Liber Albus* states was presented to Winchester by the founder, William of Wykeham. A copy (Balliol College, Oxford, MS. 235) was given to Balliol College in 1448 by Thomas Gascoigne, a priest of York.[2] A manuscript of the *Polychronicon* in the British Museum (Add. MS. 10104) was probably the copy owned by Adam of Usk, and bequeathed by him to his kinsman, Edward ap Adam.[3] Another manuscript was owned by John Macclesfield, a clerk of the privy

[1] See p. 125.
[2] f. 19.
[3] See p. 129.

seal, who had Cheshire connexions, and to whom it was re-stored by Thomas Erdeley, Abbot of St. Werburgh's.[1]

Among copies mentioned in contemporary sources are several which were given to Oxford and Cambridge colleges. Pembroke College, Cambridge, received a *Polychronicon* in two volumes given about 1390 as the gift of Richard Dunmow.[2] St. Catherine's College, Cambridge, received a copy of the *Polychronicon* from the founder.[3] Queen's College, Oxford, appears to have possessed a manuscript of the work,[4] and Merton College seems to have acquired an early copy given by Thomas of Buckingham who died about 1350.[5] It received another copy in 1498.[6]

Religious institutions are known to have possessed manu-scripts of the *Polychronicon* that no longer survive, or which can-not now be traced. The library catalogue of the Brigettine foundation at Syon contains two entries referring to copies of the *Polychronicon*.[7] The catalogue of the Austin friary at York con-tains a copy,[8] and it appears that Cobham College also pos-sessed one.[9]

Wills contain evidence of individual clerics who bequeathed their manuscripts of Higden's work. William Duffield, a canon of York, who died in 1452–3, owned a manuscript worth twenty shillings.[10] John Hurte, S.T.P., Vicar of St. Mary's, Nottingham, in his will dated 14 September 1476, left a text of the *Poly-*

---

[1] See p. 100. New College MS. 152 appears to have been owned by William North, a priest in the diocese of Bath and Wells. Trinity College, Cambridge, MS. 1293 was owned and perhaps written by Roger Walle, prebendary of Lichfield (c. 1450–60) whose rebus is in the book. It was read and annotated at Lichfield in 1575.

[2] M. R. James, *A Descriptive Catalogue of the Manuscripts in the Library of Pem-broke College, Cambridge* (Cambridge, 1905), p. xiv.

[3] M. R. James, *A Descriptive Catalogue of the Manuscripts in the Library of St. Catherine's College, Cambridge* (Cambridge, 1925), p. 6.

[4] *The Stonor Letters and Papers*, ed. C. L. Kingsford (C.S. 1919), i. 13.

[5] F. M. Powicke, *Medieval Books of Merton College* (Oxford, 1931), p. 113.

[6] Ibid., p. 223.

[7] *Catalogue of the Library of Syon Monastery*, ed. Mary Bateson (Cambridge, 1898), p. 78. (K. 4, K. 5.)

[8] 'The Catalogue of the Library of the Augustinian Friars at York', *Fasciculus J. W. Clark dicatus* (1909), no. 154.

[9] *Archaeologia*, vol. xxviii (1840), 455.

[10] T.E. iii. 133.

chronicon to St. Mary's.[1] Richard Pearson, the rector of Garforth by his will dated 4 March 1473-4, is shown to have owned a copy of the *Flores Policronicon*, which was possibly a manuscript of Higden's work.[2]

The evidence that has been brought together, though admittedly fragmentary, suggests that for a medieval text the *Polychronicon* was widely distributed. Religious houses and cathedral churches owned manuscripts, and in several cases more than one manuscript of the work. Colleges and hospitals also possessed copies. Individual clerics up and down the country, who were wealthy enough to afford a copy of what must have been a fairly expensive text, possessed one. Although there are hardly any examples of lay ownership, none the less among the educated clergy of the fourteenth century the *Polychronicon* was obtaining an almost national audience.

[1] Ibid. 221.   [2] Ibid. 208.

VII

THE FOURTEENTH-CENTURY
CONTINUATIONS

THE *Polychronicon* was particularly important in the fourteenth century for the continuations with which it was
furnished. Monastic houses that owned copies added continuations of their own to Higden's text. Several of the main
literary sources for Richard II's reign; Walsingham's early history,
the Westminster chronicle, and the chronicle of Adam of Usk,
were written as continuations of Higden's work. The earliest
continuations were concerned, however, not with the reign
of Richard II, but with the period of history from the middle
of the century, when the text of the *Polychronicon* ended,
to the final years of Edward III's reign. This was a period
when few chronicles were written. No first-class contemporary
chronicle was compiled between 1340 and 1377, and not until
1376 did the earliest writings of Walsingham appear.[1] It is therefore for a period when literary sources are scarce that the continuations of the *Polychronicon* first became important.

The *Polychronicon* was furnished at the start with a continuation that extended from the conclusion of Higden's text down to
the end of Edward III's reign. An examination of this early continuation raises immediately the problem of the concluding date
of Higden's text. In the short (CD) version Higden's text went to
1327. The later versions, A, B, and E, brought the text down to
varying dates between 1340 and 1352. When one considers these
different versions, one difficulty has always been to establish the
concluding point of the main text and the opening date of the
earliest continuation. The manuscript of the *Polychronicon* now

---

[1] See Chapter II. The *Historia Aurea* was sometimes used to cover the period
from the 1320's to the 1340's.

in the Huntington Library, offers new evidence on this problem.[1] In the Huntington copy the main text comes down to 1340 in a single script. The view that the *Polychronicon* originally ended at this point is supported therefore by what is almost certainly the author's working copy, and this conclusion is sustained by other evidence.[2] Already in the Huntington manuscript, however, there exist brief entries that extend from 1340 to 1352. From the variations of the ink the entries from 1340 to 1348 appear to have been written contemporaneously in three or four instalments, possibly by Higden himself. A final and separate entry describing the election of Pope Clement VI, and the general shortage of marketable goods is given for 1352.[3] The entries from 1340 to 1348 represent in all probability additions made by Higden to the main text of his chronicle during the decade or so after 1340. They may be regarded as Higden's own continuation to a main text which ended originally at 1340.

Higden's additional entries formed the basis of a continuation that was to extend from 1340 to 1377, constituting one of the few contemporary sources for this period of English history. The continuation was rewritten during the reign of Richard II in a number of separate and independent versions, and after the appearance of Walsingham's history it became associated with his work. The development of this early continuation is the first subject of this chapter.[4]

I

The first continuation from 1340 to 1377 with which the *Polychronicon* was furnished, was probably constructed by stages, and

[1] See V. H. Galbraith, *H.L.Q.*.
[2] The main text ends at this point in Peterhouse College, Cambridge, MS. 177; B.M. MS. Harley 1707; Exeter Cathedral, MS. 3509; Cambridge U.L. Add. MS. 3077; Royal College of Physicians MS. 398. There is a note that it ended at this point originally in B.M. MS. Laud Misc. 545; Bibliothèque Nationale, Paris, MS. 4923. *Chronicon Henrici Knighton*, i. 479, says that Higden ended at the words, 'utrimque discessum eot'.
[3] *Polychronicon*, viii. 406, n. 3.
[4] Sections (i) and (ii) are substantially as printed (with some additions and alterations) in *E.H.R.* lxxvi (1961). A table of manuscripts is given in Appendix IV.

may not have been commenced before the 1360's. It is found attached to those longer versions of Higden's main text which are named A and B.[1] The earliest surviving form of this continuation is found in the following manuscripts: Bodleian Library, MS. Ashmole 796, MS. Oriel 74, MS. Digby 201; B.M. MSS. Harley 1728-9, MS. Harley 3884, MS. Harley 4875; T.C.D. MS. 488;[2] and it has been printed by Hearne from MSS. Harley 1728-9 as pp. 421-52 in vol. ii of his edition of *Walter of Hemingford*. This continuation which will be referred to as (A) appears to have been composed in several stages. The entries from 1340 to 1352 already existed in the Huntington copy. The other stages are not easily identifiable in the completed form in which the chronicle survives, but they may be marked by the entries on episcopal elections for the 1360's and 1370's.[3] The view that (A) was composed in various stages is strengthened by the fact that alone among the recensions through which it went, it fails to mention under the entry on Richard II's birth in 1366, his later succession to the throne. (A) is a work which may have grown by accumulation in different religious houses. References to Ely, which are excised from later versions, suggest one possible source of origin.[4]

This short continuation, with its dated entries on political and ecclesiastical events, is one of the few contemporary sources for a period almost bare of literary authorities. Its main entries concern the campaigns and negotiations of the Hundred Years War, and such notable events at home as droughts and royal activities. A distinguishing feature of (A) is the frequent mention of episcopal translations. Certain entries for the 1360's may derive from the fuller chronicle of the Westminster writer, John of Reading.[5] Tait, who suggested the connexion, used, however, as the basis of his comparison, not (A), but a continuation written after 1377,

[1] See Chapter VI.
[2] A number of annals which were apparently written at Wigmore were added to the continuation in T.C.D. MS. 488. They describe events in Edward III's reign.
[3] These are given in Hearne, *Walteri Hemingford, Historia* (Oxford, 1731), ii. 425, 428, 431, 440, 442.   [4] Hearne, pp. 427, 443.
[5] Tait, *Chronicon Johannis de Reading*, pp. 46-47.

which contains entries undoubtedly taken from Reading. (A) may have used Reading, but it may equally be the source of Reading's own chronicle. All the manuscripts which contain (A) carry the text to 1377.

This original continuation formed the basis of several later versions, all of which were written during the reign of Richard II. Of these later versions the earliest appears to have been a slightly revised version of (A). This revised version, which has been taken sometimes as the first continuation,[1] was written in its present form no earlier than the reign of Richard II, and will be described as (B). Its text is substantially that printed on pp. 407–28 in vol. viii of the Rolls Series edition of the *Polychronicon* and known there as B. It is found in Gonville and Caius College, Cambridge, MS. 82 (from which Lumby printed his Rolls Series text), and MS. 249; Trinity College, Cambridge, MS. R. 4. 1 (634); Bodleian Library, MS. Bodley 358; Magdalen College, Oxford, MS. 147; B.M. Cotton MS. Nero D. ii, MS. Nero D. viii, MS. Stowe 64, Add. MS. 39236, MS. Harley 3671; Rylands Library, Manchester, Latin MS. 170; T.C.D. MS. 487.[2]

The continuation described as (B) was made after 1377, for under the birth of Richard II in 1366 it refers to his later succession to the throne.[3] In (B) when contrasted with (A) there are both omissions and additions. Most notable among the omissions are the majority of Ely references and of entries relating to episcopal translations. It may have been felt that in what was becoming a standard account of the period of history 1340–77, local references such as these no longer justified inclusion. Equally interesting is the omission in (B) of the passage at the end of (A) which described Gaunt's persecution of Wykeham when Chancellor.[4] The additions made in (B) consist in the main of entries taken from the chronicle of John of Reading. These include mention of the birth of Thomas of Woodstock, of

---

[1] Tait, op. cit., pp. 46–47.
[2] MS. Gonville and Caius 249 was a copy made for his own use by John Herryson in 1464. MS. Bodley 358 has a leaf or two missing covering the years 1352 to 1362. B.M. MS. Harley 1320 contains a fragment of this continuation.
[3] *Polychronicon*, viii. 415.
[4] Hearne, pp. 448–9.

Edward III's observance of the feast of St. George at Windsor, and of the death of the Archbishop of Armagh.[1] The influence of Reading, which Tait noted, is evident both here and in the other versions made after 1377.

The manuscripts of (B) differ only slightly among themselves. The entry on the birth of Thomas of Woodstock caused some confusion, and was inserted in different places in various copies. The entry is also found added at the foot of a folio in a manuscript of (A).[2] Apart from the Woodstock entry, and occasional discrepancies on episcopal translations, differences in the manuscripts of (B) are mainly matters of phrasing. The majority of manuscripts end at 1376 with the words 'sermonibus praedicantes'.[3]

The continuation described as (B) did not in any sense, however, become the standard continuation of the *Polychronicon*, and it has no claim to be printed as such in the Rolls Series edition. It is not the continuation found in the greatest number of manuscripts, and it represents the first stage only in the revision and expansion of (A). A second and equally important revision came with the appearance of a longer continuation, with additional entries for the 1340's and 1350's, and with rewritten entries for the early 1360's. This continuation will be described as (C). (C) which is unprinted, and which formed the basis of recensions later still, is found in the following manuscripts; National Library of Wales, MS. Brogyntyn 40; Winchester College, MS. 15; Heralds' College, London, MS. Arundel 4; Inner Temple, MS. 511. 5; B.M. Add. MS. 10104, MS. Arundel 86, MS. Royal 14. C. xii; Bodleian Library, MS. Hatton 14; Harvard University, MS. 116; Corpus Christi College, Cambridge, MS. 117; Trinity College, Cambridge, MS. R. 5. 24 (719); Christ's College, Cambridge, MS. 3; Eton College, MS. 213; Merton College, Oxford, MS. 121.[4]

---

[1] They occur in the Rolls Series edition of the *Polychronicon* viii at pp. 408, 409, 410, and in the chronicle of Reading at pp. 122, 130, 147.

[2] MS. Digby 201, f. 220ᵛ.

[3] With the exception of MS. Harley 3671 and Cotton MS. Nero D. ii which end at 1377, with 'diu postea habuerunt'.

[4] James Tait noted this fuller version in MS. Arundel 86.

On the period of the 1340's and 1350's the narrative of (A) contained only brief entries. Down to 1352 its narrative was in fact simply those entries following the main text of the *Polychronicon* that are to be found in the Huntington copy, and which from 1340 to 1348 were possibly the work of Higden himself. (B) added little to this part of the narrative. Its main additions were the entry on the birth of Thomas of Woodstock, and, after 1352, the account of Edward III's observance of the feast of St. George at Westminster. (C), which was now constructed, attempted to supply a fuller text on this period. Between the years 1343 and 1346 it added entries on the birth of Edmund at Langley, on the General Chapter of the Black Monks at Northampton, on the birth of Edward III's daughter, Mary, and on Henry of Lancaster in Gascony. The account of Poitiers was expanded and under 1349 an entry was added on Geoffrey de Chargny. On the period of the 1350's new entries included an account of the translation of the relics of Thomas of Hereford, of Simon Langham, of the death of Bradwardine, of the troubles at Oxford, and of Wykeham's building activities at Windsor. For the period of the 1360's the entries on the Great Company and the White Company were expanded.

The additional material which is found in (C) appears at first sight to bear some resemblance to entries in the chronicle of John of Reading. Entries are added, however, for the period before Reading's chronicle begins,[1] while the entries which occur in Reading occur also in a chronicle written during the reign of Edward III, and found now as part of Corpus Christi College, Cambridge, MS. 6.[2] (C) has so many of its additional entries in common with this chronicle, and the resemblance in phrasing between the two accounts is such that there can be little doubt that the two are related. (C) must be indebted to the Corpus chronicle; for whereas the Corpus chronicle was written during

[1] In B.M. MS. Cleopatra A. xvi where Reading's chronicle is found, there is an earlier section covering the years 1325–45, from which Tait printed extracts, pp. 77–99. Some of its entries appear to be taken from the (D) continuation, see p. 116.

[2] For a discussion of this chronicle *infra*, pp. 120–1.

the reign of Edward III, (C) was not compiled before 1379 when it mentions Langham's reburial at Westminster.

There are few differences between the manuscripts of (C). Corpus Christi College, Cambridge, MS. 117 contains a double entry about the drought of 1353, which arose from copying the same entry twice, once from a copy of (C) and later from a copy of (B).[1] Harvard MS. 116 contains, instead of the usual account of Wykeham's building activities at Windsor, the more critical account found in the continuation known as Rolls Series A.[2] It also gives the year of Langham's death wrongly as 1386. Eton College MS. 213 is a sister manuscript to the Harvard text and contains both these entries. The Eton copy gives also a list of Popes concluding with Urban VI.[3] This suggests that the version described as (C) was compiled before Urban died in 1389 and after 1379 when Langham's reburial at Westminster is mentioned.

The development of the main *Polychronicon* continuation did not cease at this point. (C) was based upon (B). This dependence can be seen most clearly in the text of (C) for the period after the middle 1360's when the additions cease and (C) is in effect simply a copy of (B). At some point, however, again after 1379, the need for an even fuller text was felt. (A) was brought back into use and combined with the text of (C) to form the basis of a fuller account that will be described as (D). Five manuscripts contain the text of (D): Bodleian Library, MS. Tanner 19, MS. Digby 196; Heralds' College, London, MS. Arundel 2; Magdalen College, Oxford, MSS. 97 and 190. Of these the text contained in MS. Tanner 19 reveals most clearly the process of compilation.

MS. Tanner 19 contains almost all the additional material for the period of the 1340's and 1350's found in (C). It adds, which the other manuscripts of (D) do not, a passage on the Archbishop of Armagh and his writings.[4] After 1360, however, it uses (A) and

---

[1] Corpus Christi College, Cambridge, MS. 117, f. 156.
[2] Harvard MS. 116, f. 155. The account of Wykeham in the (A) continuation is found in the *Polychronicon*, viii. 359–60.
[3] Eton College MS. 213, f. 241ᵛ.
[4] MS. Tanner 19, f. 415. This passage may derive from the chronicle of John

not (B). It copies, for example, the passages on the episcopal translations of 1366, 1372, and 1375 that are to be found in (A) and that had been excised from (B).

A confused folio in MS. Tanner 19 reveals the manner in which the compiler worked. On f. 413 the passage on the burning of the two friars at Avignon in 1354 is given twice, once in the margin, and again later in the text. The reason for the double entry is that the compiler used copies of (C) and (A). In the margin he gave the entry on the two friars at the point where it occurred in (C) whilst in the text he gave the same entry on the two friars at the slightly different point where it occurred in (A). There can be no doubt, therefore, that the compiler of MS. Tanner 19 had before him copies of (C) and (A) and built up his text from the two.

The remaining manuscripts of (D) contain a text similarly constructed from (C) and (A), but with additional entries. For the years 1343-6 these manuscripts contain new entries on the succession of the Popes, and on the succession of the abbots at Westminster.[1] For the 1350's they add an account of the jubilee at Rome taken from John of Reading.[2] After 1360, like MS. Tanner 19, they use the text of (A).

The text that is found in this group of manuscripts already bears a family likeness to the account known as 'the continuation of Murimuth', and it is in fact the ancestor of that narrative. Before it was used to make the text of 'the continuation of Murimuth', however, its narrative was once more expanded into a version now preserved in three manuscripts; Vatican Library, MS. 1959; Glasgow University, MS. Hunterian 72; and Corpus Christi College, Cambridge, MS. 21, which may be described as (E).

(E) represents what was possibly the final stage in the development of the main *Polychronicon* continuation before it was

---

of Reading (Tait, p. 147). MS. Tanner 19 omits the passage on Bradwardine which is found in other copies of this version.

[1] The entry on Abbot Henley of Westminster which is antedated by a year is copied with the same error into this portion of Cotton MS. Cleopatra A. xvi which later contains Reading. [2] *Chronicon Johannis de Reading*, p. 110.

rewritten as the so-called 'Continuation of Murimuth'. To the fuller text contained in (D), (E) once more added new entries for the 1350's and 1360's. From the chronicle of John of Reading it copied entries on the succession at St. Albans, and the appearance of the Flagellants in 1350.[1] It mentioned the marriage of John of Gaunt and the great tempest of 1360. It abbreviated entries such as those on Langham, and on Wykeham at Windsor, which had been dealt with at greater length in the earlier versions.

In some version similar to (E), the main *Polychronicon* continuation was finally rewritten in the form known as 'the continuation of Murimuth'.[2] The name of this continuation is misleading, and comes from the fact that Hall, its first editor, knew it only in Queen's College, Oxford, MS. 304, where it follows the main text of Murimuth's chronicle. Even in the Queen's College manuscript, however, it is apparent that the continuation belonged originally to a *Polychronicon*. From 1337 to 1342 the text of the continuation as printed in the edition of the English Historical Society is simply the main text of Higden.[3] Thereafter it is a rewritten version of (E) as far as 1377. As evidence that it was originally part of a seventh book of the *Polychronicon* it continues the chapter numbers of that book.[4] In fact, however, the text is also found in its original form as a *Polychronicon* continuation in the following manuscripts: B.M. MS. Harley 3877; Bibliothèque Nationale, Paris, MSS. 4922 and 4923; T.C.D. MS. 487.[5]

It seems likely that this version of the main *Polychronicon* continuation was written at St. Albans, for St. Albans is placed before Westminster in the account of the General Chapter at Northampton. Walsingham used the continuation later as a source for his 'Short History', and (with the omission of certain

---

[1] *Chronicon Johannis de Reading*, pp. 109, 112.
[2] The text of this continuation has been printed by Hall (Oxford, 1722) and Hog, *Adami Murimuthensis chronica sui temporis* (*English Historical Society*, 1846).
[3] Hog, pp. 171–3.   [4] Ibid., pp. 203, 211, 218.
[5] It is found also in B.M. MS. Royal 13, E. ix. This manuscript is earlier than MS. Queen's College 304, but it contains the later text. See V. H. Galbraith, 'Sources of St. Albans Chronicle' in *Essays to Lane-Poole*, ed. H. W. C. Davis (Oxford, 1927), pp. 379–98. Trinity College, Dublin, MS. 487 also contains the (B) continuation.

entries unflattering to John of Gaunt) in B.M. MS. Royal 13.
E. ix.[1] Whether or not this continuation was written at St.
Albans, and is the work of Walsingham, it still adds little to (E).
As already stated, it reverses the order of the presidents of the
General Chapter at Northampton; a sentence is added on the
marriage of Edward III's daughter to the Duke of Brittany; a
somewhat different version of the Battle of Neville's Cross is
given; a sentence is added on the payment made by the town of
Oxford to the university after the riots; and the order of the
entries on the tempest and John of Gaunt's marriage is re-
arranged. The verses which appear in Queen's College, Oxford,
MS. 304 on the battle of Poitiers,[2] are not present in the other
manuscripts. There can be little doubt that this text depended
upon (E), for at the foot of f. 209 in MS. Harley 3877 the order
refers back to the arrangement of that version.

In this version known as 'the continuation of Murimuth', the
text of the main *Polychronicon* continuation was used by Walsingham as one source for the retrospective portion of his *Chronicon
Angliae*.[3] Behind this source, however, lay (E), and the earlier
revisions based upon (A). It was this record of historical writing
which Walsingham inherited when he came to write his retrospective history.

II

The rise of Walsingham and the re-emergence of St. Albans as
a writing centre during the reign of Richard II inevitably influenced the development of the *Polychronicon* continuations. The
continuation described as (E) was rewritten at St. Albans and
was used by Walsingham. Other continuations that describe the
period of history from 1340 to 1377 were either written at St.
Albans, or used Walsingham's work.[4]

[1] See p. 118, note 5. It is interesting to note that B.M. MS. Otho C. ii, which
contains a portion of Walsingham's contemporary history uses the (C) form of
the *Polychronicon* continuation for the 1340's.

[2] *Adami Murimuthensis chronica*, ed. Hog, pp. 188–90.

[3] V. H. Galbraith, 'Sources of St Albans Chronicle', op. cit.

[4] The conclusions of this section and of the preceding section are set out in
Appendix IV at the end of the book.

The continuation known as (E) was not the only source which Walsingham used when he came to write his history of the years 1340 to 1377 in the *Chronicon Angliae*. He used also a chronicle, which may originally have been written as a continuation of the *Polychronicon*, but which is now found, apart from the *Polychronicon*, in three manuscripts; Corpus Christi College, Cambridge, MS. 6; Bodleian Library, MS. Rawlinson B. 152; and Trinity College, Dublin MS. 511. The chronicle, which is unprinted, is a contemporary account of the second half of Edward III's reign, and it covers much the same period (1343–76) as (E).[1] This chronicle was used to construct the main *Polychronicon* continuation. The version described as (C) has many of its additional entries for the period of the 1340's and 1350's in common with it, and the similarities of phrasing are such that there can be little doubt of the debt of one to the other. As (C) was not written until after 1379, this chronicle is almost certainly its source.[2]

The nature and provenance of this short chronicle are not easy to determine. Its narrative has items in common with the abbreviated *Historia Aurea*[3] and with Reading, but apart from these passages it is based largely upon contemporary entries. Although it is no longer found together with a main text of a *Polychronicon*, it appears to have been compiled originally as a continuation of a *Polychronicon* which ended at or about 1342, for on the opening folio of the text in the Dublin manuscript there appear, after the mention of the papal succession in 1343, the words 'vide supra in Polychronicon', referring to an originally preceding text of Higden, which gave this entry under 1342.[4]

---

[1] The chronicle is analysed by V. H. Galbraith, 'Sources of St. Albans Chronicle', op. cit. It is mentioned by Horstmann in the introduction to his *Nova Legenda Anglie* (Oxford, 1901), who ascribed it to an anonymous monk of St. Albans. The chronicle contains a preponderance of information on the 1370's, and under 1359 it shows knowledge of Wykeham's election to Winchester in 1367.

[2] See pp. 115–16. The entries on Geoffrey Chargny (1349), William Edington (1351), the scarcity of provisions (1353), the agreement between the King (1354), are very similar in the two accounts.

[3] This is printed in Ludewig, *Reliquiae Manuscriptorum Diplomatum* (Halle, 1741), pp. 86–165.

[4] See *Polychronicon*, viii. 338. The text in Trinity College, Dublin, MS. 511

Though the provenance of this *Polychronicon* continuation, as it may be called, is not known, it has associations with St. Albans. It is found either in manuscripts that belonged to the St. Albans *scriptorium* or that contained parts of Walsingham's history,[1] and, together with the main *Polychronicon* continuation, it was treated as an original authority by Walsingham when he came to write the 1340–76 portion of his *Chronicon Angliae*. If it is a St. Albans chronicle it represents a tradition of historical writing which extends across the middle of the century to the time of Walsingham.[2]

Whether or not this continuation comes from St. Albans, the influence of Walsingham's own writings is apparent in other continuations that describe the years 1340–77. That version of (E), which was almost certainly written at St. Albans, and which is known as 'the continuation of Murimuth', was used, together with an extract from Walsingham's contemporary history, to form the basis of another continuation. The text of this continuation is contained in two manuscripts: Christ Church, Oxford, MS. 89; and B.M. Add. MS. 12118. In these two manuscripts the St. Albans version of (E) is transcribed together with that section of Walsingham's contemporary history which describes the death of the Black Prince.[3] Apart from this extract

(ff. 1–87) which is ascribed in a contemporary hand to Thomas Walsingham, *precentor* of St. Albans, and which was therefore written before 1394, differs from the text in the other two manuscripts. It has additional entries from the main *Polychronicon* continuation, and one or two entries which appear only in the *Chronicon Angliae*. It may represent an early draft in the writing of Walsingham's retrospective history.

In MS. Rawlinson B. 152, before the beginning of this chronicle, the text contains the short summary of the year ('Transiit annus frugifer et fructifer') which denotes a formal continuation of Matthew Paris. The summaries for 1340 and 1342 in MS. Rawlinson B. 152 are not found in the printed texts of Walsingham. See V. H. Galbraith, *The St. Albans Chronicle, 1406–1420*, pp. l–lii.

[1] Corpus Christi College, Cambridge, MS. 6 contains a copy of the *Historia Aurea* which was presented to St. Albans by William Wintershill: V. H. Galbraith, 'Sources of St. Albans Chronicle' (op. cit.). MS. Rawlinson B. 152 and Trinity College, Dublin, MS. 511, contain portions of Walsingham's history. It should be noted that no surviving St. Albans *Polychronicon* has yet been identified.

[2] There is mention of a succession of chronicle writers at St. Albans in the fourteenth century in Amundesham, *Annales Monasterii S. Albani*, ed. H. T. Riley (R.S., 1891), ii. 303.

[3] It is printed in the *Chronicon Angliae*, p. 88, and formed part of Walsingham's 'Scandalous Chronicle' which he later excised from his main history. See p. 125.

from Walsingham, the text differs from the St. Albans version of (E) only in that it adds at the end certain lines critical of Edward III.[1]

The influence of Walsingham is evident also in the continuation that is printed in the Rolls Series edition and known there as A.[2] This continuation, which extends from 1348 to 1377 and which may have been compiled during the 1380's, used the St. Albans version of (E) and parts of Walsingham's *Chronicon Angliae*. A note in Corpus Christi College, Cambridge, MS. 197, assigns the authorship of this continuation to John Malvern, a monk of Worcester. The note which is found under the year 1344 says that Malvern wrote the continuation in the Corpus manuscript for the years after 1346: 'At this point Ranulf the monk of Chester as a matter of fact closed his chronicles. . . . After him wrote a certain monk of Worcester, John Malvern, leaving a gap of two years; possibly nothing noteworthy had occurred in them to require the labours of his pen: accordingly he proceeds thus: "On the feast of the translation of St. Thomas the Martyr".' If the author was John Malvern he is doubtless to be identified with the sacrist of that name who became Prior of Worcester in 1395.[3] In the Corpus manuscript his chronicle is followed by the *Vita Ricardi Secundi* and by the chronicle of the anonymous monk of Westminster,[4] and he can therefore be the author of the narrative only as far as 1377.

Though Malvern's chronicle borrows from the (E) continuation of the *Polychronicon*, and from the *Chronicon Angliae*, it has original material.[5] Among its more interesting entries is one on

---

[1] These lines were printed by Tait in his edition of John of Reading (p. 91). He drew attention to this version in B.M. Add. MS. 12118.

[2] viii. 355-406.

[3] The Obedientary Rolls at Worcester show that John Malvern was *Precentor* in II Rich. II (1387-8), and *Pitanciarius* the next year.

Corpus Christi College, Cambridge, MS. 197 is on paper, and may have been added to MS. Bodley 341 which is a *Polychronicon* that ends at 1327. MS. Bodley 341 has a note 'reliqua de isto Edwardo III vide infra in papero in fine libri'. I owe this information to Professor V. H. Galbraith. The best account of the manuscript is to be found in J. Armitage Robinson, 'An Unrecognised Westminster Chronicler', *Proceedings of the British Academy*, iii (1907). [4] See pp. 127-9.

[5] There are references to Worcester (*Polychronicon*, viii. 383, 387), and to

Wykeham and his building activities at Windsor which is out-spokenly critical.[1] Malvern's continuation, based on sources which were themselves written during the 1380's, achieved some popularity towards the end of the fourteenth century, and it follows the main text of a *Polychronicon* in several manuscripts.[2] In most of these manuscripts the continuation goes to 1377 (*unus puer octo annorum*), but in some an eighth book of the *Polychronicon* has been constructed from the *Vita Ricardi Secundi*.[3] The narra-tive in this eighth book carries the text to 1381, and Walsing-ham's influence is apparent in the use of the *Vita Ricardi Secundi*, which was based upon various St. Albans' accounts.[4]

While the influence of Walsingham is evident in Malvern's writing other continuations were based even more directly upon Walsingham's work. Bodleian Library, MS. Laud Misc. 529 is a *Polychronicon* which from 1342 to 1377 contains a continuation constructed from the *Chronicon Angliae*, with additions from the main *Polychronicon* continuation, and from the *Eulogium Historiarum*. Passages taken from the main *Polychronicon* continuation include the account of the meeting of the General Chapter at Northampton, and the account of Langham's career, while the *Eulogium Historiarum* supplied entries on the battle of Poitiers, and the earthquake at Rhodes.[5] For the most part, however, the narrative came from Walsingham's 'Short History'.[6] Another

places near Evesham (p. 387), and references to Henry Wakefield, Bishop of Worcester.   [1] viii. 359.
[2] University Library, Cambridge, MS. Ii. II. 24 (from which Lumby printed his text in the Rolls Series), and Dd. i. 17; Trinity College, Cambridge, MS. R. 5. 35 (726); Magdalen College, Oxford, MS. 147; New College, Oxford, MS. 152; Lincoln College, Oxford, MS. 107; Oriel College, Oxford, MS. 16; Queen's College, Oxford, MS. 307; Bodleian Library, MS. Lyell 21; B.M. MS. Royal 13. D. i; MS. Harleian 3600; Lambeth Library, MSS. 48 and 160; Gonville and Caius College, Cambridge, MS. 58; and Magdalen College, Oxford, MS. 147 has a continuation which starts as (B) and then changes to this later continuation.
[3] This is found in Cambridge U.L. MS. Ii. II. 24; Cambridge U.L. MS. Dd. i. 17; Trinity, Cambridge, MS. 726; Magdalen, Oxford, MS. 147; Queen's, Oxford, MS. 307; MS. Lyell 21.
[4] The *Vita Ricardi Secundi* is sometimes found after 1381 following some form of the main *Polychronicon* continuation. On the *Vita Ricardi* see Kingsford, pp. 23–24. See also p. 132.
[5] *Eulogium Historiarum*, ed. F. S. Haydon, pp. 223–5, 237–8.
[6] The combination of extracts from the *Chronicon Angliae* and the main *Poly-*

continuation found in Corpus Christi College, Oxford, MS. 89, a copy of the *Polychronicon* which appears to have belonged at one time to the Abbey of St. Peter at Gloucester, used Walsingham's 'Short History' to continue Higden's text. Walsingham's history was transcribed beyond 1377 and, like MS. Laud Misc. 529, the continuation in Corpus Christi College, Oxford, MS. 89 reveals the manner in which during the later fourteenth century Walsingham's writings were used to continue Higden's work.

III

The earliest *Polychronicon* continuation (A), compiled in stages during the reign of Edward III is a contemporary source for a period when few chronicles were written. This continuation was revised during the 1380's. During these years on the basis of the narrative in (A), a number of separate and independent versions were written, and in the course of time passages were added from Walsingham's work. The separate identity of these continuations was obscured because of their association with Walsingham's writings, and it is not surprising if, in certain cases, Walsingham came to be credited with their authorship.[1]

In addition to these accounts of the years 1340–77, several chronicles of Richard II's reign were written as continuations of the *Polychronicon*. These later continuations are very different from the brief entries which characterize the earliest continuations, and they are, in fact, new chronicles owing little or nothing to Higden's text. Among them one of the most important narratives is Walsingham's account of the years 1376–7, which was once found continuing a copy of Higden's text. This part of Walsingham's early history, which extended from the meeting of the Good Parliament in 1376 to the death of Edward III in 1377, has been printed as pp. 68–146 of the *Chronicon Angliae*.[2]

chronicon continuation is reminiscent of the text in MS. T.C.D. 511. The text in MS. Laud Misc. 529 is, however, much closer to the text of the *Chronicon Angliae* than is the Dublin copy.

[1] The scribes at St. Albans frequently did this. See *Chronicon Angliae*, p. xxxvi.
[2] Ed. E. M. Thompson (R.S., 1874).

Walsingham's 'Scandalous Chronicle' was strongly critical of John of Gaunt, and it was excised from his later work. The finding and reconstruction of the original text by Maunde Thompson has been described as an 'example of the finest detective work in scholarship'.[1] Three manuscripts supply the missing portion of the text for the years 1376–7; MS. Bodley 316 (a *Polychronicon*), B.M. MS. Harley 3634, and Cotton Otho, c. ii. MS. Bodley 316 is a copy of the *Polychronicon* which was presented by the Duke of Gloucester to his new foundation of Pleshey. It contains a copy of Higden's chronicle, which extends to 1342, and at one time it was followed by Walsingham's account of the years 1376–7. The manuscript can be dated fairly accurately, for Gloucester was murdered in 1397, and the chronicle contains a reference to Sir Hugh Calverley, which could only have been written after Calverley's death in April 1394. The Bodley manuscript was written therefore during the period 1394–7.

In the Bodley manuscript only two leaves (ff. 150–1) of Walsingham's 'Scandalous Chronicle' now remain. The missing folios form part of a composite manuscript, MS. Harley 3634 (ff. 137–63), where the running title 'Liber VII' at the top of the folios is one proof that these leaves formed part of a *Polychronicon*. A fuller text is to be found in B.M. MS. Cotton Otho, c. ii, but the leaves of this manuscript were badly charred during the Cottonian fire of 1731. The reason for the removal of the quires, which contained the greater part of Walsingham's contemporary history, from the Bodley manuscript, is unknown, but it was not necessarily on account of any dissatisfaction with the text on the part of the scribe. The two leaves that he left were highly compromising, and the discarded quires were used to form another chronicle in MS. Harley 3634. One possible explanation for their removal was that the scribe found the 'Scandalous Chronicle' too long for his purpose, and substituted Walsingham's 'Short History' instead.

[1] V. H. Galbraith, 'Thomas Walsingham and the St. Albans Chronicle', *E.H.R.* xlvii (1932), 12–29. I am indebted to this article for the account which follows.

There can be little doubt, however, that Walsingham did modify this part of his narrative in the course of his lifetime. B.M. MS. Royal 13 E. ix, which contains the text of Walsingham's *Chronica Majora* from 1272 to 1392, almost certainly included the whole of the 'Scandalous Chronicle' at one time, for in the Royal manuscript the leaves which contained the narrative between 1347 and 1377 have been excised, and new ones substituted. The reason for the substitution probably lay in the references to John of Gaunt, which Walsingham felt were no longer true. Walsingham's removal of this early history from his later text reveals his change in outlook over a period of years. At the beginning of Richard's reign Walsingham had regarded Gaunt with hatred and distrust but in the course of the reign his opinion changed. After 1389 Walsingham portrayed Gaunt in a more favourable light, as one who had renounced the errors of his early life.[1] As Gaunt's star rose, so that of Richard declined in Walsingham's pages, and Walsingham viewed more critically a king whom he had once hoped would unite the country and renew the war with France. Walsingham's change of mind, and his removal of that part of his history, which was critical of Gaunt, reveals the outlook of a writer 'whose personal attitude was slowly but completely transformed through a period of revolution'.[2]

Walsingham's 'Scandalous Chronicle' is an important source for the years 1376–7. His account opened with the meeting of the Good Parliament in 1376,[3] when the committees were set up and Peter de la Mare was elected Speaker.[4] He quoted the words of Gaunt against the commons, and described the impeachment of Latimer and Lyons, two of Edward III's councillors.[5] After describing the death of the Black Prince, he related the manner

---

[1] *Historia Anglicana*, ii. 194. The reason for Walsingham's early attitude to Gaunt may have been Gaunt's support of Wyclif. *Chronicon Angliae*, pp. 115–21. See Chapter VIII.

[2] V. H. Galbraith, op. cit.

[3] Other sources for the Good Parliament are the *Rotuli Parliamentorum*, ii. 321–60, and the *Anonimalle Chronicle*, pp. 79–94. For a recent account of the Good Parliament see M. McKisack, *The Fourteenth Century*, pp. 387–94.

[4] *Chronicon Angliae*, pp. 68–72.   [5] pp. 74, 76–78.

in which Gaunt had sought to settle the succession in the event of Richard's death, and mentioned the imprisonment of the Speaker, Peter de la Mare, at Nottingham Castle.[1] Wyclif's appearance at St. Paul's accompanied by representatives of the Mendicant Orders was also described in some detail, and the rising of the Londoners against Gaunt occupied several pages.[2] The death of Edward III concluded this first part of Walsingham's early history.[3]

The chronicle of the monk of Westminster was also written as a continuation of Higden's text.[4] The Westminster chronicle, which is found in Corpus Christi College, Cambridge, MS. 197, follows the continuation (1348–77) assigned to John Malvern, a monk of Worcester. If Malvern was the author of the continuation from 1348 to 1377, he had no special interest in Westminster, and his chronicle shows no first-hand knowledge of its affairs. This distinguishes his work from that of the writer of the further continuation from 1381 to 1394, which is in fact a separate account compiled by a monk of Westminster.[5] The Westminster origins of the chronicle are proved by the frequent references to Westminster in the course of the narrative. Among them is an account of Richard's visit to the abbey in September 1383 to see the relics laid up by his predecessors, while a note of the loss of the regalia at the time of Richard's coronation contains the expression, 'Igitur nostrates caveant in posterum', 'Therefore let our people take care for the future'.[6]

It is not difficult to imagine the manner in which a Westminster monk came to continue the Worcester continuation of Higden. John Malvern, as his name suggests, was almost certainly connected with Malvern. At Little Malvern there was a cell of Worcester Priory, and at Great Malvern one of Westminster Abbey. Malvern was almost certainly the place where the Worcester manuscript was copied and then transferred to

[1] pp. 92, 105. [2] pp. 118–29. [3] pp. 142–6.
[4] It is printed as vol. ix of the *Polychronicon* in the Rolls Series.
[5] J. Armitage Robinson, 'An Unrecognised Westminster Chronicler', *Proceedings of the British Academy*, iii (1907), 61–92.
[6] *Polychronicon*, ix. 66, 222–3.

Westminster. The author of this Westminster chronicle cannot be identified with any degree of certainty. Among the monks at Westminster Richard of Cirencester, who wrote the *Speculum historiale de gestis regum Anglie*, and William of Sudbury, who wrote a treatise on the regalia, are possible authors. Dr. Armitage Robinson, who proved the chronicle's Westminster origin, attributed it to John Lakyngheth, who was a candidate for the abbacy in 1380 and Warden of the Household (*Custos Hospicii*) in 1392. There is little to connect Lakyngheth with the work, however, and among the monks at Westminster William of Sudbury is the most likely author.

The historical value of the Westminster chronicle is greatest for the years 1388–92. For this period it is better than Walsingham. The Westminster chronicler held the view that in the years following the Merciless Parliament Richard never dropped his intention of revenging his friends,[1] and it is instructive to compare his view of the leading personalities of the reign with that of Walsingham. The Westminster writer regarded Gaunt as an able man, and one who exercised a steadying influence on events even before his departure for Spain in 1386.[2] He praised Richard, none the less, for his qualities and his zeal for the Church.[3] On the crisis of 1388 the chronicler used official documents. The chronicle contains the articles of impeachment against the king's councillors,[4] a diary written in French of the proceedings in parliament,[5] and the terms of a pardon for all acts committed in the course of the year.[6] Apart from this it preserves a fragment of text concerning the commission for inquiry into the royal revenue which was set up in 1386, and which provoked the first great crisis of Richard's reign.[7] The Westminster chronicler was also well informed upon London matters. Under 1388 he mentioned an attempt to mediate in the struggle between the

---

[1] *Polychronicon*, ix. 239. 'Itaque scio quid faciam amicis meis existentibus iam in partibus transmarinis.'

[2] p. 56. The chronicler says that the temporal lords feared Gaunt for his ability.

[3] See pp. 174–5.

[4] pp. 119–47.

[5] pp. 147–58. See Tout, *Chapters*, iii. 431, note 5.

[6] pp. 158–65.

[7] pp. 83–89.

victualling and the other guilds,[1] and gave a detailed account of the troubled relations between Richard and the Londoners in 1392.[2]

The chronicle of Adam of Usk was again written as a continuation of Higden's work. Usk's chronicle describes in some detail the final years of Richard's reign, and though it continues to 1421 some two-thirds of the narrative deal with the period 1397–1404.[3] The chronicle is found in B.M. Add. MS. 10104, which is an (AB) version of the *Polychronicon* with a (C) continuation to 1376. At the end is the *Chronicon Adae de Usk*, which was the work of several scribes. In the manuscript the chronicle ends in 1404, but a quire of vellum, which was discovered at Belvoir Castle among the Duke of Rutland's papers, contains supplementary leaves which carry the chronicle to 1421.[4] The manuscript of the *Polychronicon* may have been Usk's own copy, which he bequeathed to his kinsman Edward ap Adam.[5]

More is known of Usk than of many chroniclers. He was a native of Usk in Monmouthshire, and from references in his chronicle the year of his birth has been placed about 1352.[6] The lords of Usk were the Mortimers, and they decided Adam's life. Through the patronage of Edmund Mortimer, third Earl of March, he was sent to Oxford, where in 1387 he was lecturing in civil law. In 1388 and 1389 he was involved in the conflict of the Welshmen against the northern scholars.[7] Some time between 1390 and 1392 he left Oxford to practise law in the court of Canterbury, and he was advocate in the court of Arches after practising for seven years as proctor in the court.[8] Through a connexion with the Arundels, Usk was on the royal commissions of 1395 and 1396,[9] and was present at the parliament of 1399. He was a member of the commission to advise on the deposition of

---

[1] pp. 117–18.   [2] pp. 267–73.   [3] See Kingsford, pp. 32–35.
[4] *Chronicon Adae de Usk*, ed. E. M. Thompson (1904), p. v.
[5] Ibid., p. xxx.
[6] See A. B. Emden, *A Biographical Register of the University of Oxford to 1500*, vol. iii, 1937–8.
[7] *Chronicon Adae de Usk*, p. xii.   [8] *C.P.R. 1396–9*, p. 23.
[9] *C.P.R. 1391–6*, pp. 636–95.

Richard, and was in a position, therefore, to describe in some detail the circumstances surrounding the fall of the king. In 1402, owing to an episode that is not entirely clear, Usk was obliged to leave the country for Rome.[1] He spent the next few years at the papal court acting as papal chaplain and auditor of causes of the sacred palace. In 1405 the revolt in Rome against Innocent VII ended his papal career, and he journeyed to Bruges in the hope of returning to England. There he waited two years, for possibly in view of his contacts with the exiled earl of Northumberland and Glendower, he had to seek the king's pardon. In 1408 he formed a scheme with Lancaster King-of-Arms, whom he met in Paris, to cross to Wales, and obtain the king's pardon. Usk succeeded in landing at Barmouth in Merionethshire among Glendower's followers. He left Glendower and finally, after three years, obtained the pardon that he sought. He lived until 1430 without further recorded adventures.[2]

Such was the career of the man who wrote a vivid account of the final years of Richard's reign. Usk's presence at the last parliaments of the reign gives his narrative considerable value. His account of the parliament of 1397 where Richard exacted his revenge on Arundel, Warwick, and others, is given in very nearly the same words as in the *Vita Ricardi Secundi* of the monk of Evesham, which was a popularized form of Walsingham. Whether the one copied from the other, or both used the same source, their narrative may be regarded as authentic and accurate in view of Usk's presence in this parliament. In 1399 Usk joined Archbishop Arundel on his return to England with Henry, duke of Lancaster, and accompanied the invading force from Bristol to Chester. He described the march and some of the incidents on the journey including the pillaging by Henry's followers in north Wales, and Richard's surrender at Flint. In the events

---

[1] It was said that he was convicted of the theft of a horse and harness, J. H. Wylie, *History of England under Henry IV* (London, 1886), iv. 558. Professor Galbraith points out that on p. xxii of the *Chronicon Adae de Usk* it is stated that two days before taking ship Usk had found two sureties in £40 each to refrain from doing anything in the Court of Rome contrary to the Statute of Provisors. This suggests that Usk did not run away, but went to Rome on clerical preferment.

[2] See W. Llewelyn William, Adam of Usk, *Y Cymmrodor*, xxxi (1921), 135–60.

which followed Usk described a visit to the Tower, and his admission to the presence of the imprisoned king not long before Richard's deposition. He represents Richard lamenting his lot: 'My God! a wonderful land is this and a fickle; which hath exiled, slain, destroyed, or ruined so many kings, rulers, and great men, and is ever tainted, and toileth with strife and variance and envy'. Leaving Richard, 'musing on his ancient and wonted glory, and the fickle fortune of the world', Usk departed, 'much moved at heart'.[1]

Whatever credence can be placed upon this passage, which is reminiscent of Shakespeare's lines, Usk has unique value for the events of 1399. He was a member of the commission of doctors and bishops which sat to give advice on Richard's deposition.[2] He relates that in this commission the question arose whether Henry could claim the throne by descent from Henry III.[3] It was argued that Edmund Crouchback was the eldest son of Henry III, but that on account of his infirmity Edward I had been advanced to his place. Usk could not accept this argument, which the commission set aside, and he quoted several chronicles, including the *Polychronicon*, against the claim.[4] For this period of history the main criticism against Usk is that his chronology is poor. This is partly due to the fact that his chronicle was made from a series of jottings, some set down at the time, and some compiled from memory. His attitude to Richard was not unsympathetic. He described the king, 'well-endowed as Solomon, and fair as Absalom', 'cum Salamone dapsilis, cum Absalone pulcher',[5] and he regarded the crisis of his reign as caused by the king's youth.[6] Despite Richard's arbitrary actions, including the excesses of his Cheshire guards, which were described in some detail,[7] Usk appeared genuinely moved by the fate which befell him. He mentioned the omens at Richard's coronation, the loss of the coronation shoes foretelling the rise of the commons; the golden spur falling from his shoe foretelling the forces to be raised against him; and the crown falling from his head, denoting his deposition.

---

[1] *Chronicon*, p. 18a. [2] p. 29. [3] p. 30. [4] p. 31.
[5] p. 43. [6] p. 4. [7] p. 23.

Apart from these chronicles, a popular continuation which covered the reign of Richard II was the *Vita Ricardi Secundi* of the monk of Evesham. The *Vita Ricardi Secundi* gave an account of English history from 1377 to 1422, and, as already mentioned, was sometimes used to construct an eighth book of the *Polychronicon*.[1] The *Vita Ricardi Secundi* was indebted to Walsingham's history for the early period of Richard's reign, but after 1393 it contained a more independent version of events, and had little in common with the St. Albans account, the *Annales Ricardi Secundi*, which describe the years 1392–1406. It has already been noted that the account of the parliament of 1397 in the *Vita Ricardi Secundi* is almost identical with the account found in Usk's chronicle.

The last fourteenth-century continuation of the *Polychronicon* which need be mentioned is that contained in B.M. MS. Harley 3600, a *Polychronicon* that belonged to Whalley Abbey. This manuscript contains the text of the *Polychronicon* to 1340 (f. 225). At 1346 it has the Rolls Series (A) continuation, to the beginning of Richard II's reign (*finem accelerabant*), but from that period (f. 231ᵛ) to 1422 it contains an individual account of English history.[2] An entry at f. 232ᵛ, given in no other chronicle, contains an account of a deposition of Richard II in 1387–8. The chronicle says that after the battle of Radcot Bridge, Gloucester, Arundel, Warwick, and other magnates deposed Richard for three days, but because they could not agree upon the succession they restored him to the throne. As regards the truth of this account a deposition could have taken place after the defeat at Radcot Bridge, when the Appellants interviewed Richard in the Tower.[3] It is notable that during the last three days of December there are

---

[1] The only edition of the *Vita Ricardi Secundi* is that published by Hearne in 1729. See p. 123, note 3. The *Vita Ricardi Secundi* was also used as a continuation beyond 1381 in such manuscripts as B.M. MSS. Harley 3884, 4875; Bodleian Library, MSS. Digby 201, Lyell 21; Oriel College, Oxford, MS. 74.

[2] Kingsford prints the fifteenth-century portion of this chronicle, under the title of 'A Northern Chronicle, 1399–1430', pp. 279–91. Apart from the account of the deposition in 1387–8 it is identical with MS. Cotton Domit. A. xii from Richard II's reign onwards.

[3] M. V. Clarke, *Fourteenth Century Studies*, pp. 91–95.

no entries on the Close or Patent Rolls. The king's renewal of his coronation oath in the Merciless Parliament of 1388 suggests that the story in the Whalley continuation may be true. If it is, the *Polychronicon* continuation preserves the only account of this remarkable episode.

VIII

THE TRANSLATIONS AND INFLUENCE OF THE
POLYCHRONICON

THE translations of the *Polychronicon* which were made in the course of the fourteenth and fifteenth centuries increased its influence during the later Middle Ages, and transmitted a knowledge of Higden's work to a lay audience. In this form as well as in the original Latin the *Polychronicon* continued to be read until Tudor times.

I

The first translation of the *Polychronicon* was made by John Trevisa during the 1380's. The circumstances of Trevisa's life help to explain his undertaking of the work.[1] Trevisa was a Cornishman, born possibly at Trevessa in St. Enoder parish. He may well have been educated at the Collegiate Church of Glasney in Penryn, and from there or some other Cornish school he proceeded to Exeter College, Oxford, during the 1360's. He was at Exeter College between 1362 and 1365, and in 1369 he entered Queen's College, of which he became a Fellow during the 1370's. Trevisa was a Fellow of Queen's at much the same time as William Middleworth and Nicholas Hereford, both of whom were associated with the Lollard movement. Middleworth had been expelled together with Wyclif from Canterbury Hall in 1369 after the college became a monastic association, while

---

[1] I am much indebted for the following remarks on Trevisa to the articles by David C. Fowler, 'John Trevisa and the English Bible' in *Modern Philology*, lviii. 2 (1960), and 'New Light on John Trevisa', *Traditio*, xviii (1962). Professor Fowler says that the place of Trevisa's birth is not known. Carew mentions Crocadon as the Trevisa family residence in later times, ed. 1811, p. 269. Fuller says that he was born at Caradock, *Worthies* (1662), i. 204, or at Crocadon, *Church History* (1655), iv. 151.

Hereford was known as a prominent follower of Wyclif, and as a translator of the Lollard Bible. Wyclif himself rented a room in Queen's in 1374. There can be little doubt therefore that during the period of his Oxford residence Trevisa was thrown into close contact with the Wycliffite circle, and it is conceivable that during these years together with Hereford and with others he worked upon a translation of the Bible.[1]

Whatever Trevisa's views during these Oxford years, a dispute between northern and southern scholars at Queen's College that began in 1376, and was apparently concerned with the appointment of the provost, resulted in Trevisa's expulsion together with other southern scholars on account of 'unworthiness' in 1378.[2] It may be that behind this incident lay some dispute over Lollard doctrines, though on the surface it was simply a matter concerning the interpretation of the founder's rules. At some time, probably during the 1370's, Trevisa became chaplain to Thomas, Lord Berkeley, in Gloucestershire. The Berkeley family had an interest in Cornwall, and Trevisa may have owed his place at Oxford to them.[3] Between 1370 and 1387 he became Vicar of Berkeley,[4] and like Wyclif held a non-resident canonry in the Collegiate Church of Westbury-on-Trym.[5] He held the living at Berkeley until his death in 1402, and it was while serving as chaplain to Lord Berkeley that he made several of the translations for which he is chiefly remembered.

The works of Trevisa, which can be accurately dated, are the translation of the *Polychronicon*, which was completed in 1387, and the translation of the *De Proprietatibus Rerum*, which was completed in 1398.[6] Trevisa translated the *Polychronicon* at the

---

[1] The evidence for Trevisa's work upon a translation of the Bible is considered by David C. Fowler, 'John Trevisa and the English Bible' (op. cit.).

[2] Ibid., pp. 88–93.

[3] 'New Light on John Trevisa', pp. 299–300.

[4] A. J. Perry (ed.), *Dialogus inter Militem et Clericum, Richard FitzRalph's Sermon, Defensio Curatorum*, etc. E.E.T.S., no. 167 (1925).

[5] 'New Light on John Trevisa', pp. 311–13. Trevisa was probably appointed shortly before 1390.

[6] These two works were done under the patronage of Thomas IV, Lord Berkeley. In Professor Fowler's opinion Trevisa's translation of the *Gospel of Nicodemus*, the *Dialogus inter Militem et Clericum*, and Fitz Ralph's *Defensio*

request of Lord Berkeley. In the *Dialogue between a Lord and a Clerk upon Translation*, which he prefixed to his work, the justification for the translation of famous books and Scriptural texts is given in the words of the peer:

It is wonder that thou makest so feeble arguments, and hast gone so long to school. Aristotle's books and other books also of logic and of philosophy were translated out of Greek into Latin. Also at praying of King Charles, John Scott translated Deny's books out of Greek into Latin, and then out of Latin into French; then what hath English trespassed that it might not be translated into English? Also King Alured, that founded the University of Oxford, translated the best laws into English tongue, and a great deal of the Psalter out of Latin into English, and caused Wyrefrith, Bishop of Worcester, to translate Saint Gregory's books, the dialogues, out of Latin into Saxon. Also Caedmon of Whitby was inspired of the Holy Ghost, and made wonder poesies in English nigh of all the stories of holy writ. Also the holy man Beda translated St. John's Gospel out of Latin into English. Also thou wotest where the Apocalypse is written in the walls and roof of a chapel, both in Latin and in French. Also the gospel, and prophecy, and the right faith of holy church must be taught and preached to English men that can no Latin. Then the gospel, and prophecy, and the right faith of holy church must be told them in English, and that is not done but by English translation, for such English preaching is very translation, and such English preaching is good and needful; then English translation is good and needful.[1]

The question of translation was here debated in the light of the argument on the lawfulness of Biblical translation, and it is apparent that Trevisa was concerned with these considerations in his approach to the subject. It would be wrong, however, to regard Trevisa's choice of works, and in particular his choice of the *Polychronicon*, as directly connected with his Lollard sympathies. The writings which he chose to translate such as the

---

Curatorum belong to the years 1365–75, while the translation of the *De Regimine Principum* belongs in all probability to the period 1390–1400.

[1] This is quoted in A. W. Pollard, *Fifteenth Century Prose and Verse* (London, 1903), pp. 205–7.

Polychronicon and the *De Proprietatibus Rerum* were orthodox medieval writings, well known to the educated clergy of the time. It was their popularity which in the first instance almost certainly decided him to undertake the task. At the same time an interest in translation reached back in all probability to his Oxford years, and it is worth noting that at the time of the dispute in Queen's College, the southern scholars, of whom Trevisa was one, carried off with them a number of manuscripts, which included a copy of Higden's work.[1]

Trevisa began his translation of the *Polychronicon* in 1385. Though his English version never attained the popularity of Higden's Latin text, it had its own particular merits. Trevisa wrote at a time when the dialects of English varied considerably and when people in the south could scarcely understand what William of Malmesbury termed the 'uncouth' dialect of the north.[2] Higden himself spoke of the three branches of the English language, and of the 'strange bleatings and babblings' produced as a result of Danish and Norman influence.[3] To make himself understood to as wide an audience as possible Trevisa was obliged to give an extremely free rendering of his original, and in certain cases to use pairs of words to convey his meaning. In the dialogue that he prefixed to his translation he admitted that he found Higden's Latin difficult to read: 'Though I can speke, rede, and understande Latyn, there is moche Latyn in these bookes of Cronykes that I cannot understande nether thou, without studying, auisement, and lokying of other bookes'. Trevisa made occasional errors, but whatever his inaccuracies, his work had positive merits. He wrote in a vivid and lively way, with a felicity of word and phrase, and he tackled Higden's text in a spirited and forthright manner. In the course of his narrative Trevisa gave the reader his opinions on the burning questions of the day,[4] and he frequently dissented with some warmth from the statements of his authorities. His attitude to the legendary

---

[1] 'John Trevisa and the English Bible', p. 94.
[2] *Gesta Pontificum*, p. 209.   [3] ii. 158.
[4] Such as the right of secular lords to take away the superfluous goods of the 'possessioners', vi. 465–7.

history of Britain has already been mentioned;[1] elsewhere 'he falls foul of Alfred of Beverley for reckoning up the shires of England "without Cornwall", and he cannot forgive Giraldus Cambrensis for qualifying a tale with *si fas sit credere*'.[2] As regards historical information Trevisa did not add much of value to Higden's work. His additions consist in the main of brief explanations in which anecdotes point the moral, while the best-known addition is that which says that during the 1360's English began to be taught in the schools.[3] Trevisa wrote a brief continuation, of no great value, which carried the *Polychronicon* down to 1360.

Trevisa's additions to Higden's chronicle reveal, on the whole, a typical clerk of the fourteenth century, orthodox on most points of doctrine, interested like all medieval men in miracles and marvels, and strongly attached to his native district. His contribution to the *Polychronicon* was to translate it with an eye to a lay audience; and this explains his style, and his use of short paragraphs and definite statements. Yet despite its undoubted merits, Trevisa's English version never equalled the popularity of Higden's Latin text, and his work survives in only a few manuscripts. These include St. John's College, Cambridge, MS. 204, which was used by the editors of the Rolls Series edition; B.M. MS. Harley 1900; B.M. MS. Cotton Tiberius D. vii; B.M. Add. MS. 24194; B.M. MS. Stowe 65; Chetham's Library, Manchester, MS. 11379; Glasgow Hunterian MS. 367; Aberdeen University MS. 21; and Corpus Christi College, Cambridge, MS. 354. Trevisa's autograph copy is not extant, but Professor Cawley has worked out the *stemma codicum* of the surviving manuscripts as follows:[4]

---

[1] See p. 44.
[2] See the comments of Alice D. Greenwood, 'The Beginnings of English Prose', *Cambridge History of English Literature* (1908), ii. 76.
[3] ii. 161.
[4] A. C. Cawley, 'Relations of the Trevisa Manuscripts and Caxton's *Polychronicon*', *London Medieval Studies*, i, pt. 3 (1948), 463–82. In addition to the manuscripts listed by Professor Cawley other copies include Aberdeen University MS. 21, which superficially resembles St. John's College, Cambridge, MS. 204, *A Catalogue of the Medieval Manuscripts of the University Library, Aberdeen*, ed.

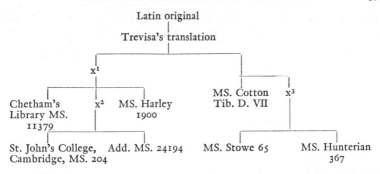

It can be seen that St. John's College, Cambridge, MS. 204; B.M. MS. Harley 1900; B.M. Add. MS. 24194; and Chetham's Library, Manchester, MS. 11379 form one group of manuscripts, while B.M. MS. Cotton Tiberius D. vii, B.M. MS. Stowe 65, and MS. Hunterian 367 form an independent group closer to the Latin original. Of this second group B.M. MS. Cotton Tiberius D. vii has been held to preserve the oldest version. In the fifteenth century when Caxton printed Trevisa's text he used a manuscript similar to B.M. MS. Harley 1900.

In addition to Trevisa's text another translation of the *Polychronicon* appeared in the course of the fifteenth century. The author of this second translation is unknown, and his work survives in a single copy (B.M. MS. Harley 2261). Like Trevisa's version this later translation followed the intermediate (AB) text of the *Polychronicon*, and from internal evidence it is probable that it was compiled between 1432 and 1450.[1] The second translation was shorter than Trevisa's. Where Trevisa expanded the *Polychronicon* and added material, the later writer curtailed the narrative. This may have been due to a change of viewpoint.

M. R. James (Cambridge, 1932), pp. 106–7, and Corpus Christi College, Cambridge, MS. 354, an imperfect copy which begins Lib. i, cap. 23 (Rolls edition, i. 199) and ends Lib. vii, cap. 22 (Rolls edition, viii. 43, line 5). See *Corpus Christi College, Cambridge. Catalogue of Manuscripts*, ed. M. R. James (Cambridge, 1912), ii. 186. Aberystwyth MS., N.L. DN. 4923 is an English version which belonged to St. Werburgh's.

[1] The remarks on this translation are indebted to Bert Leroy Kinkade, 'The English Translations of Higden's *Polychronicon*' (Illinois dissertation, 1934). The translation is printed together with Trevisa's translation in the Rolls Series edition. It ends in 1401 with an account of the spoilation of the shrine at Hales.

It is possible that the fifteenth-century translator was a man of humanist tendencies, possibly a layman, uninterested in the marvels, explanations, and repetitions that formed a part of Trevisa's text.

Of the two works Trevisa's was undoubtedly the more popular. Whatever the merits and the learning of the later writer the solitary manuscript in which his work survives is, in itself, evidence of its limited appeal. Trevisa's colloquial style was more attractive to a medieval audience, while his prejudices against monks and friars found no doubt a ready sympathy among his readers. Though Trevisa's English version never equalled the popularity of the Latin original Trevisa introduced the *Polychronicon* to a lay audience, and his translation extended the fame of Higden's work in the course of the fourteenth and fifteenth centuries.

II

The popularity of Trevisa's text among the laity can be seen from the printed editions of Caxton and Wynkyn de Worde. To his edition Caxton added a continuation which brought Trevisa's text down to the 1460's. Though these printed editions are of limited historical value, they have their place in the history of the *Polychronicon*, and through them Trevisa's version preserved a reading public until the sixteenth century.

Caxton printed his own choice of medieval writings, but among the historical works which he chose to publish were chronicles such as the *Brut* and the *Polychronicon* which had been popular during the later Middle Ages. In 1480, under the title *The Chronicles of England*, Caxton printed a version of the *Brut*, and added a continuation known as *Caxton's Chronicles*.[1] In 1480 he published chapters from Trevisa's translation of the first book of the *Polychronicon* which he called the *Descripcion of Britayne*, and two years later he printed the whole of Trevisa's text in a revised version. Caxton did not print Trevisa's work exactly as it was

---

[1] On Caxton's *Chronicles of England* and their continuation see Kingsford, pp. 113–15, 119–22.

written. He wrote that he 'somewhat haue chaunged the rude and old Englyssh, that is to wete certayn wordes, which in these days [i.e. in 1482] be neither usyd ne understanden'. He revised Trevisa's text, displaced words, and modified Trevisa's spelling. He introduced for the first time a system of punctuation into the English version. As Professor Cawley has said, 'Caxton marks off large units of thought by means of paragraph signs, and he marks off smaller, sometimes purely grammatical units [separate sentences, co-ordinate sentences, clauses, phrases] by means of commas and points. He does not consistently recognize very short units like oppositional phrases or single words, nor does he recognize consistently the large grammatical units which we call complex sentences.'[1] In this way Caxton modernized Trevisa's text for the reading public of his day. Though there are differences between the *Descripcion of Britayne* and the 1482 edition of Trevisa's text, these are small, and are accounted for by the fact that in all probability Caxton used a different manuscript of Trevisa's work when he came to prepare his later edition.[2]

The greatest historical interest attaches, however, not so much to Caxton's revision of Trevisa's text, as to the continuation which he added in the eighth book or *Liber ultimus*. This continuation extended to 1460, and has been termed 'the single work of importance of which the authorship can be traced to William Caxton'.[3] By way of introduction to his own continuation Caxton wrote, 'I haue emprysed to ordeyne this newe booke by the suffraunce of Almyghty God to contynue the sayd werk bryefly, and to sette in hystoriall thynges, suche as I haue conne gete'. In the colophon he asks pardon of his readers: 'Wher as ther is fawte, I beseche them that shal rede it to correcte it, for yf I could haue founden moo storyes I wold haue sette in hit moo; but the substaunce that I can fynde and knowe I have shortly

---

[1] A. C. Cawley, 'Punctuation in the Early Versions of Trevisa', *London Medieval Studies*, i, pt. i (1937), 116–33.

[2] A. C. Cawley, 'Relations of the Trevisa Manuscripts and Caxton's *Polychronicon*' (op. cit.).

[3] W. Blades, *Life and Typography of William Caxton* (1861), i. 215–65, printed Caxton's continuation of the *Polychronicon*. See Kingsford's remarks upon this continuation, pp. 137–9.

sette hem in this book, to thentente that such thynges as have ben done syth the deth or ende of the sayd boke of Polychronycon shold be had in remembraunce and not putte in oblyvyon ne forgetynge'. The first part of Caxton's continuation was based upon a version of the *Brut*, though he included material from the *Chronicles of England*, and the *Chronicles of London*. Caxton himself says that for this part of his narrative he could find no book of authority, 'except a lytel booke named *Fasciculus temporum* and another called *Aureus de universo*'. After 1419 his continuation was similar to the *Chronicles of England*, and in both the narrative from 1419 to 1430 was based upon a London chronicle. After 1440 the two continuations followed the *Main City Chronicle*, and were Yorkist in outlook, favourable to Humphrey, Duke of Gloucester, and hostile to Suffolk and Margaret of Anjou.

Such was Caxton's edition of Trevisa, printed at the end of the fifteenth century. The *Descripcion of Britayne* and the *Polychronicon* were reprinted within a few years by Wynkyn de Worde, while another edition of Higden's chronicle appeared in the course of the fifteenth century.[1] The successive editions of Trevisa's text illustrate not only the continuing popularity of the *Polychronicon*, but the extent to which English had become established as the first language of historical writing.

III

Whatever the influence of these translations during the later Middle Ages, the vogue of the *Polychronicon* reached its height during the second half of the fourteenth century. In the world of Latin chronicles, the *Polychronicon* was a new and exciting development, a model to be copied in some religious houses, and a text to be continued in others. Fourteenth- and fifteenth-century chronicles which quoted Higden's text include the *Fasciculi Zizaniorum*, the *Annales Rerum Anglicarum* of William of

---

[1] The *Polychronicon* was published by Wynkyn de Worde in 1495, and *The descripcion of Britayne* in 1498. There was an edition by P. Treveris at Southwerke in 1527, Pollard and Redgrave, *Short Title Catalogue* (Bibliographical Society, 1950).

Worcester, the *Liber de Illustribus Henricis* of John Capgrave, the *Speculum Historiale* of Richard of Cirencester, and the *Historia Monasterii Sancti Augustini Cantuariensis* of Thomas of Elmham. The Bridlington prophecies of John Erghome, which were written during the 1360's, derived their opening almost entirely from Higden's work.[1]

In more than one case the *Polychronicon* influenced the form of chronicles written during the fourteenth century. The *Eulogium Historiarum*, which was completed during the 1360's, was a universal chronicle constructed along the lines of Higden's work. The author, who was a monk of Malmesbury, encouraged by his abbot and in an effort to escape the tedium of monastic life which 'dulls the faculties and frustrates the striving after virtue', attempted to compile a history of the world similar to the *Polychronicon*. He opened his account[2] with the story of the Creation and traced the course of the four great empires concluding with an account of the Roman Empire, which he described in detail. The monk of Malmesbury, however, lacked Higden's learning, and he lacked also the industry that was necessary to compile a chronicle on the scale of Higden's work. Several parts of his narrative were taken from the *Polychronicon*, yet despite his debt to Higden the author of the *Eulogium* attacked him on several occasions. In the fourth book of his chronicle he criticized Higden for rejecting the popular explanation that St. Patrick had expelled venomous snakes from Ireland, and elsewhere the author of the *Polychronicon* was criticized for casting doubt upon 'historical facts', which had been clearly established by William of Malmesbury.[3]

As well as in the *Eulogium Historiarum* the influence of the *Polychronicon* can be seen in two writings concerned more particularly with British affairs, the *Historia Aurea*, and the history of John of Brompton. The *Historia Aurea*, which gave rise to a new version of the *Polychronicon*,[4] was an account of British history

---

[1] The Bridlington prophecies are discussed on pp. 146-7.
[2] Ed. F. S. Haydon, 3 vols. (R.S., 1858-63).
[3] *Eulogium Historiarum*, ii. 130-1.   [4] See p. 101.

from its origins to the 1340's. It was seven times the length of the *Polychronicon*, and was probably inspired by the earliest version of Higden's work. Up to the period of the Norman Conquest the compiler, who is said to have been John, Vicar of Tynemouth, absorbed the greater part of the *Polychronicon* into his text, though he did it in such a way as to conceal to some extent his borrowings. The *Historia Aurea* gave a massive account of British history. Similar in scope was the chronicle of 'John of Brompton', which was written during the middle years of the fourteenth century.[1] Like John of Tynemouth 'John of Brompton' used Higden,[2] but he aimed also at continuing or supplementing the work of Geoffrey of Monmouth. Beginning with the conversion of the Saxons, which Geoffrey had not treated, Brompton sought to trace English history through to the reign of Edward I. Though his chronicle stopped in 1199 with the reign of John, as far as he goes Brompton gives a fuller account of British history than Higden, and his chronicle was one of the more ambitious compilations of this period.

After the end of the fourteenth century the influence of the *Polychronicon* on historical writing declined. This may be explained by the fact that monastic chronicles were gradually replaced by other forms of historical writing. In the fifteenth century the writing of history became increasingly a secular activity taking at first the form of the town chronicle, and then, under the impact of humanist thought, the form of histories written by laymen. In this situation the limitations of the monastic chronicle rendered its influence less enduring. Even at its most effective monastic history had been the expression of a restricted viewpoint.[3] It was history written from the viewpoint of the Church, and ecclesiastical problems were those

---

[1] It is published in *Decem Scriptores*, ed. Roger Twysden (1652), cols. 725–1284.

[2] *Polychronicon*, ii. 90–96 = Twysden, cols. 956–7.

[3] It should be noted that medieval chronicles were frequently written under conditions which prohibited a personal expression of opinion on the part of the author. They were often a task laid upon a particular member of a religious community who might have little aptitude for historical composition. Their object was not to 'write history' but to keep a record of events for the benefit of a particular monastery.

which the monastic chroniclers best understood. On political and social issues they took a narrow stand, and one not calculated to appeal to a lay audience.[1] The partial view which the monastic chroniclers took of the world around them can be seen in the fourteenth-century continuations of the *Polychronicon*, and in the description that their authors gave of events such as the Peasants' Revolt and the Lollard movement. Economic interests, other than those of their own house, meant little to ecclesiastical writers of history, and as great landlords the monks were uniformly unsympathetic to the aspirations of peasants and townsmen. At St. Albans, therefore, Walsingham made little effort to understand the causes of the Peasants' Rising. His view of the aims of the rebels, which he gave in the form of Straw's confession: to kill the king and those around him, to confiscate the lands of the Church, to leave only the Mendicants (whom Walsingham did not like) to celebrate mass, and to burn London, can only be described as fiction.[2] Straw's confession, as given by Walsingham, made out the worst possible case against the rebels and is at variance with other parts of his history.[3]

If the Peasants' Revolt received partial and prejudiced treatment in the monastic chronicles, the story of the Lollard movement was told with equal bias. Walsingham painted a scurrilous picture of Wyclif and of Gaunt, who supported him during the critical years of the 1370's.[4] To the monk of St. Albans Wyclif

[1] See Walsingham's condescending treatment of John Philpot, one of the big merchant princes who put up money to fight the French, *Historia Anglicana*, i. 370, 435; ii. 115; *Chronicon Angliae*, p. 359.

[2] *Chronicon Angliae*, pp. 309–10. The Mendicants were accused of causing the rebellion, *Fasciculi Zizaniorum*, p. 293; *Chronicon Angliae*, p. 312.

[3] St. Albans was a centre of the movement. The townsmen, who were tenants of the abbey went to London to join the revolt, and returned threatening to set fire to the abbey if their demands were not met. They demanded the surrender of the charters which they believed ensured their freedom. The abbot was forced to give them what charters the abbey possessed. The serfs burst into the abbot's parlour and carried away some millstones which had been placed as a pavement at the door in memory of an ancient law-suit gained by the abbey against the town. Walsingham describes these and other events in detail. *Historia Anglicana*, i. 458 ff. For a recent account of the Rising see M. McKisack, *The Fourteenth Century*, pp. 406–23.

[4] *Chronicon Angliae*, pp. 115–21, 281–3, 335–45.

was 'the instrument of the devil, the enemy of the Church, the confounder of the people, the idol of heretics, the mirror of hypocrites, the begetter of schism . . .'.[1] Walsingham was equally hostile to Gaunt, and his view of all who supported Wyclif can be seen in his comment on the University of Oxford in this period: 'Oh, Oxford, Oxford, how low hast thou fallen from the heights of wisdom and learning. For, whereas thou wast formerly wont to unravel the doubts and perplexities of the whole world, now, darkened by a cloud of ignorance, thou dost not fear to doubt the things which it does not become any one to doubt even among lay Christians.'[2]

In the ecclesiastical chronicles we see 'through a glass darkly' into the world of the fourteenth century, and only a little of the depth of contemporary social and political problems comes through in their writings. Events were judged with regard to the interests of the Church. In addition ecclesiastical authors wrote in a language and according to conventions not easily understood by a lay audience. The political prophecies of John Erghome, an Austin friar of York, illustrate the esoteric world of the ecclesiastical author.[3] Writing within the framework of a prophetic narrative which he ascribed to the saintly John of Bridlington, Erghome retold historical facts, yet the principal object of his work was not to write history, but to encourage Edward III to resume his wars in France. Events and people were judged with this in mind, and the prophecy ended with the 'reign' of the Black Prince for a time when he was firmly established as the King of France. Erghome's work, with its concealed meanings, and its prophetic machinery, was dedicated to Humphrey de

<hr />

[1] *Historia Anglicana*, ii. 119.
[2] *Chronicon Angliae*, pp. 173–4.
[3] For a study of political prophecy see Rupert Taylor, *The Political Prophecy in England* (1911). On the Bridlington prophecies Sister Helen Margaret Peck's, Chicago Ph.D. dissertation (1930) 'The Prophecy of John of Bridlington' contains an interesting analysis. The prophecies are printed by T. Wright in *Political Poems and Songs* (R.S., 1859), i. 123–215. They are quoted by the Canon of Bridlington, Walsingham, and Adam of Usk. On Erghome's books see M. R. James, 'The Catalogue of the Library of the Augustinian Friars at York', *Fasciculus Ioanni Willis Clark dicatus* (1909).

Bohun, but it was a type of writing more easily understood by an ecclesiastic than a lay reader.

IV

Approaching contemporary issues in this way, monastic writings expressed the outlook of a world which was very different from that of the laymen who wrote history during the fifteenth and sixteenth centuries. Yet, despite the secularization of history, something of the universal outlook of medieval times lived on among the writers and antiquaries of the Tudor age, and it would be a mistake to regard Higden's chronicle as utterly alien to the histories of a later day. In the style of universal histories Tudor writers opened their chronicles at the Creation or some similar point.[1] The *Cronycle of Fabyan* (1516) began with the Creation, Stowe's *Summarie of English Chronicles* (1565) started with the Flood, and Holinshed began his *Chronicles of England, Scotland and Ireland* (1587) with Noah. The medieval encyclopaedic tradition also survived into Tudor times. Camden included all manner of information in his *Rerum Anglicarum et Hibernicarum Annales*, and in the same way that Higden began his history with a description of the world Holinshed opened his *Chronicles* with Harrison's description of Britain.

In the spate of universal histories that appeared in the course of the sixteenth and seventeenth centuries none was more popular than Raleigh's *History of the World* (1614), which went through ten editions before the Restoration.[2] A comparison between Raleigh's *History* and the *Polychronicon* reveals the advance in historical method that had been achieved in the course of two

[1] On Renaissance histories see W. K. Ferguson, *The Renaissance in Historical Thought* (1948); T. E. Mommsen, 'Petrarch's Conception of the Dark Ages' in *Medieval and Renaissance Studies*, pp. 106–29; D. Hay, 'Flavio Biondo and the Middle Ages', *Proceedings of the British Academy*, xlv (1959), 97–129; and the comments in C. A. Patrides, *The Phoenix and the Ladder*.

[2] For Raleigh's *History of the World*, which was never completed, C. Firth, 'Raleigh's History of the World', *Proceedings of the British Academy*, viii (1917–18), 427–46; T. N. Brushfield, 'Sir Walter Ralegh and his History of the World', *Reports and Transactions of the Devonshire Association*, xix (1887), 389–418; *Raleghana*, pt. vi, *Reports and Transactions of the Devonshire Association*, xxxv (1904), 181–219.

centuries. Raleigh used, in a manner impossible to a medieval scribe, the accounts of classical historians to describe the political problems and the political personalities of the ancient world. He drew modern parallels, illustrating from the struggle between England and Spain the importance of sea power at the time of the wars between the Romans and the Carthaginians.[1] Yet whatever the differences between Raleigh's history and Higden's chronicle, both works came from the same tradition. They were universal chronicles which gave a Christian and providential view of history. To both Higden and Raleigh universal history was one facet of the Divine Order, and the similarity of their approach reveals the continuity in thought between medieval and Renaissance times. In transmitting medieval ideas to the Tudor age writings like the *Polychronicon* had played their part. Though it had long ceased to exercise any direct influence upon the forms of historical writing, Higden's chronicle was still read in the sixteenth century. It was consulted by Elizabethan divines, and by statesmen such as Cecil.[2] It was used by Tudor chroniclers and antiquaries. Because it portrayed the universal trend of history, and because a belief in universal history still survived, the *Polychronicon* retained the interest of a later age.

[1] *History*, ii. 351, 359–62.
[2] William Cecil owned a copy of Trevisa's text, and at the end are notes in his hand. The manuscript was offered for sale by Frank Hammond in 1959.

IX

CONCLUSION

THE importance of the *Polychronicon* is immediately apparent in the pattern of chronicle writing throughout the century. In contrast with the separate and independent accounts of history written during the reign of Edward II, the second half of the fourteenth century is predominantly the age of the '*Polychronicon* continuation'. To the monks who wrote chronicles the *Polychronicon* had become the standard account of early history. What were the reasons for its unprecedented success?

Much of the answer to that question lies in the quality of Higden's work. The *Polychronicon* was not competing with the majority of contemporary chronicles such as the writings of Walsingham. Where Walsingham and others aimed at giving a record of contemporary events, the *Polychronicon* possessed a wider literary and antiquarian appeal. From the standpoint of the contemporary reader it was a literary masterpiece. Written at enormous length and with considerable scholarship, the *Polychronicon* was a mine of information on a great number of subjects, and an essential reference book for the cleric of the time. It was because of its intrinsic merits that copies were manufactured at such an unprecedented rate between 1350 and 1450, and were to be found in monasteries, cathedrals, and even in the possession of laymen. The Duke of Gloucester gave a copy of the *Polychronicon* to his chantry college at Pleshey in the 1390's, and bequests received by the library of the Guildhall during the fifteenth century from the wealthier merchants of London include copies of Higden's work.[1] It was the triumph of the *Polychronicon* that, though written in Latin, it had such an immediate appeal.

[1] Sylvia Thrupp, *The Merchant Class of Medieval London* (Chicago, 1948), pp. 162–3.

The form of Higden's work recommended itself to the audience of the time. The *Polychronicon* was an encyclopaedia, mainly historical but with a great deal of information on the geography of the world. As Caxton's edition of 1480 shows, the geographical description of Britain remained of particular interest throughout the fifteenth century. This was a part of the work which appealed to both ecclesiastic and layman. Undoubtedly, however, a large part of the appeal of the *Polychronicon* came from its account of ancient history. Higden traced in detail the fortunes of Rome from the time of its foundation down to the decline of the empire in the West. Though this part of his chronicle met with success it is doubtful whether in compiling his narrative Higden felt that he was opening a new chapter in historical writing. Vincent of Beauvais had written in the same way in France during the thirteenth century. The medieval encyclopaedic tradition within which Higden wrote lent itself to this fuller treatment of ancient history. 'The study of classical authors and ancient history grew naturally out of the teaching of patristic as part of theology, and out of the preparation of supplements to encyclopaedias.'[1] Higden none the less was the first chronicler in England to write at such length and with such evident interest about the Roman past.

Important as Higden's achievement was, however, it is doubtful whether the *Polychronicon* would have enjoyed the success it did had not the interests of the educated clergy also been changing during this period. Whether it be called pre-humanist or not, a growing interest in the classical authors and in ancient history was undoubtedly present among the educated clergy. The court at Avignon encouraged classical studies. The work of Trevet, though written within a medieval tradition, was indicative of the 'classicizing' trend. If in England the Oxford Franciscans appear to have had no obvious successors, scholars like De Bury were not alone in their concern with ancient authors, and both Bradwardine and Burley used classical material in their writings. In the field of literature an increasing number of poems and prose

[1] *English Friars*, p. 63.

works drew on classical antiquity and used classical themes. Antiquity came to the educated clergy of the fourteenth century in many forms, and if it came in the form of the lecture commentary and the chronicle it was present none the less.

It was an audience, therefore, increasingly interested in the ancient world that read the *Polychronicon* with such enthusiasm during the latter part of the fourteenth century. The vogue of the *Polychronicon* was at first mainly among the educated clergy. Copies of Higden's work, some of them beautifully illuminated,[1] were to be found in monasteries, and in cathedrals up and down the land. So popular in fact was the chronicle, and so great was its success among the clergy, that it was translated into English for the benefit of a lay audience. That this was done was due to the interests of John Trevisa. Yet for all the merits of his translation the *Polychronicon* remained essentially an ecclesiastical history, a Latin book written by a Benedictine monk for monks and secular clerics, and Trevisa's English version never equalled the popularity of the Latin text.

Such was the story of the *Polychronicon*, the most original chronicle to come out of fourteenth-century England, and one of the last important chronicles of the medieval world. In the fourteenth century the world was still profoundly medieval, the monasteries remained the chief centres of historical studies, and the monks still wrote the kind of history which appealed to the most-educated audience of the day. In its learning and its wider perspectives, no less than in its miracles and its marvels, the *Polychronicon* mirrored the outlook of the educated clergy of the time.

[1] To give a few examples: New College, Oxford, MS. 152 has the initials of the books illuminated; B.M. MS. Harley 3877 has the initials to the books ornamented; MS. Harley 4875 has illuminated initials; Paris MS. Lat. 4922 has an elaborate first page where the initial *P* shows the Holy Trinity, and in the bottom left-hand corner is portrayed a monk at prayer; B.M. Add. MS. 12118 has illuminated borders.

APPENDIX I

LIST OF LATIN MANUSCRIPTS OF THE
POLYCHRONICON

This list of manuscripts is indebted to the list compiled by
Sir R. A. B. Mynors

Manuscript	Provenance	Text
Boston:		
Harvard University (College Library):		
Lat. 116		Late XIV cent.
Brussels:		
Bibliothèque Royale:		
MS. 3096		XV cent.
MS. 3097	St. Augustine's, Canterbury	XIV cent.
Cambridge:		
Cambridge University Library:		
MS. Dd. I. 17		XIV cent.
Dd. VIII. 7		XIV cent.
Ee. II. 22		Late XIV cent.
Ii. II. 24	St. Augustine's, Canterbury	XIV–XV cent. (Rolls A)
Ii. III. 1	Christ Church, Canterbury	XIV cent. (Rolls E)
Add. 3077		XIV cent.
Christ's College:		
MS. 3		XV cent.
Corpus Christi College:		
MS. 21	Hospital of St. John the Evangelist, Cambridge	Late XIV cent.
117		XIV–XV cent.
164	Wells Cathedral Chapter	XIV cent. Books I–II only
259		XIV cent.

Manuscript	Provenance	Text
Gonville and Caius College:		
MS. 58		XV cent.
82		XV cent. (Rolls B)
249	John Herryson (1464)	XV cent.
St. John's College:		
MS. 12	Hyde Abbey. Written by John Lutton (1386?)	Late XIV cent. (Rolls D)
Peterhouse College:		
MS. 177		XV cent.
Trinity College:		
MS. R. 4. 1		XV cent.
R. 5. 24 (719)		XV cent.
726		XV cent.
1293	Roger Walle, prebendary of Lichfield (*c.* 1450–60)	XV cent.
Trinity Hall:		
MS. 25		Late XIV cent.
Dublin:		
Trinity College:		
MS. 486	Austin Friars, London	XV cent.
487		XV cent.
488		XV cent.
Edinburgh:		
National Library of Scotland:		
Advocates MS. 33. 4. 12		XV cent.
Eton College:		
MS. 213	Witham, Charterhouse of the Holy Cross	XV cent.
Exeter Cathedral:		
MS. 3509	Exeter cathedral	Late XIV cent.
Glasgow:		
Hunterian Library:		
MS. 72		XIV–XV cent.
223		XIV cent.

Manuscript	*Provenance*	*Text*

London:

British Museum:

Add. MS. 10104	Adam of Usk (*c.* 1352–1430)	Late XIV cent.
10105	Glastonbury (1512)	XIV cent. Wants Books I, II, and part of III
12118		? Early XV cent.
15759	Norwich cathedral	XIV cent.
39236		XV cent.
Arundel MS. 86	Written by John Lutton. He wrote St. John's College, Cambridge, MS. 12. Bath	XIV–XV cent.
Cotton MS. Julius E. viii		XV cent.
Nero D. viii		XV cent.
Egerton 871	John Macclesfield (1416–17)	XIV–XV cent.
Harley MS. 655		XIV cent.
1320		XV cent.
1707		XV cent.
1728–9	Nicholas Shaxton, Bishop of Salisbury (1535–56)	XV cent. Originally one volume
1751	Oxford, Queen's College?	XIV cent.
3600	Whalley abbey	XV cent.
3671	Hospital of St. John the Baptist, Exeter	XV cent.
3673		XV cent.
3877		XV cent.
3884		XV cent. Wants first chapters
4875		XV cent.
Royal MS. 13. C. iii		XV cent.
13. D. i	London, St. Peter, Cornhill	XIV cent.

Manuscript	Provenance	Text
Royal MS. 13. E. i	Lincoln Cathedral	XIV cent.
14. C. ix	Ramsey, Benedictine abbey	XIV cent.
14. C. xii	Hospital of St. Thomas of Acon, Cheapside	XIV cent.
14. C. xiii	Norwich, Benedictine cathedral priory	XIV cent.
Stowe MS. 64		Early XV cent.

College of Arms:

Arundel MS. 2		XIV–XV cent.
4		Late XIV cent. Wants first three quires

College of Physicians:

MS. 398		XIV cent.

Inner Temple:

MS. 511–15	Francis Babington, rector of Lincoln College (1559)	XV cent.

Lambeth Library:

MS. 48		Late XIV cent.
104	Exeter cathedral	Late XIV cent.
112		XIV cent.
160		XV cent. Part printed in *Chronicon Angliae*
181		XIV cent.

Los Angeles:

Huntington Library:

MS. 132	St. Werburgh's (*c.* 1330–60)	XIV cent. Author's manuscript (?)

Lincoln Cathedral·

MS. 85		XIV cent.
109		XV cent.

Manuscript	Provenance	Text
Manchester:		
Rylands Library:		
Latin MS. 170		XV cent. Wants Book I
217	St. Mary, Dublin (*c.* 1431)	Mid-XV cent.
218		XV cent.
Oxford:		
Balliol College:		
MS. 235	Thomas Gascoigne (1448)	XIV–XV cent. Wants part of Book VII
236	Duke of Buckingham (1444–60)	Mid-XV cent.
Bodleian Library:		
Ashmole MS. 796		XV cent.
Bodley MS. 316	College of Holy Trinity, Pleshey. Written 1394–7	XIV cent.
341	Westminster	XIV cent.
358		XV cent.
359		XIV cent. Wants Books VI and VII
Digby MS. 201		XV cent.
Douce MS. 138		XV cent.
Laud Misc. MS. 529		XV cent.
545	Franciscan convent, London	XV cent.
Laud MS. 619	Fountains	XV cent.
Hatton MS. 14	Charterhouse of Jesus of Bethlehem, Sheen	XIV cent.
Lyell MS. 21	Abingdon	Late XIV cent.
Rawlinson B. MS. 179		XV cent. Wants first four chapters

Manuscript	Provenance	Text
Rawlinson B. M.S. 191	Christ Church, Canterbury	XIV cent. Wants first four chapters
Tanner MS. 19		XV cent.
170	Gloucester, Austin priory	XIV cent.
Christ Church:		
MS. 89		XV cent.
Corpus Christi College:		
MS. 83	Llanthony	XIV–XV cent.
89	St. Peter's Abbey, Gloucester	XV cent.
Lincoln College:		
MS. 107		? XIV cent.
Magdalen College:		
MS. 29		XV cent. Wants part of Book VII
97		XV cent.
147	St. Sepulchre's, Newgate (1449)	XV cent.
181	Dunstable	XIV cent. (Rolls C)
190		XV cent.
Merton College:		
MS. 118	Robert Stoneham (1409)	XIV–XV cent.
121		XV cent.
New College:		
MS. 152	William North, Bath and Wells	XV cent. Beginnings of Books III, IV, VI missing
Oriel College:		
MS. 16		XIV–XV cent.
74		XV cent.

Manuscript	Provenance	Text
Oxford (cont.)		
Queen's College:		
MS. 307	St. Augustine's, Canterbury	XV cent.
University College:		
MS. 177	Barnwell Priory	Late XIV cent.
Paris:		
Bibliothèque Nationale:		
MS. Lat. 4922	Writing similar to MS. Bodley 316. Norwich cathedral	? XIV cent.
4923		XIV cent.
12502		XV cent. Books I–IV only
15014	St. Victor of Paris	XV cent. Books I–III only
Rome:		
Vatican Library:		
MS. Vat. Lat. 1959		XIV cent.
Taunton:		
Somerset County Museum	Richard Godwyn (fifteenth century), Keynsham. Austin abbey	Late XIV cent.
Valencia:		
Valencia Cathedral:		
MS. 89		XIV cent.
Wales:		
National Library:		
Brogyntyn MS. 40		XIV cent.
Winchester College:		
MS. 15	William of Wykeham	XIV cent.
27		XV cent. Wants part of Books I and VII

SELECTED LIST OF FRAGMENTS OF THE
POLYCHRONICON

Manuscript	Text

London:

British Museum:

Cotton MS. Nero D. ii — This is a volume of historical collections. At f. 204 after the *Commendacio lamentabilis in transitu magni regis Edwardi* it has the *Polychronicon* text from 1307 to 1377. The notes in the margin are in the hand of Polydore Vergil.

MS. Lansdowne 239 — This has 4 ff. on the reigns of Edward II and III from a *Polychronicon* continuing the chronicle of Walter of Guisborough.

MS. Sloane 289 — This has Book I at ff. 1–54.

Lambeth Library:

MS. 99 — Excerpts from Book I at ff. 158–86.

Oxford:

Bodleian Library:

Digby MS. 82 — An abbreviation of Book I.

196 — A paper book of historical collections. At f. 111 it has Book VII to *diu postea habuerunt.*

218 — This has fragments of Books VI and VII.

Rawlinson B. MS. 154 — A fragment of Book I.

Maidstone Museum — Kent Archaeological Society's Library. A wrapper of an autograph manuscript of Sir Roger Twysden's *Certayn Consideration upon the state of England.* The end of Book II and the beginning of Book III.

APPENDIX II

TRANSLATION OF SELECTED PASSAGES OF THE *POLYCHRONICON*

On the Civil War between Caesar and Pompey (iv. 188–206)

CLEOPATRA, the daughter of Ptolemy Dionysus (Auletes) ruled over the Egyptians for twenty-two years, that is to say two years before Caesar, five years under Caesar, and fifteen years under Octavius Augustus. The civil war between Caesar and Pompey, his father-in-law, began in this way: after the labours of ten years in which he had conquered Gaul, Germany, and Britain, Caesar asked for a triumph or the honours which such victories merited, but Pompey, Cato, and Marcellus the consul resisted this, and ordered that he should disband his army and return to Rome.[1] And by the order of the consul Marcellus, Pompey was sent to take charge of the legions which were at Liceria. Because of this rebuff, Julius Caesar advanced with his army against his own country. While there were many offices at Rome, some of which lasted for a year, and some for two years, the greatest among them was the office of dictator, which was to last for five years.[2] At first there was one dictator, but with the growth of the Republic there came to be three, so that if perchance a dispute arose between two of them, the third would settle it. It happened that these three, Pompey, Caesar, and Marcus Crassus were dictators at the same time, and that Pompey, because he was old and had finished active service, remained to defend the state. Crassus who had been sent to subdue the Parthians was captured by a trick and killed. Caesar was sent to the west and stayed there for five years conquering the Gauls and the Allobroges. After that, sustained by his own authority, he extended his term of office for another five years, during which he conquered the Britons and again conquered the Gauls. When he had reached the Alps on his return to Rome, he commanded Pompey, whose daughter he had married, to prepare

[1] Eutropius, vi. 19.   [2] Suetonius, *Julius*, caps. 27, 28.

a triumph for him. Pompey, however, with the consent of the senate, refused him this on account of his audacity in extending his term of office, whereupon Caesar, who was furious, hastened to Rome to attack Pompey. Pompey fled in fear to Greece with the senate and the consuls, and there renewed war against Caesar.[1] Caesar, however, entered the city which was as if deserted and broke into the public treasury. He took four thousand one hundred and thirty pounds of gold, and ninety thousand pounds of silver, and distributed it among his soldiers.[2] Counterfeiting peace, he personally filled evey office at once. Then he made for Spain where he destroyed Pompey's three strongest armies along with their leaders. After that he went to Greece and fought Pompey. In the first battle Caesar was defeated and put to flight, but because night came down Pompey did not wish to follow. Whence Caesar said that Pompey did not know how to be victorious, and that he himself could have been defeated only on that day. They fought in Thessalia where Pompey's line of battle consisted of forty thousand foot, six hundred cavalry on the left wing, and five hundred cavalry on the right wing, and all the resources of the east with the nobility of the senate, the praetors, and the consuls. Caesar in his battle line had not fully thirty thousand foot, and a thousand cavalry. When battle eventually began the army of Pompey fled, its camps were scattered, and Pompey himself fled to seek help from the young Ptolemy, the king of Egypt, to whom he had been appointed tutor by the senate. But the king following fortune and not friendship, had Pompey slain, and sent his head and his ring to Caesar. On seeing these Caesar burst into tears. Soon Caesar sailed for Alexandria but Ptolemy prepared ambushes. Constrained by the force of the enemy which pressed on, Caesar boarded a skiff which was soon weighed down and submerged through the weight of those who followed. Caesar swam the distance of two hundred paces until he reached a ship with one hand which was holding documents raised. When shortly he was forced into a naval battle with great ease he either sank or captured the king's fleet. But because the citizens of Alexandria begged for the life of their king, Caesar agreed, warning him that he should have recourse to the friendship of Rome rather than the fortunes of arms against her.

---

[1] Eutropius, vi. 19.   [2] Orosius, vi. 15.

As soon as Ptolemy was freed, however, he waged war on Caesar but was quickly destroyed together with his army. Caesar then granted the realm to Cleopatra with whom he stayed for two years in a state of debauchery. At this time he corrected the calendar, and devised the idea of the intercalary day in the leapyear.[1] For the Romans, like the Hebrews, up to the time of Numa Pompilius began the year from March. Although Numa Pompilius added January and February to the year, which was already in a state of confusion, the year remained uncorrected until the time of Caesar. In his honour the month of Quintulus, which was the fifth after March, was afterwards called Julius, either because it was in that month that he was born or because he had gained some great victory then. For a similar reason the sixth month was called Augustus in honour of Augustus Caesar. Returning from Egypt Caesar defeated Pharnaces, the son of Mithridates, who had aided Pompey against him, and had him put to death. He then returned to Rome and made himself consul for the third time. From there he went to Africa where he defeated in addition to Juba himself, the King of Mauretania, the noble leaders Scipio and Porcius Cato who eventually committed suicide. Seneca in his twenty-sixth letter,[2] and *Policraticus*, Book VII, last chapter, say of this Cato that he drank poison, and fell on his sword, and so yielded up his spirit, that he might not live to see Caesar reign. Also Seneca, *De Providentia*, cap. 2: 'Cato did not survive freedom, nor freedom Cato.' Also another Roman history says that Cato was not killed in the battle between Caesar and Pompey, but that having heard of the death of Pompey, he read Plato's book on The Immortality of the Soul, and wounded himself, though his friends sought to dissuade him. Physicians came and brought poultices, but after they had gone, he reopened his wounds and died. Nor is this act excusable in Cato, no matter how learned and famous he was. In the first place because his friends who were wise men dissuaded him; secondly because he did not recommend this course to his son, but rather persuaded him to live under the victorious Caesar; and thirdly because he killed himself out of envy, not wishing to endure the glory of a victorious Caesar. And so it appears that Cato killed himself rather out of weakness to avoid misfortune than out of virtue to

---

[1] Huguccio, *Janus*.   [2] 24th Letter.

avoid base deeds. It should be noted that there had been many Cato's among the Romans. One was Cato, the quaestor, who brought Ennius the poet from Tarentum to Rome. Another was Mennius Cato[1] who fought nobly against the Greeks under the command of Aemilius Paulus. Another was Marcus Porcius Cato, called Uticensis, who killed himself at Utica in Africa, and of whom we have been speaking. And possibly this was Cato the Censor, of whom Jerome speaks in the Epistle to Nepocianus, that when an old man he neither despaired nor was ashamed of learning Greek. He was a philosopher of the Stoic school who made a great moral treatise called *Ethica Catonis*, from which is taken that little book in metre which schoolboys read. After a year Caesar returned to Rome and made himself consul for the fourth time, and immediately set out for Spain where the sons of Pompey were preparing great wars.[2] In the last of these Caesar was so nearly defeated that as his troops were in flight he wished to kill himself, lest after such military glory he should fall as an old man into the hands of children, for he was fifty-six years old. In the end, however, after gathering his forces together he defeated the enemy. After he returned to Rome he had himself called emperor, and there for three years and seven months he began to act with marked lack of moderation contrary to the tradition of Roman freedom. He was the first of all the leaders of Rome to be called emperor and Caesar[3]—emperor from the exclusive dominance of his unrivalled monarchy, Caesar because he had been taken from the womb of his mother when she was dead. His successors were called emperors and Caesars, and even Augusti on account of their exalting of the State. When therefore Caesar dispensed at his own whim the offices which formerly had been allocated by the people, when he would not rise when the senate came to him, and performed other unaccustomed and tyrannical acts, then two hundred and sixty senators and knights of Rome conspired against him, and particularly two by the name of Brutus.[4] When Caesar came to the Capitol on the senate's meeting he was killed after being stabbed twenty-three times.

[1] This is M. Porcius Cato Licinianus.
[2] Eutropius, vi. 20.
[3] Isidore, *Etymologiae*, ix. 3.
[4] Cf. Eutropius, vi. 25.

On Caesar, the first Roman Emperor (iv. 208-22)

As Caesar was going to the Capitol he received letters fore-casting his death, the bearer of the letters saying that if he entered the assembly that day he would die. Caesar said to him, 'At this time I will consult a soothsayer, after the meeting I will look at the letters.' A soothsayer was summoned who on the kalends of Julius the death foretold [*sic*]. Caesar said, 'The kalends are today, but I am still alive.' The soothsayer replied to him, 'The kalends are now, but they are not yet past. I hope that I may be found to lie.' Then Caesar turning to the Capitol was slain with gladiators' swords on the kalends of March. No wound appeared on his body,[1] but the letters were found in his hand after his death. The hundredth day before the death of Caesar lightning struck the statue of Caesar in the forum, and obliterated the letter C from Caesar.[2] The night before his death the windows of his chamber were flung open with such a great noise that Caesar leaping up from his bed thought the house was going to fall. The day following his death three suns appeared in the east, which gradually came together in one solar body, signifying by this that the lordship of the threefold world would come together in one monarchy, or rather that the knowledge of God that is Three in One should be made known to the whole world. Also an ox spoke to a ploughman in the suburbs of Rome saying that it was being driven in vain, 'for in a short time man will be missing rather than oxen or wheat'. Also on the Julian column, which is now called the needle of Peter by pilgrims, where Caesar's ashes were placed, a verse was written:

> Once Caesar you were mighty as the earth,
> But now a little urn holds all your worth.

Many people wrote in praise of Caesar. For according to the sixth book of Eutropius [*sic*] on the day when Caesar entered the city no one was punished. He also caused his soldiers to wear costly armour, so that they might defend themselves through fear of such a loss. He was a man whom no-one excelled in battle. Under his leadership eleven hundred and ninety-two thousand enemy were killed,

---

[1] See the end of the previous chapter.
[2] Petrus Comestor, *Lib. ii Machab.*, cap. xvi.

not counting the civil wars the dead of which he was unwilling to record. Caesar fought fifty times in pitched battle. And yet no one wrote more swiftly, or read more speedily. He was accustomed to dictate four letters at once, and those whom he overcame by arms he conquered through mildness. There was no day in the tumult of war when he did not write, read, or practise oratory. Julius Caesar, whose hand was no less apt with the pen than the sword,[1] who governed the State better than anyone, in the whole of his rule ordered only one man to be slain, that is to say Domicius, to whom he had previously granted his life, but when he later saw him fighting against him a second time though he had forsworn arms in the civil war, he said to his soldiers, 'It is enough that I have spared the life of this ungrateful man once.' He had never so much hatred against anyone but that given the occasion he could abandon it.[2] Caesar was a man of great patience. For the soldiers at the time of his triumph in Rome said in his hearing and without provoking his anger, 'Caesar triumphs, who has conquered the Gauls, but why is there no triumph for Nicomedes, the king of Bithynia, who has conquered Caesar?', for Caesar was said to be excessively friendly towards him. Cicero is said to have remarked to Caesar, 'Hail, king and queen', and again, 'Hail, queen of Bithynia, you were a woman of all men, now you are made a man of all women.' When Caesar was troubled by his baldness, as the hair receded, he drew his hair forward from the crown to the forehead.[3] A Roman soldier rebuked for cowardice before him replied to Caesar, 'O, Caesar, it would be easier to put hair on your head, than that I should have done anything cowardly in the Roman army.' Likewise when there were scandalous writings about him, and comic songs were spread about to disparage him, he bore it patiently. When someone reproached him for his ancestry on his mother's side, saying he was a breadmaker, he concealed his feelings by laughing. Therefore Cicero said in his praise, 'Caesar did not know how to forget anything except injuries.' Caesar came to the school of Cicero.[4] When Cicero rose to meet him Caesar stopped him saying, 'Do not rise to me; wisdom is greater than power.' Cicero replied, 'Shall I not rise to the conqueror of the world?' But Caesar said, 'You have obtained a better

---

[1] Pliny, *Natural History* vii. 25.
[2] Suetonius, *Julius*, caps. 49, 50.
[3] *Policraticus* (ed. Webb), iii. 14.
[4] Pliny, *Natural History*, vii. 31.

garland than extending the boundaries of Roman power.' From his words on this occasion Caesar caused to arise a law that no-one holding or reading a book should rise to anyone. Accius the poet did not rise to Caesar when he came to the college of poets. Asked if he was superior to such majesty he replied, 'The inferior should rise to the superior, equal meets equal on terms of equality, but wisdom has precedence over everybody', which saying Caesar approved. Also two children were brought before Caesar, one male and the other female, the pair of them most like one another, and after Caesar had looked at them for some time he sent them on their way with many presents, 'So go you in step together and control the very depth of your hearts that they be as one; let not unclean kissing nor branches of ivy, nor the seductive murmurs of the dove, have power over your association. Live you together like with like and free from deceit.'[1] The conspiracy of Catiline was detected and condemned in the noble consulship of Cicero. Neither the noble birth of the guilty man, nor the eloquence of so great a patron as Caesar appealing for mercy could help the defendent when Marcus Cato advocated the contrary. Marcus Cato and Julius Caesar were two outstanding men, almost equal in birth, years, and eloquence.[2] They were alike in greatness of spirit, but different in fame. Cato was great for the uprightness of his life, Caesar for his magnificence and liberality. One was famed for his austerity, the other for his generosity. Caesar was praised for his gifts, Cato for being lavish with nothing. In Caesar was a refuge for the needy, in Cato a punishment of the wrongdoer. To Caesar, it was pleasant to work, to keep watch, to neglect his own, to refuse nothing which he could do, to contrive a new war, and to desire triumphs. For Cato it was zeal for moderation, constancy, and gravity (which was pleasant); he strove not with wealth against the rich, nor with partisanship against the factious, but with courage against the strong and with modesty against the gentle, to be rather than to appear good. And so the less he sought fame the more he attained it. After the death of Cassibellanus in Britain and his burial in York, his nephew Tenuantius the duke of Cornwall, the son of king Lud, and the brother of Andragius succeeded him. For Andragius himself went with Caesar to Rome.

[1] The passage is in verse.
[2] Sallust, *Catilina*, caps. 53, 54.

On the Archbishoprics (ii. 110–18)

There were three archbishoprics in England in the time of Lucius, the first Christian king, that is at London, at York, and at Caerleon, the city of the legions in Glamorgan.[1] Twenty-eight bishops who were then called *flamines* were subject to these archbishoprics. To the archbishop of London belonged Cornwall, and the whole of England (Loegria) up to the Humber; to the archbishop of York belonged the whole of Northumberland from the bend of the Humber together with the whole of Scotland; and to the city of the legions was subjected the whole of Wales then with its seven bishops, and now distinguished by four suffragan bishops, and divided from England by the Severn. Although in the time of the Saxons the blessed Gregory granted the privilege of the archiepiscopate to London, none the less Augustine who was sent by Gregory, by the persistent attentions of his host the king Ethelbert, and captured by affection for the citizens of Canterbury, moved the archbishopric to Canterbury after the death of Gregory where it has remained to this day, except that for a certain time Offa, king of the Mercians, enraged with Canterbury, took the primacy away from them, and with the approval of pope Adrian, who was perhaps swayed by gifts, invested Aldulph,[2] bishop of Lichfield, with the archiepiscopal pallium, for his time. The primacy was restored by King Cenwulf. The archiepiscopal dignity has remained at York from the origins until the present day, although Scotland withdrew from its obedience in the course of time. The metropolitan see was transferred from the city of the legions to Menai which is situated in the west of Wales by the Irish sea in the time of Saint David in the reign of King Arthur.[3] From that time until the time of archbishop Sampson there were twenty-three archbishops. At last when the yellow pestilence which they call jaundice was breaking out throughout Wales archbishop Sampson taking the pallium with him, went to Brittany, and presided over the see of Dôl. From which time until the days of Henry I there were twenty-one bishops at Menai, which is called St. David's, who were without the pallium either through

[1] Alfred of Beverley, *Annales sive Historia*, p. 97. The passage is very much changed.
[2] *Rectius*, Hygeberht.   [3] *Itinerarium Cambriae*, ii. 1.

slothfulness or poverty. At all times, however, until then all the bishops of Wales were consecrated by the bishop of Menai, and he himself was similarly consecrated by the other Welsh bishops and the suffragans. They did nothing in acknowledgement of or subjection to another church. Succeeding bishops, however, at the pressing command of the king, received consecration from Canterbury. As a sign of whose consecration and subjection, Boniface, archbishop of Canterbury in the time of Henry II, discharging the office of ambassador of the cross, was the first of the archbishops of Canterbury to have mass solemnly celebrated in every cathedral church in Wales. But today there are only two primates in the whole of England, Canterbury and York. Thirteen English bishops and four Welsh ones are subject to Canterbury. York strictly speaking has only two suffragans, namely Carlisle and Durham. Concerning the successive institutions to all the sees some matters must be touched on in order. It is to be noted that in the early English church the bishops established their seats in places which were unimportant though very suitable for the life of contemplation and devotion. In the time of William the Conqueror it was laid down by a decree of canon law that bishops should move from towns to cities. So it came about that the see of Dorchester moved to Lincoln, Lichfield to Chester, Thetford to Norwich, Sherborne to Salisbury, Wells to Bath, Cornwall to Exeter, and Selsey to Chichester. Of the southern bishops. The bishop of Rochester has no parish, but is the chaplain of the archbishop of Canterbury. From the time of its institution by St. Augustine of Canterbury to the present day the place of the see has not changed. The bishop of Chichester, who has authority only over the South Saxons and the Isle of Wight, had his see at Selsey, which is called the island of sea calves, in the time of archbishop Theodore, and it lasted for three hundred and thirty-three years under twenty bishops from Wilfred, who was the first, to Stigand, who was the last. Then Stigand, at the command of William the Conqueror, transferred his see from Selsey to Chichester.

On the languages of the natives (ii. 156–62)

It is clear that there are as many different languages as peoples in this island. The Scots, however, and the Welsh, in so far as they have not intermixed with other nations, have retained the purity of their native speech, unless perhaps the Scots took something in speech from living together with the Picts, with whom they once dwelt as allies. The Flemish who live in the west of Wales have abandoned their barbarous speech, and speak Saxon well enough. Likewise the English although in the beginning they had a language of three branches, namely southern, midland, and northern, as coming from three Germanic peoples, nevertheless as a result of mixture, first with the Danes and then Normans, by a corruption of their language in many respects, they now incorporate strange bleatings and babblings. There are two main causes for their present debasement of the native language, one, that children in the schools against the practice of other nations are compelled since the coming of the Normans to abandon their own tongue and to construe into French, and, secondly, that children of the nobility are taught French from the cradle and rattle. Because of this peasants wishing to be similar, and so that they may appear to be more notable by this, make every effort to Frenchify their speech. It is a remarkable thing that in one little island the native language of the English should be pronounced in so many different ways, while the language of the Normans, which was imported, is so uniform. Concerning the tripartite language of the Saxons which has persisted up to now among a few rural people, the easterners are more like the westerners in speech (as situated under the same clime of heaven) than the north is like the south. Wherefore the Mercians, or Middle English, absorbing the two extremes, understand the north and south much better than the north and south understand one another. The whole of the Northumbrian dialect, especially in York, is so uncouth that we of the south can scarcely follow it. I think this is because they live so close to barbarians, and also because of the remoteness from those parts of the kings of England, who move mainly in the south, and come to the north only with a great army.[1] The reasons why they spend more time in the south than in the north may be the richer soil, the larger number of people, the better cities, and the more suitable harbours.

[1] *Gesta Pontificum*, p. 209.

On the creation of Adam (ii. 218–24)

Adam the first man was formed from the slime of the earth in the field of Damascene outside Paradise on the sixth day of the world. He was taken to Paradise, but after sinning the same day, was expelled from Paradise after noon. And so he fell from a condition of innocence to a state of misery. Man in his first beginnings might have taken sweet foods in the house of God, but he desired forbidden things, and trying what was forbidden he fell from the heights to the depths, from light to filth, from dwelling to exile, from home to wanderings, from delight to wailing, from praise to distress, from jest to strife, from love to hate, from success to retribution, from safety to weakness, from provision to need, from grace to blame, from peace to punishment, from friendship to hatred. This Adam in the fifteenth year of his life begot Cain and Calmana, his sister. And in the fifteenth year after that, which was the thirtieth year of his life, Adam begot Abel and Delbora, his sister, but after the death of Abel his parents mourned him for a hundred years. According to the Jews Adam begot Seth in the hundred and thirtieth year of his life and lived for eight hundred years after this, but the writers of the Septuagint and Isidore, *Etymologies*, Book V, say that Adam was two hundred and thirty years before the birth of Seth and lived for seven hundred years more. And so Adam lived in all, nine hundred and thirty years, and after his death was buried in Ebron, which is Kirjath Arba, because it means the City of Four, on account of the four patriarchs who are buried there, that is to say Adam, Abraham, Isaac, and Jacob.

In the hundred and fifth year of his life Seth begat Enos, and lived eight hundred years after this, but the writers of the Septuagint say that Seth was two hundred and five when he begat Enos and lived seven hundred and seven years after that.

APPENDIX III

THE AB AND CD VERSIONS CONTRASTED

Rolls Edition	Text
I, p. 2	The Prologue, 'Post praeclaros . . . posteris derivarunt', is added in the AB version.
pp. 8–18	The remainder of the chapter after 'Quod dum sodalibus' is expanded in AB from four sentences in the CD version.
p. 28	The remainder of Chapter III, 'Deinde secundus . . . populo Dei', is expanded in the AB version.
p. 34	The section on the ages of the world, 'Ubi est sane . . . ab Incarnatione Christi', is added in the AB version.
p. 40	At the end of Chapter IV in certain manuscripts of CD there is a passage on the Cinque Ports. The CD version begins Chapter V 'De orbis divisione. Julius Caesar' etc.
pp. 60–64	The AB version adds extracts from Bede, *De Naturis Rerum*, and a note by Higden on the Caspian.
pp. 66–74	The AB version adds a passage on the position and rivers of Paradise from the *De Proprietatibus Rerum*. The description of Paradise in CD begins at p. 74.
pp. 108–14	The AB version adds a passage on Mount Sion, the Mount of Olives, and Calvary, which quotes Huguccio, *Derivationes* (Cambridge U.L. MS. Ff. 5. 34; f. 67.)
pp. 120–8	The AB version rearranges the chapter on Canaan.
pp. 164–6	The AB version adds the passage on Aeneas and Dido (see p. 77).
pp. 178–80	The AB version adds a passage on Constantinople.
pp. 200–2	The AB version adds two paragraphs on Apulia and Calabria.
p. 206	In the AB version Chapter XXV opens 'Auctores tradunt quod in Tuscia . . . '.
pp. 266–8	The AB version adds a passage on France with extracts from the *De Civitate Dei*, ii. 5 and the *Aeneid*, viii. 660.

Rolls Edition	*Text*
pp. 288–98	The AB version adds a new chapter, 28, where the CD version has 'De Gallia dicit Eutropius', and a paragraph on Burgundy.
pp. 302–18	The AB version has a rewritten narrative in Chapter 30, *De Insulis Maris Magni*, and adds a paragraph on Corsica (pp. 304–6).
II, p. 38	The AB version omits a passage from Bede's *Ecclesiastical History*, iv. 16.
p. 58	The AB version adds a passage on King Bladud and the city of Bath = Geoffrey of Monmouth, *Historia Regum Britanniae*, ii. 10.
p. 66	The AB version has a passage on the city of Dumbarton. Bede, i. 12; Geoffrey of Monmouth, ii. 7.
pp. 86–90	The AB version has an expanded account of the provinces and counties of England.
p. 224	The AB version omits a passage on Noah and the Flood.
pp. 390–4	The AB version adds to the early history of Egypt and the Amazons.
p. 432	The AB version adds a passage on Aeneas and Dido (see p. 77).
III, pp. 58–62	The AB version adds a passage on Romulus and the Sabine women. *De Civitate Dei*, iii. 13, 15.
p. 86	The AB version adds a passage on Tarquinius Priscus from *Ab Urbe Condita*, i. 40.
pp. 90–92	The AB version adds a passage on Jechonias = Matthew i. 11.
pp. 164–6	The AB version has a passage on Tarquin from *De Civitate Dei*, iii. 14.
pp. 188–212	The AB version has a rewritten chapter, 'De vita et philosophia Pythagorae', from John of Wales, *Compendiloquium*, ff. clxx, clxxi.
p. 238	The AB version omits a passage on Constantinople.
pp. 250–2	The AB version adds a passage on the laws of Solon.
pp. 274–94	The AB version has a rewritten chapter on Socrates, with additions from *Compendiloquium*, ff. cxliv–clvi.
p. 298	The AB version adds a passage on Furius Camillus from *Policraticus*, iv. 7.
pp. 340–58	The AB version has a considerably expanded chapter on Plato, *De vita et sententiis Platonis philosophi*, with extracts from *Compendiloquium*, ff. clxiii–clxv.

Rolls Edition	Text
pp. 358–72	The AB version has an expanded chapter on Aristotle from *Compendiloquium*, f. clxiii.
pp. 374–8	The AB version adds a passage on the battle at the Caudine Forks from *Ab Urbe Condita*, ix. 2–4.
p. 418	The AB version omits a paragraph on Alexander and the siege of Tyre which is in CD.
p. 450	The AB version omits a passage describing the Caucasus.
p. 452	The AB version omits the story of the man to whom Alexander gave a city, which is compared to that of Antigonus and the Cynic who asked for an obol. See Cary, *The Medieval Alexander*, pp. 86, 360–1.
p. 454	The AB version has the title for Chapter 29, 'Qualiter Alexander esset ad Bragmanarum insulam', where CD has 'Epistola Dindimi'.
IV, pp. 22–24	The AB version adds a passage on Roman methods of fighting.
pp. 24–26	The AB version rewrites a passage on Pyrrhus.
p. 48	The AB version omits a passage from Eutropius on the Gauls.
pp. 62–68	The AB version adds a long passage from Livy and other sources on Rome at the time of the Second Punic War. *Ab Urbe Condita*, xxvi. 35–36.
pp. 98–102	The AB version expands the end of Chapter 34 on Roman stage plays and Seleucus Soter. Some of the information is found at the end of Chapter 36 (p. 130) in CD.
pp. 150–70	The AB version has a rewritten narrative for Chapter 39, 'De Mario, Sulla et Mithridate Ponti rege', and has a lengthy addition (pp. 154–60) on Marius.
pp. 188–206	The AB version expands Chapter 41, 'De bello civili quod gesserunt Caesar et Pompeius', with additions from Seneca, *De Providentia*, Chapter 2.
p. 244	The AB version transfers a passage on Virgil from Isidore, *Etymologiae*, x. 44, to the Prologue, i. 10–12.
pp. 332–40	The AB version expands the beginning of Chapter V, 'De Christi vita et miraculis et quaedam de Johanne Baptista', which is very brief in CD, and which has the account of the chronology of Christ's life (p. 344) at the end.

Rolls Edition	*Text*
V, p. 256	The AB version at the end of Book IV omits a long passage on Vortigern which quotes Bede, *Ecclesiastical History*, i. 13.
pp. 256–78	The AB version has a rewritten narrative of the first chapter of Book V, and it omits a long passage on St. Germanus (pp. 270–2).
p. 306	The AB version omits a passage on Hengist and his descendants.
p. 330	The AB version omits a passage on Arthur having conquered Gaul, 'ibidem dicitur quod Arthurus per novem annos Galliam sibi subjugavit . . .'.
p. 340	The AB version has a rewritten narrative of the early West Saxon kings.
p. 408	The AB version omits a passage on the monks of Bangor.
VI, p. 4	The AB version omits a passage on St. Birinus.
p. 72	The AB version omits a passage on St. Birinus and his successor.
p. 78	The AB version adds a passage on Benedict Biscop from the *Gesta Regum*, i. 59.
pp. 82–84	The AB version rewrites a passage on Oswy.
p. 122	The AB version adds a passage on Agilberht, bishop of the West Saxons, from Florence of Worcester. *Chronicon ex Chronicis*, i. 24.
pp. 134–6	The AB version adds an account of Ripon and Theodore of Tarsus from Florence of Worcester, *Chronicon ex Chronicis*, i. 37.
pp. 218–26	The AB version adds a long section on Bede which paraphrases the *Gesta Regum*, i. 60.
pp. 270–2	The AB version adds an account of Cynewulf and Offa from Florence of Worcester. *Chronicon ex Chronicis*, i. 59.
pp. 280–4	The AB version adds a long passage on the kings of Mercia from the *Gesta Regum*, i. 94.
p. 298	The AB version adds a passage on Charles the Bald from the *Gesta Regum*, i. 110.
p. 322	The AB version omits a short passage which states that the imperial dignity remained with the Germans until the time of Frederick II.
p. 328	The AB version adds a passage on the sons of Lothair from the *Gesta Regum*, i. 111.

Rolls Edition	Text
pp. 342–4	The AB version adds a passage on Edmund, king and martyr, from the *Gesta Regum*, i. 265.
pp. 366–70	The AB version adds a long passage on Rollo and the siege of Chartres from the *Gesta Regum*, i. 138.
pp. 436–40, 442, 466–70	The AB version adds passages on Anlaf, the rebellion in Northumberland, and Edgar, from the *Gesta Regum*, i. 143, 142, 177.
VII, p. 8	The AB version omits a passage on the succession at Canterbury.
p. 12	The AB version omits a passage on the institution of monastic chapters at Winchester and Worcester.
p. 18	The AB version omits a passage at the end of Chapter 10 on Edgar and the Danes.
pp. 18–30	The AB version has an expanded chapter, 'De Edgaro rege', and quotes passages from the *Gesta Regum*, i. 179, 180.
pp. 30–36	The AB version expands the opening of Chapter 12, 'De regibus Anglorum', with an account of the reign of Edward from the *Gesta Regum*, i. 181, 184, 185.
pp. 66–78	The AB version adds a long passage on Sylvester II from the *Gesta Regum*, i. 193–5.
pp. 122–6	The AB version adds a passage on William of Normandy from the *Gesta Regum*, i. 211.
pp. 142–8	The AB version adds an account of the Emperor Henry III from the *Gesta Regum*, i. 205.
pp. 174–6	The AB version substitutes an account of Godwin from the *Gesta Regum*, i. 241.
pp. 180–6	The AB version adds an account of Edward and Godwin from the *Gesta Pontificum*, pp. 35, 36, 179; and of Siward from Florence of Worcester.
pp. 198–204	The AB version adds a long passage on the Roman citizen, Lucianus, from the *Gesta Regum*, i. 256.
pp. 208–12	The AB version adds a passage on Berengar.
pp. 214–28	The AB version adds a long section on Harold and the death of Edward the Confessor, which forms the beginning of Chapter 28. It is taken from Henry of Huntingdon, Book VI, and the *Gesta Regum*, i. 246, 280.
pp. 230–44	The AB version has a long account of the Battle of Hastings, which occupies most of Chapter 29,

Rolls Edition	Text
	while the CD version has only a brief description. The account in AB comes from Henry of Huntingdon, Book VII, and the *Gesta Regum*, ii. 299.
pp. 306–8	The AB version adds a passage on the Carthusians.
pp. 314–18	The AB version adds a description of William from Henry of Huntingdon, Book VI.
pp. 324–8	The AB version adds an account of Rufus from the *Gesta Regum*, ii. 324.
p. 360	The AB version gives a revised account of the foundation of the monastery at Chester.
pp. 364–80	The AB version puts in an account of Wulstan from the *Gesta Pontificum*, pp. 278–87. In the CD version it is inserted at p. 214.
pp. 382–4	The AB version adds a passage on Ranulf Flambard from the *Gesta Regum*, ii. 368.
pp. 394–404	The AB version adds a long passage at the beginning of Chapter 10 on the Cistercians from the *Gesta Regum*, ii. 380–2.
pp. 410–14	The AB version adds a passage on the death of Rufus from the *Gesta Regum*, ii. 377.
pp. 416–28	The AB version adds almost the whole of Chapter 12, 'Henricus primus rex Angliae Robertus dux Normanniae', from the *Gesta Regum* ii. 461, 470; *Gesta Pontificum*, p. 258.
pp. 454–6	The AB version adds a note on the death of Florence of Worcester, 'cuius litterato labore plurimum adaucta est praesens historia'.
VIII, p. 34	The AB version omits a passage concerning Chester.
pp. 66–68	The AB version adds a passage on Baldwin of Worcester.
pp. 142–4	The AB version omits a passage on the primacy of Canterbury and York.
pp. 170–6	The AB version adds a passage on John.
pp. 272–80	The AB version adds a long section on the succession to the throne of Scotland.
p. 324	The CD version ends at 'ecclesia libertatem'.

Note. Only the most notable examples of the differences between the two texts have been given.

APPENDIX IV

TABLES OF *POLYCHRONICON* CONTINUATIONS

The *Versions of the* Polychronicon

(i) A great many of the manuscripts containing the AB version add a form of the main continuation which ends either in 1376 with 'sermonibus praedicantes' or in 1377 with 'diu postea habuerunt'. There are manuscripts of this AB text, however, which possess no continuation: (1) B.M. MS. Royal 14. C. ix, Add. MS. 15759; Glasgow University, MS. Hunterian 223; Bodleian Library, MS. Douce 138; Valencia Cathedral, MS. 89, end at 1344. (2) Balliol College, Oxford, MS. 236 ends at 1346. (3) Bodleian Library, MS. Tanner 170 ends at 1347. (4) Trinity College, Dublin, MS. 486 ends at 1356.

(ii) The version of the *Polychronicon* named E in the Rolls Series edition, derived directly from the Huntington text, and survives in only a few manuscripts. It was furnished with no continuation beyond 1352. The text to 1352 was printed in the Rolls Series edition from University Library, Cambridge, MS. Ii. III. 1.

(iii) The shorter versions of the *Polychronicon*, named C and D in the Rolls Series edition, extended only to 1327. They were furnished with no standard form of continuation, but in certain copies the *Historia Aurea* was used as a continuation as far as the 1340's: Rylands Library, Manchester, Latin MS. 218; Cambridge U.L. MS. Dd. viii. 7; B.M. MS. Royal 13. E. i.

TABLE I

Manuscript Versions of the Polychronicon Continuation, *1340–77*

Written during the reign of Edward III	Written during the reign of Richard II			
(A)	(B)	(C)	(D)	(E)
(Printed in Hearne, *Walteri Hemingford*, ii. 421–521, from MSS. Harley 1728–9)	(Printed in Rolls Series, *Polychronicon*, viii. 407–28 from Gonville and Caius Coll., Camb, MS. 82 (Rolls B))	(Not printed)	(Not printed)	(Not printed)
MS. Harley 3884	Gonville and Caius Coll., Camb, MS. 249	MS. Brogyntyn 40	MS. Tanner 19	MS. Vatican Lat. 1959
MS. Harley 4875	Trinity Coll., Camb, MS. R. 4. 1	Winchester Coll., MS. 15		MS. Hunterian 72
Trinity Coll., Dublin, MS. 488	MS. Bodley 358	MS. Arundel (Heralds) 4	MS. Arundel (Heralds) 2	C.C.C., Camb, MS. 21
		MS. Inner Temple 511. 5		
	Magdalen Coll., Oxf, MS. 147	B.M. Add. MS. 10104	MS. Digby 196	
	MS. Nero D. II	MS. Arundel 86	Magdalen Coll., Oxf, MS. 97	
		MS. Royal 14. C. xii	Magdalen Coll., Oxf, MS. 190	
MS. Asholme 796	MS. Nero D. VIII	MS. Hatton 14		

MS. Digby 201	MS. Stowe 64	MS. Harvard 116
		MS. Eton Coll. 213
Oriel Coll., Oxf., MS. 74	B.M. Add. MS. 39236	C.C.C., Camb., MS. 117
	MS. Harley 3671	Trinity Coll., Camb., MS. R. 5. 24
	MS. (Latin) Rylands 170	Christ's Coll., Camb., MS. 3
	Trinity Coll., Dublin, MS. 487	Merton Coll., Oxf., MS. 121

TABLE II

St. Albans' Influence on Polychronicon Continuations, 1340–77

Written during the reign of Edward III	Written during the reign of Richard II				
	Based on main Polychronicon continuation			Based more directly on Walsingham's writings	
Continuation 1343-76 (probably written at St. Albans)	'Continuation of Murimuth' (based on (E) and probably written at St. Albans)	'Continuation of Murimuth' and extract from Walsingham's contemporary history	Rolls Series A Continuation (using Chronicon Angliae as well as 'Continuation of Murimuth')	Using principally the Chronicon Angliae	Using Walsingham's Short Chronicle 1328-88
(Not printed)	(Printed in Hog, Adami Murimuthensis, pp.174-227, from Queen's Coll., Oxf., MS. 304)	(One additional passage printed by Tait in Chronicon Johannis de Reading, p. 91)	(Printed in Polychronicon, viii. 355-406, from Camb. U.L. Ii. II. 24 (Rolls A))	(Not printed)	(The text of Walsingham's Short Chronicle is printed in the Chronicon Angliae omitting 1370-82)
MS. Rawlinson B. 152	Paris MS. Lat. 4922	Christ Church, Oxf., MS. 89	Camb. U.L. Dd. i. 17	MS. Laud Misc. 529	C.C.C., Oxf., MS. 89
Trinity Coll., Dublin, MS. 511	Paris MS. Lat. 4923	B.M. Add. MS. 12118	Trinity Coll., Camb., MS. 726		
	MS. Harley 3877		Magdalen Coll., Oxf., MS. 147		
			New Coll., Oxf., MS. 152		

C.C.C., Camb, MS. 6	MS. Royal 13, E. ix (written at St. Albans, and with passages omitted)	Lincoln Coll., Oxf., MS. 107
		Oriel Coll., Oxf., MS. 16
		Queen's Coll., Oxf., MS. 307
		MS. Royal 13. D. i
	Trinity Coll., Dublin, MS. 487	MS. Harleian 3600
		MS. Lambeth 48
		MS. Lambeth 160
		Gonville and Caius Coll., Camb, MS. 58
		MS. Lyell 21

APPENDIX V

WRITINGS BY HIGDEN AND WRITINGS ATTRIBUTED TO HIM

CERTAIN of these survive in manuscript, but others are mentioned in medieval catalogues only. Among the works most likely to be by Higden are:

I. 1. *Speculum Curatorum.*

This exists in B.M. MS. Harl. 1004 (incomplete); MS. Balliol College 77;[1] Cambridge U.L. Mm. i. 20; and MS. Durham B. iv. 36. *Incipit*: 'Cum circa duo potissime'. The initials of the first eighty chapters read 'Cestrensis monachus frater Ranulphus compilavit hoc speculum anno Domini MCCC quadragesimo'.

2. *Pedagogium artis grammaticae.*

This work is referred to in the catalogue of Syon Abbey, where it formed part of MS. Syon A. 4.[2] It is described there as 'Prima pars pedagogici compilati a Radulpho Higdon de Ordine sancti Benedicti'.

In his *Bibliotheca Britannico-Hibernica* (London, 1748), p. 403, Tanner refers to this manuscript.

3. *Ars kalendarii.*

This forms part of Magdalene College, Cambridge, MS. 23, which contains the chronicle of Martinus Polonus.[3] The tract by Higden commences at f. 23ᵛ,

'Tractatus qui dicitur ars kalendarii ranulphi monachi cicestr.' *Incipit*: 'Artem kalendarii ecclesiastici nosse', and ends 'inspiciendos derelinquo'.

---

[1] R. A. B. Mynors, *Catalogue of the Manuscripts of Balliol College, Oxford*, p. 62.
[2] *Catalogue of Library of Syon Monastery*, ed. Mary Bateson (Cambridge, 1898), p. 2.
[3] *Manuscripts in the Library of Magdalene College, Cambridge* (Cambridge, 1909), ed. M. R. James, p. 50.

Followed by tables 36ᵛ, 37ᵛ, 38. The recto of 37 is blank. A tract by Ranulph Higden, *In literam kalendarii*, is mentioned by Bale but the *incipit* is not given (*Index*, 336). The contents of this volume are similar to those of K 28 in the Library of Syon Monastery, which is St. John's College, Oxford, MS. i. 11.

4. *Ars Componendi Sermones*.

This exists in MS. Harley 866; MS. Bodley 5; MS. Bodley 316; MS. Auct. F. 3. 5. The work is in the library catalogue of St. Mary's, Leicester (2 f. *de thematis*). The initials of the chapters read 'Ars Ranulphi Cestrensis'.

1. MS. Bodley 316, f. 176. After a copy of the *Polychronicon*. *Incipit*: 'Rectitudo intencionis'. At end: 'Explicit ars componendi sermones. Nota quod littere capitanee huius artis syllabatim inuicem tantum sonant Ars Ranulphi Cestrensis.'

2. MS. Bodley 5, f. 1. The *Ars componendi sermones* of Ranulph Higden, without title or author's name. The first part of the preface is lost. The letters of the first chapters give the author's name. The text begins 'me sinit Deus uota tua'.

3. MS. Auct. F. 3. 5, f. 9. *Incipit*: 'Ad preeminentem huius artis laudem'. At end: 'Explicit tractatus artis predicatorie de compilacione domini Ranulphi (Higden) de ordinacione sermonum'.

5. *Sermones*.

MS. Latin Rylands 367.[1] This is a vellum manuscript of the fifteenth century. ff. 322+1. *Expositum omnium epistolarum evangeliorumque festivalium sanctorum secundum Radulphum de Attone (Ranulph Higden)*.

II. Other works which have been attributed to Higden include two collections of *Distinctiones*, which are excerpts from the Scriptures or a form of commentary compiled apart from the Gloss to explain various interpretations of Scripture.

---

[1] *The Bulletin of John Rylands Library*, xii. 2. 600, ascribes this to Higden.

1. *Distinctiones Cestrensis monachi.*

Worcester Cathedral MS. F. 128,[1] ff. 125. *Incipit*: 'Abicere secundum' and ends 'Zelus'.

It should be noted that *Abicere* to *Zelus* is the *incipit* and *explicit* of Simon Bolaston's *Distinctiones* in the Merton College Library (nos. 547, 977).[2]

2. *Distinctiones.*

MS. Lambeth 23.[3] *Alexander Neckam super cantica* etc. At ff. 202–50 it contains *Distinctiones Cistrensis valde utiles*. Incipit: 'Apparuit gratia dei. ad titum. Apparicio Christi triplex est.' Attributed to Ranulph Higden by Bale (*Index*, 336) and by Tanner who mentions this manuscript, *Bibliotheca*, p. 403. The text of this is also found in Worcester Cathedral MS. F. 80 f. 209.[4] Incipit: 'Apparuit gratia dei, ad titum. Apparicio Christi' etc.

3. *Abbreviationes Chronicorum.*

This exists in B.M. MS. Cotton Tiberius E. viii, and in the following copies of the *Polychronicon*: Corpus Christi College, Cambridge, MS. 21; Winchester College, MS. 15; the Taunton County Museum MS. 1, Vat. Lat. MS. 1959. Tanner mentions that Higden wrote the *Abbreviationes Chronicorum*: *Bibliotheca*, p. 403. It is entitled *Chronica bona et compendiosa de Regibus Anglie tantum, a Noe post diluvium usque in hunc diem conscripta a Ranulpho Higdeno Cestrensi monacho, qui vixit anno gratiae 1358.*[5]

---

[1] J. K. Floyer and S. G. Hamilton, *Catalogue of Manuscripts in Chapter Library of Worcester Cathedral* (Worcester, 1906), p. 66.

[2] F. M. Powicke, *The Medieval Books of Merton College* (Oxford, 1931), p. 255.

[3] M. R. James and C. Jenkins, *Catalogue of Manuscripts at Lambeth Palace* (Cambridge, 1930), p. 38.

[4] Floyer and Hamilton, pp. 40–41. [5] *Polychronicon*, I. xii.

BIBLIOGRAPHY

THIS is a selective list of the more important and relevant works used in the course of this study. Other items will be found cited in full in the footnotes.

PRINTED TEXTS OF MEDIEVAL CHRONICLES AND LITERARY SOURCES

Annales Cestrienses, ed. R. C. Christie (Record Society of Lancashire and Cheshire, 1887).

Anonimalle Chronicle, ed. V. H. Galbraith (Manchester, 1927).

AUGUSTINE, *De Civitate Dei,* 2 vols., ed. Dombart and Kalb (*Bibliotheca scriptorum graecorum et romanorum,* Teubner, 1928–9).

BEAUVAIS, VINCENT OF. *Speculum Historiale* (Balthazaris Belleri, 1624).

BEVERLEY, ALFRED OF. *Historia de gestis regum Britanniae,* ed. T. Hearne (Oxford, 1716).

Brut, or the Chronicles of England, ed. F. W. D. Brie (Early English Text Society, 1906–8).

CHANDOS, *Life of the Black Prince,* ed. M. K. Pope and E. C. Lodge (Oxford, 1910).

Chester Plays, ed. H. Deimling and G. W. Matthews (Early English Text Society, 1892, 1914).

Chronica Johannis de Reading et Anonymi Cantuariensis, ed. J. Tait (Manchester, 1914).

Chronicles of the Reigns of Edward I and II, ed. W. Stubbs, 2 vols. (Rolls Series, 1882–3).

Chronicon Galfridi le Baker de Swynebroke, ed. E. M. Thompson (Oxford, 1889).

Chronique de la traïson et mort de Richard II, ed. B. Williams (English Historical Society, 1846).

Chronique de Richard II (1377–99), ed. J. A. C. Buchon (Collection des chroniques nationales françaises, xxv, supplément II, Paris, 1826).

COMESTOR, PETER. *Historia scholastica,* Migne, *Patrologia Latina,* cxcviii.

CRÉTON, *Histoire du roy d'Angleterre Richard,* ed. J. A. C. Buchon (Collection des chroniques nationales françaises, xxiv, 1826).

Dieulacres Chronicle, ed. M. V. Clarke and V. H. Galbraith (*Bulletin of John Rylands Library,* xiv, 1930).

English Chronicle 1377–1461, ed. J. S. Davies (Camden Society, 1856).

Eulogium Historiarum sive temporis, ed. F. S. Haydon, 3 vols. (Rolls Series, 1858–63).

Fasciculi Zizaniorum magistri Johannis Wyclif cum tritico, ed. W. W. Shirley (Rolls Series, 1858).

Flores Historiarum, ed. H. R. Luard, 3 vols. (Rolls Series, 1890).

FREISING, OTTO OF, *Historia de duabus civitatibus*, ed. A. Hofmeister (*Scriptores Rerum Germanicarum in usum scholarum*, Hanover and Leipzig, 1912).

French Chronicle of London, ed. G. J. Aungier (Camden Society, 1844).

GALE, T. *Historiae Britannicae Scriptores XV* (Oxford, 1691). Excerpts from the *Polychronicon*.

Germanicarum Rerum Quatuor Celebriores Vetustioresque Chronographi (Basle, 1559). The first two books of Marianus Scotus.

Giraldi Cambrensis Opera, ed. J. S. Brewer, J. F. Dimock, G. F. Warner, 8 vols. (Rolls Series, 1861–91).

GUISBOROUGH, WALTER OF. *Chronicle*, ed. H. Rothwell (Camden Society, 1957).

Historia de rebus Glastoniensibus, ed. T. Hearne (Oxford, 1726).

Kirkstall Abbey Chronicles, ed. J. Taylor (Thoresby Society, 1952).

KNIGHTON, HENRY. *Chronicon*, ed. J. R. Lumby, 2 vols. (Rolls Series, 1889–95).

Lanercost Chronicle, ed. Joseph Stevenson (Edinburgh, 1839).

LANGTOFT, PIERRE DE. *Chronicle*, ed. T. Wright, 2 vols. (Rolls Series, 1866–8).

Liber Luciani de Laude Cestrie, ed. M. V. Taylor (Record Society of Lancashire and Cheshire, 1912).

MALMESBURY, WILLIAM OF. *Gesta Pontificum*, ed. N. E. S. A. Hamilton (Rolls Series, 1870).

—— *Gesta regum*, ed. W. Stubbs, 2 vols. (Rolls Series, 1887–9).

MEAUX. *Chronicle of*, ed. E. A. Bond, 3 vols. (Rolls Series, 1866–8).

MONMOUTH, GEOFFREY OF. *Historia regum Britanniae*, ed. A. Griscom (London, 1929).

MURIMUTH, ADAM. *Chronica sui temporis*, ed. T. Hog (English Historical Society, 1846).

—— *Continuatio chronicarum 1303–47*. Robert of Avesbury, *De gestis mirabilibus regis Edwardi tertii*, ed. E. M. Thompson (Rolls Series, 1889).

NEQUAM, ALEXANDER. *De naturis rerum*, ed. T. Wright (Rolls Series, 1863).

OROSIUS, PAULUS. *Historiarum adversus paganos libri vii*, ed. K. F. W. Zangemeister (*C.S.E.L.* iv, Vienna, 1882).

PAULUS DIACONUS, *Historia Langobardorum*, ed. G. Waitz (*M.G.H. scriptores rerum*, 1878).

Philobiblon Ricardi de Bury, ed. M. Maclagan (Oxford, 1960).

Political Poems and Songs, ed. T. Wright, 2 vols. (Rolls Series, 1859–61).

Polychronicon Ranulphi Higden, ed. Churchill Babington and J. R. Lumby, 9 vols. (Rolls Series, 1865–86). Vol. ix contains the chronicle of the monk of Westminster.

RALEIGH, SIR WALTER. *History of the World* (London, 1677).

SALISBURY, JOHN OF. *Policraticus*, ed. C. C. J. Webb (Oxford, 1909).

Scalacronica, ed. J. Stevenson (Edinburgh, 1836).

SEVILLE, ISIDORE OF. *Etymologiae*, ed. W. M. Lindsay, 2 vols. (Oxford, 1911).

St. Albans Chronicle, 1406–1420, ed. V. H. Galbraith (Oxford, 1937).

The Story of England, ed. F. J. Furnivall, 2 vols. (Rolls Series, 1887).

TWYSDEN, R. *DecemScriptores*(London, 1652). It contains John of Brompton.

USK, ADAM OF. *Chronicle*, ed. E. M. Thompson (Oxford, 1904).

Vita Edwardi Secundi, ed. N. Denholm-Young (Nelson, 1957).

Vita Ricardi Secundi, ed. T. Hearne (Oxford, 1729).

WALES, JOHN OF. *Compendiloquium* (Lyons, 1511).

WALSINGHAM, THOMAS. *Chronicon Angliae*, ed. E. M. Thompson (Rolls Series, 1874).

—— *Gesta Abbatum*, ed. H. T. Riley, 3 vols. (Rolls Series, 1867–9).

—— *Historia Anglicana*, ed. H. T. Riley, 2 vols. (Rolls Series, 1863–4).

—— *Ypodigma Neustriae*, ed. H. T. Riley (Rolls Series, 1876).

WORCESTER, FLORENCE OF. *Chronicon ex chronicis*, ed. B. Thorpe, 2 vols. (English Historical Society, 1848–9).

MODERN WORKS

BAGROW, L. *Die Geschichte der Kartographie* (Berlin, 1951).

BEAZLEY, C. R. *The Dawn of Modern Geography*, 3 vols. (London, 1897–1906).

BLADES, W. *The Life and Typography of William Caxton*, 2 vols. (London, 1861–3).

BOUTARIC, E. 'Vincent de Beauvais et la connaissance de l'antiquité classique au treizième siècle', *Revue des questions historiques*, XVII (Paris, 1875).

BRIE, F. W. D. *Geschichte und Quellen der mittelenglischen Prosachronik, 'The Brut of England' oder 'The Chronicles of England'* (Brie) (Marburg, 1905).

BROWN, ARTHUR. 'A Tradition of the Chester Plays', *London Medieval Studies*, vol. ii, pt. 1 (1951).

BURNE, R. V. H. *The Monks of Chester* (London, 1962).

CAREY, G. *The Medieval Alexander* (Cambridge, 1956).

CAWLEY, A. C. 'Punctuation in the Early Versions of Trevisa', *London Medieval Studies*, vol. 1, pt. 1 (1937).

—— 'Relations of the Trevisa Manuscripts and Caxton's *Polychronicon*', *London Medieval Studies*, vol. i, pt. 3 (1948).

CHAMBERS, E. K. *The Medieval Stage*, 2 vols. (Oxford, 1903).
—— *English Literature at the Close of the Middle Ages* (Oxford, 1947).
CLARKE, M. V. *Medieval Representation and Consent* (London, 1936).
—— *Fourteenth Century Studies* (Oxford, 1937).
COLLINGWOOD, R. G. *The Idea of History* (Oxford, 1946).
COMPARETTI, D. *Vergil in the Middle Ages*, trs. E. F. M. Benecke (London, 1895).
CRAIG, HARDIN. *The Enchanted Glass* (Oxford, 1930).
—— *English Religious Drama of the Middle Ages* (Oxford, 1955).
CROMPTON, J. 'Fasciculi Zizaniorum', *Journal of Ecclesiastical History*, xii (1962).
CRONE, G. R. *The Hereford Wall Map* (Royal Geographical Society, 1949).
CURTIUS, E. R. *European Literature and the Latin Middle Ages* (London, 1953).
DEAN, J. R. 'The Earliest Known Commentary on Livy', *Medievalia et Humanistica*, iii (1945).
DENHOLM-YOUNG, H. *Collected Papers on Medieval Subjects* (Oxford, 1946).
DUHEM, P. *Le Système du monde*, 10 vols. (Paris, 1913–59).
—— *Études sur Léonard de Vinci*. 3 vols. (Paris, 1955).
EDWARDS, J. G. 'Ranulf, Monk of Chester', *E.H.R.* xlvii (1932).
EMDEN, A. B. *A Biographical Register of the University of Oxford* (Oxford, 1957–9).
FERGUSON, W. K. *The Renaissance in Historical Thought* (Cambridge, Mass., 1948).
FONTAINE, JACQUES. *Isidore de Séville et la culture classique dans l'Espagne wisigothique* (Paris, 1951).
FOWLER, D. 'John Trevisa and the English Bible', *Modern Philology*, lviii. 2 (1960).
—— 'New Light on John Trevisa', *Traditio*, xviii (1962).
GAIRDNER, J. *Early Chronicles of Europe: England* (London, 1879).
GALBRAITH, V. H. 'Sources of the St. Albans Chronicle', *Essays Presented to R. Lane-Poole* (Oxford, 1927).
—— 'The *Historia Aurea* and a French *Brut*', *E.H.R.* xliii (1928).
—— 'Thomas Walsingham and the St. Albans Chronicle', *E.H.R.* xlvii (1932).
—— 'John Seward and his Circle', *Medieval and Renaissance Studies* (1943).
—— *Roger Wendover and Matthew Paris* (Glasgow University Publication, 1944).
—— *Historical Research in Medieval England* (London, 1951).
—— 'The Chronicle of Henry Knighton', *Fritz Saxl Memorial Essays* (*F.S.*) (London, 1957).
—— 'An Autograph Manuscript of Ranulf Higden's *Polychronicon*', *Huntington Library Quarterly* (*HLQ*), xxiii (1959).

GHELLINCK, J. DE. *Littérature latine au Moyen Âge* (Paris, 1939).

GWYNN, AUBREY. *The English Austin Friars in the Time of Wyclif* (Oxford, 1940).

—— *Essays Presented to*, ed. J. A. Watt, J. B. Morrall, F. X. Martin (Dublin, 1961).

HALL, F. W. 'An English Commentary on Ovid', *Classical Quarterly*, xxi (1927).

JAMES, M. R. 'Magister Gregorius de Mirabilibus Urbis Romae', *E.H.R.* xxxii (1917).

—— 'The Catalogue of the Library of the Augustinian Friars at York', *Fasciculus Ioanni Willis Clark dicatus* (Cambridge, 1909).

JONES, D. *The Church in Chester 1300–1540* (Chetham Society, third series, 1956).

KEELER, LAURA. *Geoffrey of Monmouth and the Late Latin Chroniclers 1300–1500* (University of California Press, 1946).

KENDRICK, T. D. *British Antiquity* (London, 1950).

KER, N. R. *Medieval Libraries of Great Britain* (Royal Historical Society, 1941).

KIMBLE, G. H. T. *Geography in the Middle Ages* (London, 1938).

KINGSFORD, C. L. *English Historical Literature in the Fifteenth Century* (Kingsford) (Oxford, 1913).

KINKADE, B. L. 'The English Translations of Higden's *Polychronicon*' (Illinois dissertation, 1934).

KRIEHN, G. 'Studies in the Sources of the Social Revolt in 1381', *American Historical Review*, vii (1901).

LAISTNER, M. L. W. *The Intellectual Heritage of the Early Middle Ages* (Ithaca, 1957).

LANGLOIS, C. V. *La Connaissance de la nature et du monde au Moyen Âge* (Paris, 1911).

LAWRENCE, C. H. *St. Edmund of Abingdon* (Oxford, 1960).

LEGGE, M. D. *Anglo-Norman in the Cloisters* (Edinburgh, 1950).

LEHMANN, P. J. G. 'Mittelalterliche Büchertitel', *Sitzungsberichte der Bayerischen Akademie der Wissenschaften* (1948 and 1953).

—— *Erforschung des Mittelalters*, 5 vols. (Leipzig and Stuttgart, 1941–62).

MCKISACK, M. *The Fourteenth Century* (Oxford, 1959).

MILLER, K. *Mappae Mundi. Die ältesten Weltkarten*, iii (Stuttgart, 1895).

MOMMSEN, T. E. *Medieval and Renaissance Studies* (Cornell, 1959).

MYNORS, R. A. B. 'The Latin Classics Known to Boston of Bury', *Fritz Saxl Memorial Essays* (F.S.) (London, 1957).

—— *Catalogue of the Manuscripts of Balliol College, Oxford* (Oxford, 1963).

OAKESHOTT, WALTER. 'Some Classical and Medieval Ideas in Renaissance Cosmography', *Fritz Saxl Memorial Essays* (F.S.) (London, 1957).

OWST, G. R. *Preaching in Medieval England* (Cambridge, 1926).

—— *Literature and Pulpit in Medieval England* (New edition, Oxford, 1961).

—— '*Sortilegium* in English Homiletic Literature' in *Studies Presented to Sir Hilary Jenkinson*, ed. J. Conway Davies (London, 1957).

PANTIN, W. A. *English Church in the Fourteenth Century* (Cambridge, 1955).

PATRIDES, C. A. *The Phoenix and the Ladder* (California, 1964).

PECK, SISTER HELEN MARGARET. 'The Prophecy of John of Bridlington' (Chicago Ph.D. thesis, 1930).

PERRIN, M. L. *Über Thomas Castelford's 'Chronik'* (Boston, 1890).

POLLARD, A. F. 'Authorship and Value of the *Anonimalle Chronicle*', *E.H.R.* liii (1938).

POWICKE, F. M. *Stephen Langton* (Oxford, 1928).

—— *The Medieval Books of Merton College* (Oxford, 1931).

RICKERT, E. 'King Richard II's Books', *Library*, xiii (1933).

ROBINSON, J. ARMITAGE. 'An Unrecognized Westminster Chronicle', *Proceedings of the British Academy*, iii (1907).

RUSHFORD, MC. N. 'Magister Gregorius de Mirabilibus urbis Romae', *Journal of Roman Studies*, ix (1919).

SALTER, F. M. *Medieval Drama in Chester* (University of Toronto Press, 1955).

SMALLEY, BERYL. *English Friars and Antiquity in the Early Fourteenth Century* (*English Friars*) (Oxford, 1960).

STENTON, F. M. 'The Roads of the Gough Map', *The Map of Great Britain circa A.D. 1360, Known as the Gough Map*, ed. M. J. S. Parsons (Oxford, 1958).

TATLOCK, J. S. P. *The Legendary History of Britain* (California, 1950).

TAYLOR, J. 'The French *Brut* and the Reign of Edward II', *E.H.R.* lxxii (1957)

—— 'The Development of the *Polychronicon* Continuation', *E.H.R.* lxxvi (1961).

TAYLOR, RUPERT. *The Political Prophecy in England* (New York, 1911).

TOUT, T. F. *Chapters in the Administrative History of Medieval England* (Tout, *Chapters*) 6 vols. (Manchester, 1923–35).

ULLMAN, B. L. 'A Project for a New Edition of Vincent of Beauvais', *Speculum*, viii (1933).

VAUGHAN, R. *Matthew Paris* (Cambridge, 1958).

WEISS, R. 'The Study of Greek in England during the Fourteenth Century', *Rinascimento*, ii (1951).

WALTER, J. Th. *L'Exemplum dans la littérature religieuse et didactique du Moyen Âge* (Paris, Toulouse, 1927).

WRIGHT, J. K. *The Geographical Lore of the Time of the Crusades* (New York, 1925).

INDEX